Short-title catalogue of
BOOKS PRINTED IN THE
GERMAN-SPEAKING
COUNTRIES
and of
GERMAN BOOKS PRINTED
IN OTHER COUNTRIES
from 1455 to 1600
now in the
British Library

SUPPLEMENT

THE BRITISH LIBRARY
1990

© 1990 The British Library Board

Published by
The British Library
Great Russell Street, London WC1B 3DG

British Library Cataloguing in Publication Data

British Library
  Short-title catalogue of books printed in the German-speaking countries and of German books printed in other countries from 1455 to 1600 now in the British Library. Supplement.
  1. Books printed before 1601. Books in German — Catalogues, indexes
  I. Title II. Paisey, David III. British Museum
  011'.44

ISBN 0-7123-0207-7

Typeset by Bexhill Phototypesetters, Bexhill-on-Sea
Printed in Great Britain on permanent paper ∞ at the St Edmundsbury Press

CONTENTS

Preface

Additions	1
Amendments to the 1962 catalogue	71
Replacement of books destroyed during the War of 1939–45	93
Index I: Printers and publishers in the Supplement	97
Index II: Consolidated index of towns with dates of printers' and publishers' activity	123
— — False and fictitious names	141

PREFACE

The British Library's holdings of books printed in the German-speaking countries are notably rich from all periods, and well deserve the continuous enhancement which a generous acquisitions policy has been able to provide. The short-title catalogue of German books printed between 1455 and 1600 in the possession of the British Library's predecessor, the British Museum Library, was published by the Trustees in 1962. The present Supplement begins with a catalogue of the more than 1300 books which have either been added to the library since 1962, or been found to have been omitted by oversight from the previous work. This is followed by a list of amendments to the original entries, by a list of those books destroyed in the War of 1939–45 which have been replaced since 1962, by an index of printers and publishers in the Supplement, and by a consolidated index of towns in both works, with the names of printers and publishers arranged chronologically by the dates of their activity as represented in the British Library collections.

This Supplement has largely been compiled according to the same principles as the 1962 catalogue. It should be noted, however, that works in the Department of Prints and Drawings of the British Museum are no longer included. Works from the Henry Davis Collection have, in place of pressmarks, references to Mirjam M. Foot's catalogue of that collection: *The Henry Davis Gift,* vol. 2: *A catalogue of North-European bindings* (London 1983). Those books of uncertain date published ca. 1600 which are not included here will be found in the British Library's catalogue of German books of the seventeenth century, now nearing completion.

The catalogue has been compiled by Mr. D. L. Paisey of our German

Section, who was also responsible for selecting most of the new sixteenth-century purchases listed here. He is greatly indebted to Dr. Helmut Claus, Director of the Forschungsbibliothek Gotha, for help in identifying the printers of several of the books of the earlier sixteenth century. Mr. John Goldfinch of our Incunable Section provided assistance with a number of the entries for fifteenth-century books.

May 1989

J. M. SMETHURST
Director General
Humanities and Social Sciences
British Library

ADDITIONS

A

A., H.I.B.A.L.D.E.H. Comœdia HIBALDEHA von einem Edelman, welcher einem Abt drey Fragen auffgegeben. [By Henry Julius, Duke of Brunswick-Wolfenbüttel.] *Bey Johan: Francken: Magdeburgk,* [1599?] 8°. T.1827(9)

Abcontrafactur. Abcontrafactur eines Heidnischen Künigs sampt Weib vnd eim Kind. *s.n.* [1595.] *s.sh.* fol. Cup.651.e.(60)

Abell, Thomas. Invicta veritas. *Eng. Luneberge,* 1532. 4°. *The imprint is false; printed by Martin de Keyser at Antwerp.* G.1236; C.25.c.4(impf.)

Abraham, *the Patriarch.* Ein schön new Liedt, von den dreyen Patriarchen Abraham, Isaac, vnnd Jacob. *Valentin Neuber: Nürnberg,* [ca.1555?] 8°. C.175.i.31(64)

Abusiva. Aurelij Augustini liber de xij.abusiuis seculi. [*Georg Husner: Strasburg,* ca.1475.] fol. IB.1016

Achilles Tatius, *the Rhetorician.* De Clitophontis & Leucippes amorib. libri VIII. *Tr.* L.A. Cruceius. *Per Ioannem Heruagium: Basileæ,* 1554. 8°. C.109.m.47

Acronius, Johannes. Miraculorum quorundam descriptio. *Per Iacobum Parcum: Basileæ,* 1561. 8°. C.136.ee.17

Adam. Ein klag Liedt vom Fall Adams vnd Heua. [By Johann Kymeus.] *Valentin Neuber: Nürnberg,* [ca.1555?] 8°. C.175.i.31(4)

— Ein new geistlich Lied von erschaffunge des Menschen, vnd vom fall Adams vnd Eue. *Durch Nicolaum Knorrn: Nürmberg,* [ca.1565?] 8°. C.175.i.31(69)

Aenigma. Ænigma timorumenon in lutum sanguine maceratum. [By Matthaeus Wesenbecius.] *s.l.* 1573. 4°. 11409.f.41

Aepinus, Joannes. Pinacidion de Romane Ecclesię imposturis. [*Georg Richolff: Hamburg,* 1530.] 8°. 1606/1105

Aeschylus. Septem ad Thebas duces. *Tr.* Joannes Caselius. *Gr. & Lat. Ex officina Stephani Myliandri: Rostochij*, 1581. 4°. 1608/5184

Affelmann, Joannes. Vir politicus. *Apud Guilielmum Antonium: Hanouiæ*, 1599. 12°. 1568/8071

Agapetus, *Diaconus.* Opusculum ad Iustinianum boni principis complectens officia. *Tr.* Menradus Moltherus. *In officina Henrici Granij: Haganoæ*, 1527. 8°. 1606/1042

Agricola, Johann, *of Eisleben.* Confession vnd bekentnis vom Gesetz Gottes. *Durch Hans Weissen: Berlin,* 1540. 4°. C.136.ee.37

Agrippa, Henricus Cornelius. De incertitudine & vanitate scientiarum declamatio. [*Eucharius Cervicornus: Cologne,*] 1536. 8°. 1506/397

— [De nobilitate foeminei sexus.] Von fürtrefflichkeit des weiblichen Geschlechts. *Tr.* Balthasar Mencelius. *Gedruckt durch Paul Gräbern: Hall in Sachsen; in vorlegung Johann Francken: Magdeburg,* 1597. 4°.
RB.23.a.334

Alardus, *Amstelredamus.* Parasceue ad sacrosanctam Synaxin. Pie precationes [by Cornelius Crocus]. *Apud Petrum Quentell: Coloniæ,* 1532. 8°.
C.131.ff.7

— Selectæ aliquot similitudines. *Ioannes Gymnicus: Coloniæ,* 1539. 8°.
Davis II,31

Albert, *Cardinal, Archduke of Austria.* Kurtzer Begriff was Albrecht, Ertzhertzog zu Oesterreich im Niderlandt aussgericht hat. *Tr.* Conrad Löw. *Wilhelm von Lützenkirchen: Cölln,* 1596. 4°. 1477.bb.41

Alberus, Erasmus. Von den Zeichen des Jüngsten Tags ein schön Lied. [*Georg Rhau: Wittenberg,*] 1548. 4°. C.107.bb.71

— Widder die verfluchte lere der Carlstader. *Bei Anthonio & Walthero Brenner: Newenbrandenburg,* 1556. 4°. Cup.404.b.19

Albinus, Petrus. Meissnische Land vnd Berg-Chronica. 2 pt. *Bey Gimel Bergen: Dressden,* 1590. fol. *A reissue of the edition in STC (p.17).*
C.141.aa.6

Alesius, Alexander. Expositio prioris epistolæ ad Timotheum. (In alteram ad Timotheum expositio.) 2 pt. [*Georg Hantzsch: Leipzig,*] 1550, 51. 8°.
1578/4063

Alexander [Farnese], *Duke of Parma.* [An engraving of the funeral procession of the Duke of Parma at Brussels, 25 Dec. 1592, with verses in German and French.] *s.n.* [1592.] *s.sh. obl.* fol. 504.l.10(11)

Alsace. Reueillematin, von dem traurigen zustande im Elsass. *s.l.* 1592. 4°.
1509/1703

Altdorf. — Schola Altdorfiana. Hymenæus Altorphinæ Academiæ in nuptias Andreæ Knichen et Catharinæ Vesembeciæ. [By various authors.] *Paulus Kaufmann: Noribergæ,* 1600. 8°. MS.Egerton 1540(3)

Althamer, Andreas. Catechismus. *Künigund Hergotin: Nürmberg,* 1530. 8°.
C.143.f.9

— Conciliationes locorum scripturæ. *Laurent: Seuberlich: Vitebergæ,* 1597. 8°.
1159.f.14

Amandus, Georgius. Wye eyn geistlicher Ritter streytten sall. [*Jörg Gastel: Zwickau,*] 1524. 4°. 3908.e.18

Amerbachius, Georgius. Threnodia de morte Caroli. V. *Apud Sebaldum Mayer: Dilingæ,* [1558.] 4°. 1568/8996

Amerbachius, Vitus. Tres epistolæ de rebus grauibus [by Jacobus de Clusa and Joannes ab Aych]. *Ed.* V. Amerbachius. *Philippus Vlhardus: Augustæ Rheticæ,* [1548.] 8°. 1578/1827

Amman, Jost. Künstliche Figuren von allerlai Jag vnd Weidtwerck. *Martin Lechler in verlegung Sigmund Feyerabends: Franckfort am Mayn,* 1582. 4°. MS. Egerton 1208

Amsdorff, Nicolaus von. Das Johannes Wigandus vnbillich meine vermanung an die von Magdenburgk straffet. *Durch Joachim Walden: Magdeburgk,* 1564. 4°. 1509/3844

Anbildung. Anbildung der Höllen. [A woodcut, with verses.] *s.n.* [ca. 1600?] *s.sh.* fol. 1328.l.9(2)

Andreae, Conrad, *pseud.* [i.e. **Conrad Vetter.**] Der demütige Luther. *Wolffgang Eder: Ingolstatt,* 1595. 4°. 1608/2879

Anhalt. — George III., *Prince.* Vnderricht wie die Pfarherrn das volck in diesen geschwinden zeiten zur buss vermanen sollen. *Valentin Bapst: Leipzig,* 1546. 4°. 1578/2806

Anisius, Michael. Carmen consolatorium ad Guilielmum, comitem Palatinum Rheni. *[Closterdruckerei:] Tegernsee,* 1580. 4°. C.107.de.8

— Siben Catholische Predigen wider dem Türcken. *Adam Berg: München,* 1599. 4°. Cup.407.g.4

Annius, Joannes. Glosa super Apocalypsim. *Retro Minores: Colonie,* 1497. 4°. IA.5152

Annotatio. Annotatio seu Breviarium rerum memorabilium. *Per Valentinum Kobian: Turrelaci,* 1530. 4°. C.117.ff.17

Antichrist. Ein Rechen Büchlin vom EndChrist. [By Michael Stifel.] *Durch Georgen Rhaw: Wittemberg,* 1532. 8°. C.175.i.41

Antonius, *de Parma.* Postilla super euangelia dominicalia. *Per me Ioh'e3 Koelhoff de lubeck: Colonie,* 1482. fol. IB.3546

Apostles' Creed. Der heilig Christlich Glaub, in eyner newen melodey. *Valentin Neuber: Nürnberg,* [ca. 1555.] 8°. C.175.i.31(26)

Aristotle. [*Ethica Nicomachea.*] Questiōes Johānis versoris super libros ethicorum et textus. [*H. Quentel: Cologne,* 1494.] fol. IB.4880(impf.)

— [*Supposititious Works.*] [Problematum sectiones duædequadraginta. Problematum Alexandri libri 2.] *Tr.* Theodorus Gaza. [*Andreas Cratander: Basileæ,* 1537.] fol. 1505/54(2)(impf.)

Arithmetica. Arithmetice liliū triplicis practice. [By Johannes Huswirt?] [*Cornelis de Zierikzee: Cologne,*] 1511. 4°. C.132.b.29

Arnhem. Ein schreckliche Geschicht von einem grawsamen Kindt, welches geboren worden zu Arnhem. *Daniel Ewald: Cöln,* 1576. 8°. 11515.aa.11

Ars. Artis auriferæ quam chemiam vocant volumen secundum. *Typis Conradi Vualdkirchii: Basileæ,* 1593. 8°. 1578/8004

Artomedes, Sebastianus. Poëmata. *Ex officina typographica Johannis Beyeri: Lipsiæ,* 1590. 4°. 11405.c.4

Arznei. Ein bewerte Ertzney allen krancken. *See* B., L.

— Ein tröstlich artzeney wyder die newen kranckheit, die Engelisch schwayssucht genant. *Hanns Stüchs: [Nuremberg,* 1529?] 8°. 1578/8279

Asclepius Barbatus, Nicolaus. Oratio causas expulsi ducis Vuirtenbergēsis continens. *Per Franciscum Rhodum: Marpurgi,* [1534.] 4°. 1609/5725

— Sortium Vergilianarum sententiae ex quattuor poetis selectæ. *Andreas Kolbius: Marpurgi,* 1545. 8°. 1578/7064

Astrolabes. [Four woodcut sheets of astrolabes and sundials.] [*Nuremberg?*] 1545[–50?] *s.sh.* fol. Tab. 597.d.1(1,4–6)

Astrolabium. Astrolabium columnare. [Woodcuts.] [*Nuremberg?*] 1550. *s.sh.obl.* fol. Tab. 597.d.1(2)

Athanasius, *Saint,* Libri contra idolatriam gentium [and other works]. *Ed.* Johann Bugenhagen. *Per Nicolaum Schirlentz: Wittembergæ,* 1532. 8°.
1606/1406

— In psalmos opusculum. [With works by other authors.] *Mathias Schürerius:* [*Strasburg,*] 1508. 4°. C.175.h.10

Auctus, Mathias. Ein kurtzer Vnnterricht, wie sich die Armen zur zeit der Pestilentz beschutzen sollen. [*Andreas Winkler:*] *Breslaw,* 1542. 4°.
7561.de.10

Augsburg. [*Official Documents.*] Der Vnderkeuffel Ordnung. [*Augsburg,* 1550.] 4°. C.190.aaa.12

— [*Appendix.*] Christliche vnnd nöttige vermanung der Aussthailer des heyligen Allmusen zu Augspurg. *Valentin Schönigk; Augspurg,* 1586. 4°.
1568/4705

Augsburg, *Diocese of.* —**Synod.** Statuta diocesana. *Per Syluanum Otmar: Auguste,* 1517. fol. C.186.c.6

Augustine, *Saint.* [*De spiritu et littera.*] De spiritu et litera. *Apud Heronem Alopecium: Coloniæ,* 1527. 8°. *Another edition of that in STC (p.54).*
1506/47(1)

— [Supposititious Works. — **Soliloquia.**] Liber soliloq̄orū. [*Arnold Ther Hoernen: Cologne,* 1471 or 1472.] 16°. IA.3136

Austria. — **Ferdinand,** *Archduke.* Instruction, wie sich die Schuelmaister verhalten sollen. [16 Dec. 1586.] *s.n.* [1586.] fol. 1565/84

B

B., G., *Probst zu Berlin.* Ein prophetische Buspredigt für die jenigen, so Christum mit dem Antichrist verfolget haben. *s.n.* [ca. 1550.] 4°.
1578/1439

B., J. In disem Spruch wirdt kurtz verhört, was der Tobi sein Sun hab glert. J.B. [i.e. Jörgen Brentel.] *Melcher Kriegstein: Augspurg,* 1546. 4°.
11515.b.6

B., L. Ein bewerte Ertzney allen krancken. Darnach 4. Psalmen. L.B. *Valentin Neuber: Nürnberg,* [ca. 1555?] 8°. C.175.i.31(72)

Bacháček, Martin. Donati declinationum paradigmata. *Lat., Czech & Ger. Iohannes Schuman: Pragæ,* 1591. 8°. C.114.r.27(1)

Bairo, Pietro. De medendis humani corporis malis enchiridion. *Apud Petrum Pernam: Basileæ,* 1560. 8°. 1651/81(2)

Baldesano, Guglielmo. Stimuli virtutum adolescentiæ libri tres. *Tr.* Joannes Busaeus. *Sumptibus Arnoldi Mylij: Coloniæ,* 1594. 12°. 1606/201

Barbatia, Andreas. Cōsiliū si Eugenius papa potest facere duos episcopos in vna diocesi. [*Strasburg?,* ca. 1495.] 4°. IA.2580

Barlow, William, *Bishop.* The boke Reade me frynde and be not wrothe. *See* R., L.
— A proper dyaloge between a gentillman and a husbandmā. *See* Dialogue.
Barnes, Robert. Vitæ Romanorum Pontificum. *Apud Iosephum Clug: Vitebergae,* 1536. 8°. 1568/6488
Bartholomaeus [Arnoldi], de Usingen. Libellus in quo respondet confutationi Egidij mechlerij. [*Matthes Maler:*] *Erphurdie,* 1524. 4°. RB.23.a.866
Basil, *Saint, Archbishop of Caesarea.* [*Selections.*] Ex Basilio Magna Ecclesiarum status præsentis hypotyposis. *Tr.* Simon Stenius. *Gr. & Lat.* [*Hieronymus Commelinus:*] *Heidelbergæ,* 1593. 4°. 1607/406
Basilius, *Salvendensis. See* Salfeld, B.
Basle. [*Appendix.*] Christliche vnd trewhertzige Warnung der Pfarrherren vnd Theologen zu Basel von einer Schmachpredigt. *Basel,* 1599. 4°.
1367.i.35(3)
Bauern. Bawren Rathschlag vber den neuwen Kalender. *s.l.* 1585. 4°.
11522.e.39
Bauhinus, Joannes. De plantis absynthii nomen habentibus. Tractatus de absynthijs Claudii Rocardi. [*J. Foillet:*] *Montisbeligardi,* 1593. 8°.
450.b.27
— Historia noui fontis balneique Bollensis. 3 pt. *Apud Iacobum Foilletum: Montisbeligardi,* 1598. 4°.
1171.i.1(2); 462.b.23(impf.);233.k.34(impf.)
— Traicte des animauls aians aisles. [*J. Foillet:*] *Montbeliart,* 1593. 8°. 1507/1702
Bavaria. [*Separate Laws.*] Instruction für alle Pfleger vnd Landtrichter, was sy zu abstellung des schedlichen mordprennens anordnen sollen. [*Adam Berg: Munich,* 1565.] fol. D.CE.6
Bebelius, Henricus. [*Two or more Works.*] Opera. 2 pt. *In ædibus Thomæ Anshelmi: Phorce,* 1509. 4°. C.127.c.13
Beccadelli, Antonius, *Panormita.* [De dictis et factis Alphonsi.] Der Regiments Personen Lustbuch. *Bei Cyriaco Jacob: Franckforth am Mayn,* 1545. 4°. C.107.bb.25
Bede, *the Venerable, Saint.* [*Commentaries on the Bible.*] [In septem Epistolas canonicas commentaria.] [*Melchior von Neuss: Cologne,* 1534.] 8°.
C.110.b.30(impf.)
Bel. Ein new Liedt, vom Abgott Bell. *Valentin Newber: Nürnberg,* 1566. 8°.
C.175.i.31(60)
Berckenmeyr, Joerg. Eyn Register der heyligen Götlichen geschrifft. *See* Bible. — *Appendix.* [*Concordances.* — *German.*]
— Zwen schön Sprüch. [*Matthäs Franck: Augsburg?,* ca.1560?] 8°.
C.175.i.31(37)
Berckringer, Michael. Ein gaystlichs Lied, darinn die vrsachen des jaṁers der Christenheit Gott werden furgetragen. Sampt dem andern Psalm. *Bey dem Mattheo Francken: Augspurg,* [ca.1560?] 8°. C.175.i.31(63)
Bericht. Bericht auff dis bilde, von wegen des Aderlassens. *Durch Hansen Khol: Regenspurg,* [1555.] *s.sh.obl.* fol. 1865.c.20(3)
Bernard, *Saint, Abbot of Clairvaux.* Tractat⁹ d̃ planctu beate marie. [*Printer of Dictys: Cologne,* 1470?] 4°. IA.3321a

Bertrandus, *de Turre Cura, Cardinal.* [Sermones de tempore et de sanctis una cum quadragesimale epistolari.] pt. 1,2,4. [*Printer of Jordanus:*] *Argētine,* [1500?]–02. 4°. IA.2080(impf.)
Betti, Francesco. Risposta di M. Girolamo Mutio ad una lettera di F. Betti. [With Betti's text.] [*Peter Perna: Basle,* 1560?] 16°. 223.a.39
Beyer, Dominicus. Vorantwerunge eyner klage an hertzogen Karolum. [*Nickel Schirlentz:*] *Vuittemberg,* 1523. 4°. C.175.i.29
Beyr, Leonhard. Artickel vnd beschlusred widder die Artickel Conradi Wimpina. [*Nickel Schirlentz:*] *Vuittemberg,* 1526. 4°. 3906.b.27
Bible. [*German.*] Biblia. *Tr.* M. Luther. pt. 1. *Joh. Schwertel: Wittemberg,* 1575. 4°. Davis II, 344
— [*Spanish.*] La Biblia. *Tr.* Cassiodoro de Reyna. [*Thomas Guarin: Basle,*] 1569. 4°. *With the device of the compositor, Samuel Apiarius.* 676.c.2
— [*Selections.* — *German.*] Brunne des Lebens. [Extracts from the Bible.] *Valentin Bapsts Erben: Leipzig,* 1558. 8°. MS. Egerton 1572(1)
— **Pentateuch.** [*Latin.*] Rabani Mauri commentaria in Numeros, Deuteronomium. [With the text.] *Iohannes Praël: Coloniæ,* 1532. 8°. 1578/2504
— **Psalms.** [*Latin.*] Psalterium et hymnarius. [*Johann Prüss: Strasburg,* ca. 1498.] 4°. IA.1789(impf.)
— — — [Psalter with hymns.] [*Johann Prüss: Strasburg,* ca. 1500.] 4°. IA.1750(impf.)
— — — Paraphrasis Psalmorum poetica. *Tr.* G. Buchanan. *Iosias Rihelius: Argentorati,* 1575. 8°. Davis II, 51.
— — [*German.*] Der Psalter deutsch. *Tr.* M. Luther. [*Lukas Cranach & Christian Doering:*] *Wittenberg,* 1524. 8°. C.190.d.20(5)
— — [*Selections.* — *Latin.* — *Penitential Psalms.*] Psalmodiæ Dauidis septem, quas pœnitentiales uocant. *Tr.* Sebastianus Solidus. *Ioannes Carbo & Egidius Aquila: Viennæ Pannoniæ,* 1548. 8°. 1607/5106
— — — Psalmi pœnitentiales heroico metro redditi [by Laurentius Pogau]. *Iohannes Meisner: Magdeburgi,* 1600. 4°. 1578/388
— — [*Selections.* — *German.*] Zwey geyistliche schöne newe Lieder. Das erste auss dem 25. Psalm. Das ander auss dem 144. Psalm. *Hans Kholer: Nürnberg,* [ca. 1565?] 8°. C.175.i.31(50)
— — [*Selections.* — *German.* — *Single Psalms.*] Der xxij. Psalm. Durch Joh. Funck. Mehr zwey geistliche lieder. *Valentin Neuber: Nürnberg,* [ca. 1555?] 8°. C.175.i.31(44)
— — — Der XXIII. Psalm [*tr.* Hans Kolb]. Darbey das Gratias [by Georgius Aemilius]. *Hans Koler: Nürmberg,* [ca. 1565?] 8°. C.175.i.31(68)
— — — Der LXIII. Psalm, in gesangs weiss gestelt, durch Ambrosium Wilflingseder. *Valentin Newber: Nürmberg,* [ca. 1555?] 8°. C.175.i.31(48)
— — — [XC.] Das Gebet Mosi. *Tr.* Johann Spangenberg, *ed.* Wolffgangus Greff. *Durch Georgium Bawmann: Erffurdt,* 1558. 8°. C.175.i.31(46)
— — — [XCI.] Der 19.[91.] Psalm̃ [*tr.* Sebaldus Heyden]. Ein ander Lied [by Johann Freder]. [*Friedrich Gutknecht: Nuremberg,* ca. 1550?] 8°. C.175.i.31(61)(impf.)
— — — Der XCI. Psalm [*tr.* Sebaldus Heyden]. *Valentin Newber: Nürmberg,* [ca. 1555?] 8° C.175.i.31(62)

— — — Der XCI. Psalm Dauids gebettsweise gestellet: durch Timotheum Kirchnerum. *Johan Spies: Heydelberg,* 1583. 8°. C.104.dd.68(2)
— — — Der CIII. Psalm [*tr.* Johann Poliander]. Mehr drey schöner geistlicher Lieder. *Valentin Newber: Nürnberg,* [ca.1555?] 8°. C.175.i.31(47)
— **Proverbs.** [*Latin.*] Solomonis sententiæ. *Tr. & com.* P. Melanchthon. 2 pt. [*Johann Knobloch:*] *Argentorati; per Iohannem Secerium: Haganoæ,* 1525. 8°.
Davis II,326(1)
— — Liber Prouerbiorum Salomonis. *Tr.* Friedrich Dedekind. *Ex officina typographica VVolffgangi Kirchneri: Magdeburgæ,* 1574. 8°. RB.23.a.277
— **Ecclesiastes.** [*Latin.*] In librum qui Ecclesiastes inscribitur Ludouici Lauateri commentarius. [With the text.] *Apud Christ. Froschouerum: Tiguri,* 1584. 8°. 1509/4664
— **Isaiah.** [*English.*] The Prophete Isaye. *Tr.* George Joye. *Balthasar Beckenth: Straszburg,* 1531. 8°. The imprint is false; printed by Martin de Keyser at Antwerp. C.143.cc.16
— **Ecclesiasticus.** [*Greek.*] Sententiæ Iesu Siracidæ. *Tr.* Joachimus Camerarius. *Per Ioannem Oporinum: Basileæ,* 1551. 8°. 1578/5661
— — [*Latin.*] Liber Iesu Syrach. *Tr.* Justus Jonas. *Ex officina literaria Petri Seitz: Vitembergæ,* 1538. 8°. 1568/8856
— **New Testament.** [*German.*] Das New Testament. *Tr.* M. Luther. *Durch Johannem Feyerabend, in verlegung Peter Fischers: Franckfurt am Mayn,* 1591. 12°. 1506/231
— — [*Hungarian.*] Vi Testamentum Magiar nieluen. *Tr.* J. Sylvester. *Stainhofer Gaspar: Beczben,* 1574. 4°. C.128.c.2
— — [*Serbocroatian.*] [First part of the New Testament, in Glagolitic characters.] *Tr.* P. Truber, A. Dalmatin, S. Consul. [*Ivan Ungnad: Urach; Tübingen,* 1562.] 4°. Davis II,338
— **Epistles.** [*Latin.*] Paraphrases Erasmi in aliquot Pauli epistolas. *Apud Io. Frobenium: Basileæ,* 1522. 8°. Davis II,22
— — — D. Hieronymi Eusebii in omnes D. Pauli epistolas commentarij. [With the text.] *Apud Ioannem Gymnicum: Coloniae,* 1531. 8°. 1568/5456
— — — Theophylacti in omnes D. Pauli epistolas enarrationes. [With the text.] *Tr.* Christophorus de Persona. *Ex officina Eucharij Ceruicorni, impensis Godefridi Hyttorpij: Coloniæ,* 1532. 8°. 1607/2291
— — — Primasii in omnes D. Pauli epistolas commentarij. [With the text.] *Ioannes Gymnicus: Coloniae,* 1538. 8°. Davis II,300
— **Liturgical Epistles and Gospels.** [*Polyglott.*] Εὐαγγέλια καὶ ἐπιστολαὶ ἑλληνιστὶ καὶ ῥωμαϊστί. *Ioannes Paur: Œniponti,* 1591. 8°. 1607/3376
— .— [*Latin.*] In Euangelia quæ diebus dominicis et festis proponuntur annotationes Philippi Melanthonis. [With the text.] *Ex officina Iohannis Lufft: VVitebergæ,* 1555. 8°. MS.Egerton 1182
— — [*German.*] Postilla von Sontag nach Epiphanie biss auff den sechsten Sontag darnach. Martinus Luther. [With the text.] [*Paul Kohl: Regensburg,*]1525. 4°. 1608/4182
— — — Postilla. Zusammen getragen durch Hieronymum Mencelium. [With the text.] 3 Tl. *Abraham Lamberg: Leipzig,* 1596. fol. C.143.dd.2
— — [*Low German.*] Kercken Postilla. Doct. Mart. Luth. [With the text.] *Hans Krafft [for] Samuel Seelfisch: Wittemberg,* 1563. fol. C.127.i.5

— — [*Lithuanian.*] Postilla. Per Jana Bretkuna. 2 pt. *Jurgis Osterbergeras: Karaliaucziuie*, 1591. 4°. C.37.f.29
— **Corinthians.** [*German.*] Die erste (ander) Epistel Sanct Pauli an die Corinthier ausgelegt durch Cyriacum Spangenbergk. [With the text.] *Durch Vrbanum Gaubisch: Eisleben*, 1561,64. fol. 1575/536(2)
— **Galatians.** [*Latin.*] Enarratio Epistolæ Pauli ad Galatas, prælecta a Georgio Maiore. [With the text.] *Iohannes Lufft: VVitebergæ*, 1560. 8°. 1509/3122
— — — In Epistolam S. Pauli ad Galatas annotationes Iohannis VVigandi. [With the text.] *Hæredes Iohannis Cratonis: VVitebergæ*, 1580. 8°.
1578/1529
— **Timothy.** [*Latin.*] Enarratio Epistolæ Pauli primæ (secundæ) ad Timotheum, prælecta a Georgio Maiore. [With the text.] 2 pt. *Ex officina Iohannis Lufftij: VVitebergæ*, 1563,64. 8°. 1509/3120
— **Appendix.** [*Concordances.* — *Latin.*] Concordantiæ maiores Sacræ Paginæ. 2 pt. *Apud Paulum Gotzium: Argentorati*, 1530. fol. 1605/650
— — — [*German.*] Eyn Register der heyligen Götlichen geschrifft. [By Jörg Berckenmeyr.] Zum andern mal. [*Gabriel Kantz: Altenburg,*] 1525. 8°.
C.190.d.20(4)
— — [*English.*] A compendious olde treatyse shewynge howe that we ought to haue ye scripture in Englysshe. [By John Purvey?] *Hans Luft: Marlborow*, 1530. 8°. *The imprint is fictitious; printed by Johannes Hillen (Hoochstraten) at Antwerp.* C.25.d.16(1)
— — [*Miscellaneous.*] Auctoritates vtriusq̃ testamēti. [By N. Hanapus.] [*Petrus de Olpe: Cologne*, ca.1477.] fol. IB.4210
— — — Ein preyslied Götlichs worts durch Exempel der schrifft. *Valentin Newber: Nürnberg*, [ca.1555?] 8°. C.175.i.31(9)
— — — Zwey schöne newe geistliche Lieder, auss Göttlicher schrifft. [By M.R. Müntzer.] *Valentin Newber: Nürnberg*, [ca.1555?] 8°.
C.175.i.31(70)
— — Psalms. Zwey schöne geistliche Lieder, das erste, auss dem 56. oder 104.Psalm [by Nicolaus Hermann]. *Valentin Newber: Nürnberg*, [ca.1560?] 8°. C.175.i.31(56)
— — New Testament. [*Miscellaneous.*] Ein aller nüczlichsts büchlin vber die vier Euangelisten sampt dē büchlin d' Appostlēwirckung. *Durch Hanss Eckhartten: Spyer*, 1525. 8°. C.175.i.31(24)
Binnfert. Gründlicher vnd eigentlicher Bericht einer Historien, so sich im Dorf Binnfert zugetragen hat. *See* Strawe, Cuntz.
Binsfeldius, Petrus. Enchiridion theologiæ pastoralis. *Per Joannem Fabrum: Brunntruti*, 1599. 8°. 1607/3457
Bischoff, Melchior. Ausslegung des Euangelii am Tage der Opfferung Christi im Tempel. *Michael Schmuck: Schmalkalden*, [1575.] 4°.
C.107.bb.84(2)
— Eine Christliche Leichpredigt vber die Leiche Vuilhelmi, Bernhardts von Hutten Sönleins. *Michael Schmuck: Schmalchaldiae*, 1577. 4°.
C.107.bb.84(1)
— Eine tröstliche Predigt von der Tauffe. *Michael Schmuck: Schmalkalden*, 1577. 4°. C.107.bb.84(3)
Blum, Hans. Quinque columnarum exacta descriptio. *Apud Christophorum Froschouerum: Tiguri*, 1550. fol. 559*.f.2

Blum, Nicolaus. Eine tröstliche Leichpredigt bey der Sepultur der Frauen Barbara, Herzogin zu Liegnitz und Brieg. *Durch Nicolaum Schneider: Liegnitz*, 1595. 4°. 1560/4413

Bock, Georgius. Lucubrationes. *Per Henricum Petrum: Basileæ*, 1540. 4°. 1213.m.7(3)

Bodenstein, Andreas. Dyalogus von dem missprauch des Sacraments Jesu Christi. [(sig. A) *Hieronymus Höltzel: Nuremberg;* (sigg. B–F) *Georg Erlinger: Bamberg*, 1524.] 4°. C.175.ff.12

Boekel, Johan. Oratio funebris de Iulio Duce Brunouicens. et Lunæburg. *Iacobus Lucius: Helmæstadii*, 1589. 4°. 1578/391

Boethius, Anicius Manlius Torquatus Severinus. De consolatione philosophie. *Com.* Thomas Aquinas. Johānes Gerson De consolatione theologie. *J. Koelhoff: [Cologne,]* 1488. fol. IB.3600(impf.)

Bokelius, Cornelius. Themata de hydrope. *Præs.* Franciscus Parcovius. *Resp.* C. Bokelius, Elisaeus Leschius, Jacobus Alstenius. *Iacobus Lucius: Helmaestadii*, 1596. 4°. 1179.b.1(7)

Bologna. — Universitá di Bologna. — Natio Germanica. Migratio Germanorum ex Academia Bononiensi. *Ex officina Ludouici Lucij: Heidelbergae*, 1562. 4°. 1568/6152

Boltz, Valentinus. Illuminierbuch künstlich alle Farben zumachen. *Durch Herman Gülfferichen: Franckfurdt am Mayn*, 1551. 8°. 1560/4188(1)

Bongars, Jacques. Quaestio parricidii a Iohanne Chastel attentati in Henricum IV. *Parisiis*, 1595. 4°. *The imprint is false; printed in Germany.* 4380.aa.48(1)

Bornmann, Zacharias. Astra. Alle Bilder des Himmels. *Bey Georgio Bawman: Bresslaw*, 1596. 4°. 8561.dd.9(impf.)

— Astrolabium tetragonum. *Ger. Durch Georgium Bawman: Bresslaw*, 1595. 4°. 1560/990(impf.)

Botzhemius Abstemius, Joannes. Zwey schöne, newe, geystliche Lieder. Das erst: Ich rüff dich hyṁlischer Vatter an. *See* Lieder.

Boudinius, Joannes. Vita Christi. *Tr.* Valentin Leucht. *Ger. Durch Johannem Gymnicum: Cölln*, 1593. 4°. 1560/2645(1)

Brantius, Johannes. Epithalamium Ioannis Casimiri. *Ioannes Maior: [Heidelberg,]* 1570. 4°. 11405.bbb.9

Bredekauu, Franciscus. De schola Elisae prophetae oratio. *Petrus Seitz: VVitebergæ*, 1570. 4°. 1568/8009

Breining, Joerg. Ein schöns Lied, von Götlicher Maiestat. *See* Lied.

Brentel, Joergen. In disem Spruch wirdt kurtz verhört. *See* B., J.

Briegerus, Julius, *pseud.* Flores Caluinistici decerpti ex vita Roberti Dudlei. *Apud Ioannem Baptistam Zangarum: Neapoli*, 1585. 8°. *The imprint is fictitious; printed by Maternus Cholinus in Cologne.* 1354.a.25(2); G.11821

Brightwell, Richard, *pseud.* [i.e. **John Frith.**] A pistle to the Christen reader. [With texts by Luther and Melanchthon.] *Hans luft: Marlborow*, 1529. 8°. *The imprint is fictitious; printed by Johannes Hillen (Hoochstraten) at Antwerp.* C.37.c.41; C.37.b.53(impf.)

Brinkelow, Henry. The lamētacyon of a Christen. *See* Christian.

Brunfels, Otto. Uereum [sic] Dei multo magis expedit audire, quam Missam. [*Johann Schott: Strasburg*, 1523.] 4°. C.127.g.28

Brunnenfelser, Simon. Ein Christlich Gebett der Kirchen zu Strassburg.
Wolffgang Eder: Ingolstatt, 1586. 4°. 3911.aa.58(7)

Brunswick. — Ministers. Christliches Bedencken auff D. Maiors Repetition.
Durch Andream Petri: Eisleben, 1568. 4°. C.117.ff.19

Brusch, Caspar. Monasteriorum Germaniæ præcipuorum centuria prima.
Apud Alexandrum & Samuelem Vueyssenhornios: Ingolstadii, 1551.
fol. 1575/162

— Sacelli regii encomion. *Philippus Vlhardus: Augustæ Rheticæ,* 1551. 4°.
1568/4706

Bryssgawer, Martin. Wie man Christlicher weysz beichten sol. [*Johannes
Schwan: Strasburg,* 1524.] 4°. 3906.k.8(1)

Bucchingerus, Michael. Tyrocinium de sacro altaris mysterio. *s.l.* 1554. 8°.
4324.aaa.20

Bucer, Martin. Entschuldigung der diener am Euangelio Jesu Christi zu
Franckfurt. *See* Frankfort-on-the-Main. — Ministers.

Bucoldianus, Gerardus. Ein kurtze erzelūg von einem Döchterlin, welliches
sein lebē fürt ohne Speyss vnd tranck. *Tr.* Sixt Birck. *Hainrich Stainer:
Augspurg,* 1542. 4°. 1578/8590

Budé, Guillaume. De contemptu rerum fortuitarum libri tres. *Io. Soter: apud
inclytam Coloniam,* 1521. 8°. 1568/5230

Buechinger, Michael. *See* Bucchingerus.

Buentingus, Godeschalcus. Gründliche Erklerung der sieben letzten Wort
Jesu Christi. *Durch Friderich Hartman:* [*Frankfort on the Oder,*]1598. 4°.
1578/6319

Bugenhagen, Johann. Vermanung an alle Pfarherrn der gantzen Chur. *Johan
vom Berg & Vlrich Neuber: Nürmberg,* [1544.] 4°. 1568/8795

Bullinger, Heinrich. Gägensatz vnnd kurtzer begriff der Euangelischen vnd
Bäpstischer leer. *Christoffel Froschouer: Zürych,* 1551. 8°. RB.23.a.2775

Burchardi, Ulricus. Hortulus musices. [*Melchior Lotter: Leipzig,* 1514.] 4°.
Hirsch I.93

C

Caelius, Michael. Von der Kinder Tauffe ein Sermon. *Vrban Kaubisch:
Eisleben,* 1558. 4°. 1570/2617

— Wie der Probst zu Prage vnd Meyssen die Euangelischen prediger liegen
heyst. [*Nickel Schirlentz: Wittenberg,* 1524.] 4°. C.175.b.25

Caesius, Georgius. Alter vnd newer Schreibkalender auff das Jar M.D.XCIII.
Valentin Fuhrmann: Nürnberg, [1592.] 4°. 1509/2181

Calendarium. Calendarium simul et pietatis, et sanitatis. [By Joannes
Diemmairus?] [*Johann Burger: Regensburg?*] 1588. 8°. C.107.c.65(2)

Calepinus, Ambrosius. Dictionarium octo linguarum. Onomasticum
propriorum nominum [by Conrad Gesner]. 2 pt. *Per Sebastianum
Henricpetri: Basileæ,* 1584. fol. 1605/592

Calerus, Albertus. Extract eines Schreibens auss Spandaw. *Durch Andream
Hantzsch: Mülhausen,* 1595. 4°. 1193.e.25

Calvinius, Joannes, *Professor.* Lexicon iuridicum. *Apud hæredes Andreæ
Wecheli, Claud. Marnium & Ioan.Aubrium: Francofurti,* 1600. fol. 1605/306

Camerarius, Joachimus, *the Elder.* Ἀριθμολογία ἠθική cum interpretatione latina. *Andreas Schneider typis Voegelianis: Lipsiæ,* 1571. 8°. 1568/185
— Elementa rhetoricæ. *Per Ioannem Oporinū: Basileæ,* 1545. 8°. RB.23.a.1752
Camillus, Egidius. Ephemerides ad meridianū Viencñ. [An almanac for 1521.] *Per Jodocum Gutknecht: Nüremberge,* [1520.] *s.sh.* fol.
C.160.dd.2(impf.)
Caminaeus, Balthasar. De vita ac laudibus Lamperti Distelmeieri oratio. [*Andreas Eichorn:*] *Francofurti,* 1590. 4°. 10708.c.13
Campian, Edmund. [Rationes decem.] Zehen wolgegründte Vrsachen, warumb man bey dem Catholischen Glauben bleiben soll. *Ed.* Vitus Miletus Gamundianus. *Durch Andream Reinheckel: Neyss,* 1594. 8°.
1509/3121
Cana. Ein schön Liedt, von der Hochzeit zu Cana. [By Cyriacus Spangenberg.] *Valentin Newber: Nürnberg,* [ca.1550?] 8°. C.175.i.31(34)
Candidus, Johannes, *pseud.* [i.e. **Johann Cnipius.**] De cœna Domini veritas catholica. *Iohannes Meier* [*for Matthaeus Harnisch*]: *Heidelbergæ,* 1575. 8°.
1509/2752
Capito, Wolfgang Fabricius. [De pueris instituendis.] The true belief in Christ and his sacraments. *See* Jesus Christ.
Carinthia. Christliche einfeltige bekendtnus der Euangelischen Prediger in Kerndten. *s.l.* 1566. 4°. 3906.c.28
Carthusia. So der mensch zu dem heiligen Sacramēt wil gan das gebett geñ Carthusia. *Tr.* Ludwig Moser. [*Michael Furter: Basle,* 1506?] 8°.
1131 1606/1131
Carvaialus, Lodovicus. De restituta theologia liber vnus. *Ex officina Melchioris Nouesiani: Coloniæ,* 1545. 4°. 1609/2813
Casa, Giovanni della, *Archbishop.* Galateus. [*Tr.* Nathan Chytraeus.] Libellus de officijs inter amicos. *Apud Andream Wechelum: Francofurti,* 1580. 8°.
1568/8425
— [*Appendix.*] Il catalogo de libri, li quali sono stati condannati da Giouan della casa & d'alcuni frati. *Com.* Pietro Paolo Vergerio. [*Christoph Froschauer: Zürich,*] 1549. 4°. 619.d.8
Caselius, Joannes. Ad Casparem Rotermundium epistola παραινετική. *Ex officina Principis: Bardi Pomeraniae,* 1596. 4°. 1608/5542(8)
— Ad Mathiam de Schulenburgk παραινητικὸς [*sic*]. *In ac. Iul.: Helmæstadij,* 1595. 4°. 1608/5542(6)
— Ἐπιτάφιος Elisabethæ Bureniae. *Iacobus Lucius: Helmaestadii,* 1593. 4°.
1608/5542(5)
— Henrico Belouio et Elisabethæ Schrammiæ sponsis. *Stephanus Myliander: Rostochii,* 1583. 4°. 1608/5542(2)
— Ill.mo principi Vlrico duci Megapolitano gratulatur Joan.Caselius. *Typis Stephani Myliandri: Rostochii,* 1588. 4°. 1578/387
— Ἰουλῖον ad Henricum Iulium, Episcopum Halberstad. *Gr. & Lat. Ex officina Myliandrina: Rostochii,* 1596. 4°. 1608/5542(7)
— Laudatio Elisabethæ ab Heiligen. *Typis Stephani Myliandri: Rostochii,* 1584. 4°. 1608/5542(3)
Catechism. A breife catechisme and dialogue betwene the husbande and his wyfe. *Tr.* Robert Legate. *Wesell,* 1545. 8°. *The imprint is false; printed by Steven Mierdman at Antwerp.* 1018.h.4

11

Celichius, Andreas. Doctrina de peccato originali. *Ex officina Augustini Ferberij, impensis Francisci Omichij & Vuarneri Langij: Gustrouij,* 1582. 4°.
1560/158

Cesar, Hermannus. Epistola ad Buschium [With other matter.] [*Wolfgang Stöckel: Leipzig,* 1505.] 4°. C.190.aa.14

Chaimis, Bartholomaeus de. Interrogatorium siue cōfessionale. *Per Petrū schoiffer: in urbe Magūtia,* 1478. 4°. *A variant of IA.226.*
IA.225(impf.)

Champ: Cocolappo, Altzifolus Narratus a, *pseud.* Mein dienst, mit wenig freundlichem grus zuuor. [A comic prescription.] *s.n.* [ca.1580?] *s.sh.* 4°.
1865.c.20(3★)

Charles V., *Emperor of Germany.* [*Appendix.*] Eyn ermanung an die Keyserliche Maiestat des Euangeliums halben. *s.l.* 1546. 4°. *An edition different from those in STC (p.*192). 1578/1824

Charles Frederick, *Prince of Juliers, Cleve and Berg.* In immaturam Caroli Friderici mortem elegia funebris. *See* D., I.L.

Charopus, Andreas. Pæan de Diuo Leopoldo. *Ex officina Michaëlis Zimmermanni: Viennæ Austriæ,* 1564. 4°. 1608/5296

Chasseneux, Barthélemy de. Catalogus gloriæ mundi. *Apud Georgium Coruinum, impensis Sigismundi Feyerabendi: Francofurti ad Mœnum,* 1579. fol. 1489.d.5

— Consuetudines ducatus Burgundiæ commentariis illustratæ. *Ex officina Nicolai Bassæi, impensis Sigismundi Feyrabend: Francofurti,* 1574. fol.
1605/496

Châteillon, Sébastien. Dialogi IIII. *Per Theophil. Philadelph.: Aresdorffij,* 1578. 16°. *The imprint is fictitious; printed at Basle by Peter Perna.* 1492.f.12

Chimarrhaeus, Jacobus. Panis quotidianus animæ. *Apud Henricum Falckenburg, typis Lamberti Andreæ: Coloniæ,* 1590. 12°. 1568/9012

Christian. Erinnerung wes sich ein Christ by absterbung siner mitbrüder trösten soll. [By Otto Werdmüller.] *By Jacobo Gessner: Zürych,* 1564. 12°. 1509/2039(1)

— The lamētacyon of a Christen agaynst the cytye of London. [By Henry Brinkelow.] *Nurenbergh,* 1545. 8°. *The imprint is false; printed by Steven Mierdman at Antwerp.* C.25.d.16(4)

— Ein new geystliches Lied, vom wesen eins waren Christen. *Durch Mattheum Francken: Augspurg,* [ca.1560?] 8°. C.175.i.31(11)

Christian I., *Elector of Saxony.* Kurtze Beschreibung dess Process so bey Hertzogen Christiani Begrebniss gehalten worden. *Bey Nickel Voltzen: Franckfurt an der Oder,* 1592. 4°. C.117.ff.18(impf.)

Christian IV., *King of Denmark and Norway.* Was bey der Cronung Christiani des IIII. sich zugetragen hat. *s.l.* 1596. 4°. 1578/5053

Christian Devotion. [Feürzeüg Christenlicher andacht.] *Jobst Gutknecht: Nürnberg,* [1539.] 8°. C.104.dd.68(1)(impf.)

Christian Faith. Confessiones Fidei Christianæ tres. 3 pt. *Ex officina Petri Brubachii: Francoforti,* 1553. 4°. 1578/1297

Christian Life. Das Christenlich Läben. [By Otto Werdmüller.] *Bey Jacobo Gessner: Zürych,* 1564. 12°. 1509/2039(2)

— Ein geistlich Lied dariñ, was zu einem waren Christlichen leben gehörig, begriffen. *See* W., B.

Christian Marriage. Kurtze vnd einfeltige Anleittung, wie man eine Christliche Ehe werben sol. *s.l.* 1592. 8°. 1578/2378

Christian Songs. Drey geistliche vnd Christliche Lieder. *s.n.* [ca. 1560?] 8°.
C.175.i.31(23)

Christians. Ein schön new geystlich Lied, von schlaff vnd aufferstehung der Christen. [By Caspar Franck.] *Valentin Newber: Nürnberg,* [ca. 1555?] 8°.
C.175.i.31(22)

Christliche Ehe. *See* Christian Marriage.

Chuntz, *von Oberndorff, pseud.?* Dialogus ader ein gespreche. wieder Doctor Ecken Buchlein. [*Wolfgang Stöckel: Leipzig,* 1520.] 4°. C.141.c.5

Chytraeus, David. De lectione Herodoti. (De secundo libro Herodoti. — De lectione tertii libri. — In Melpomenen. — De quinto libro. — De sexto libro. — In Polymniam. — In Vraniam. — In Calliopen.) 9 pt. [*Heirs of Ludwig Dietz; Stephan Möllemann: Rostock,* 1559–61.] *s.sh.* fol.
586.k.19(2)

— Oratio habita, cum gradus doctoris theologiæ Cyriaco Simoni decerneretur. *Iacobus Lucius: Rostochii,* [1575.] 8°. C.107.df.39

Chytraeus, Nathan. De philosophica animi tranquillitate prælectiones. *Typis Stephani Myliandri: Rostochii,* 1592. 4°. 1578/4661

Cicero, Marcus Tullius. [*Two or more Works.*] De officiis libri tres. De amicitia [and other works]. *Apud Christophorum Froschouerum: Tiguri,* 1560. 8°. 1607/2935

— [*Selections.*] Medulla Tulliana. *Ed.* Martin Hayneccius. *Imprimebat Michael Lantzenberger, impensis Henningi Grosii,* 1595(1594★). 8°. C.106.e.21

— [*Supposititious Works.*] Ad C.Herennium rhetorica. *Ed.* Reinhardus Lorichius. *Hæredes Christ. Egenolphi: Francoforti,* 1563. 8°. 1578/1425

— — Synonyma. Stephani Flisci artificiosa eloquentia. *Per Heinricum Gran: Hagenau; impensis Joānis rynman:* [*Augsburg,*] 1518. 4°. 1609/2887

Cilicius, Christianus, *Cimber, pseud.* [i.e. **Heinrich Rantzau.**] Belli Dithmarsici descriptio. *Per Bernhardum Iobinum: Argentorati,* 1574. 8°.
C.183.aa.10(1)(impf.)

Civilius, Marcus. Eine freidige vermanung, zu klarem bekentnis Jhesu Christi. *Pref.* M. Flacius. *Michel Lotther: Magdeburgk,* 1550. 4°. 3906.c.30

Cleber, Eusebius. Ein warhaffte vnderweisung von der person Christi. (Besonderer anhang.) 2 pt. *s.l.* 1575. 4°. 1608/2488

Clencherus, Petrus. De Athanasio Symbolo disputationes tres. *Henricus Aquensis: Wirceburgi,* 1590. 4°. 1568/168

Clichtoveus, Jodocus. Homiliarum tripartitarum pars prima (secūda). 2 pt. Ex officina Eucharij [*Cervicorni*]: *Coloniæ,* 1535. 8°. Davis II, 27, 18

Clostromarius, Martinus. *See* Klostermair.

Cnipius, Johann. *See* Candidus, Johannes, *pseud.* [i.e. J. Cnipius.]

Coccius, Marcus Antonius, *Sabellicus.* [Exempla.] De memorabilibus factis dictisque exemplorum libri X. *Henricus Petrus: Basileæ,* 1533. 8°.
1578/4664

Codicillus, Petrus. Wokabulář. *Lat., Czech & Ger. Typis Danielis Adami: Pragæ,* 1586 (1587★). 8°. C.118.r.27(3)

Codomannus, Laurentius. Gründtliche Eyntheilung der Zehen Gebott Gottes. *Johann Spies: Franckfurt am Mayn,* 1585. 4°. 1560/2683

Colinus, Matthaeus. *See* Collinus.
Collecten. *See* Kollekten.
Collibus, Hippolytus à. Princeps. De nobilitate positiones LXII. Palatinus. 2 pt. *Apud Guilielmum Antonium: Hanouiæ*, 1595. 8°. 1578/8071
Collinus, Matthaeus. Elegia de natali Iesu Christi. *Per Iosephum Clug: Vitebergæ*, 1540. 4°. 11409.g.36
— Nomenclatura rerum familiariorum. *Lat., Czech & Ger. U Jana Kantora: w Starém Mieste Pražském*, 1555. 8°. C.114.r.26(1)
Cologne. — Universität Köln. Noui Collegii theologici Agrippinensis descriptio. [The statutes, and other material.] *Apud Ludouicum Alectorium, & hæredes Iacobi Soteris: Coloniæ*, 1578. 4°. C.104.d.35
Colonne, Guido delle. Historische Beschreibung von der Statt Troia. *Tr.* David Förter. *Jacob Foillet: Mümpelgart*, 1599. 8°. 12450.b.42
Comedia. Comedia. *Ed.* Balthasar Ludwici. *Per Jacobum Thanner: Liptzigk*, 1507. 4°. 1474.bb.18
Confession. [The humble and vnfained confessiō of the belefe of certain poore banished men. By John Poynet?] *Nicholas Dorcastor: Wittonburge*, 1554. 8°. *The imprint is fictitious; printed in London? by John Day?*
C.25.b.32(impf.)
Conradus, *de Zabernia.* Ars bene cantādi. *p Fridericum hewman: Magūtie*, 1509. 8°. Hirsch I.131
Conradus, *Noricus. See* Tockler, Conrad.
Copp, Joannes. Practica deutsch auff das iar M.CCCCC.xxi. *Wolffgang Stöckel: leypssgk*, [1520.] 4°. C.106.d.26
Cordiale. Quattuor nouissima cum exemplis. *p Henricum Quentell: Colonie*, 1500. 4°. IA.4729
Coturnossius, Gulielmus. Megistes. *Egidius Aquila: Viennae Austriae*, 1552. 4°. 11408.ee.28
Crato, Adamus. Geheimnuss der Türcken. 2 pt. *Paul Donat, in vorlegung Ambrosij Kirchners: Magdeburgk*, 1596. 8°. C.107.bb.89
Creissius, Joannes. Ornatissimo iuueni Ioanni Creissio et Elisabethae Myliae sponsis gratulantur amici. *Typis Iacobi Lucij: Helmæstadij*, 1591. 4°.
1608/5542(4)
Creutziger, Caspar, *the Elder.* De maxilla Samsonis oratio. *In officina Iosephi Klug: Vitebergae*, 1546. 8°. 1509/3821
Creutziger, Caspar, *the Younger.* Propositiones. *Iohannes Crato: Vitebergæ*, 1561. 8°. 1509/3820
— Propositiones theologicæ repetentes summam docrinæ de iustificatione. *Clemens Schleich & Antonius Schöne: VVitebergæ*, 1570. 4°. 1560/2684
Crolachius, Henricus. Isatis herba. *Iacobus Gessnerus: Tiguri*, [1563.] 8°.
966.b.39(2)
Cronberg, Hartmuth von. Ein Christlich Schrifft an alle Grafen vnd alle eynwoner der Cronen zū Behem. [*Michael Buchführer: Erfurt*, 1523.] 4°.
C.190.a.17
Crugerius, Pancratius. Oratio de difficultate scholastici muneris. *Typis Sciurianis: Francofordiæ ad Viadrum*, [1589.] 4°. RB.23.a.2310
Crusius, Johann. Isagoge ad artem musicam. *Typis Christophori Lochneri & Iohann.Hofmanni: Noribergæ*, 1592. 8°. Hirsch I.136

— [Isagoge ad artem musicam.] *Typis Gerlachianis: Noribergæ,* 1593. 8°.
1042.d.60(impf.)

Crusius, Martinus. Grammaticæ Græcæ cum latina congruentis pars prima & altera. 2 pt. *Ambrosius Fritsch: Gorlicii,* 1592. 8°. 1607/3286

Cube, Johann von. Gart der gesuntheit. [*Michael Furter: Basle,* ca.1496.] fol.
IB.37803

Cujacius, Jacobus. Ad Africanum tractatus VIIII. *Apud Ioannem Gymnicum: Coloniae Agrippinae,* 1588. 8°. 1607/5764

Culina. Culina opinionum. *Ger. s.n.* [ca.1590?] *s.sh. obl.* fol. 1750.b.29(79)

Culman, Leonhard. Zuchtmeister für die jungen Kinder. *In verlag Hans Grimmen: Strassburg,* 1546. 8°. C.107.bb.75

Culsamerus, Johannes. Aduersus Barptholomei Vsingi libellum confutacio. *Per Michaelem Buchfurer: Erphordie,* 1523. 4°. 1608/4422

— Eyn wiederlegung etzliche Sermon von Bartholomeo Vsingen. [*Matthes Maler:*] *Erffurdt,* 1522. 4°. 1568/8327

Curtius, Jacobus. Εἰκαστων lib. III. *Hæredes Arnoldi Birckmanni: Coloniæ,* 1554. 8°. 877.c.16

Curtius, Valentinus. Erklerung aus Gottes Wort, vnd kurtzer bericht der Herren Theologen, welchen sie der sechsischen Stedten Gesandten zu Lüneburgk gethan haben. [Signed: V.Curtius and others.] *Durch Donatum Richtzenhayn: Jhena,* 1561. 4°. C.117.ff.11

D

D., I.L. In immaturam Caroli Friderici mortem elegia funebris. *Petrus Warneri: [Emmerich,* 1575.] 4°. 837.h.3(23)

Dalnerus, Andreas. Tractatus de seditione. *Typis Leonhardi Formicæ: Viennæ Austriæ,* 1599. 4°. 8005.c.12

Damasus, *Pope, Saint.* Historia diui Apollinaris. *In officina Petri Quentell: Coloniæ,* 1526. 4°. 4824.cc.13

Dati, Agostino. [Elegantiolae.] In eloquentiæ præcepta libellus. *In ædibus Eucharii Ceruicorni: Coloniæ,* 1522. 4°. C.117.ff.20

Decembrius, Angelus. Politiæ literariæ libri septem. *Henricus Steynerus: Augustæ Vindelicorum,* 1540. fol. 631.l.6

Decimator, Henricus. Syluæ quinquelinguis vocabulorum et phrasium. *Ed.* Valentin Schindler & Zacharias Palthenius. *Ex officina Paltheniana, sumtibus Nicolai Bassæi: Francofurti,* 1596. 8°. 1568/1358

Dedekind, Friedrich. Grobianus. De morum simplicitate. *Per Iohannem Eichorn: Franc. ad Viadrum,* 1549. 8°. C.190.a.16

Demetrius, *Phalereus.* Περι ἑρμηνειας. *Ed.* Joannes Caselius. *Typis Stephani Myliandri: Rostochii,* 1584. 8°. 1578/3980

Denss, Adrian. Florilegium omnis generis cantionum ad testudinis tabulaturam accommodatarum. *Gerardus Greuenbruch: Coloniæ Agrippinæ,* 1594. fol. K.3.m.20

Dialogue. A proper dyalogue between a gentillman and a husbandmā. [By William Barlow.] *Hans Luft: Marborow,* 1530. 8°. *The imprint is false; printed by Johannes Hillen (Hoochstraten) at Antwerp.* C.37.a.28(5)

Dickius, Leopoldus. Aduersus impios Anabaptistarum errores iuditium. *Apud Iohan. Sec[erium]: Haganoæ,* 1530. 4°. RB.23.a.1820

Diemmairus, Joannes. De criminibus, eorumque poenis, aphorismus iuris.
Ioannes Burger: Ratisponae, 1568. 8°. C.107.e.65(3)
— Declaratio resolutiua Aphorismi iuris, de criminib. puniendis. *Iohannes Burgerus: Ratisponæ,* 1570. 8°. C.107.e.65(4)
Dietmannus, Gaspar. Sacrosanctum extremæ vnctionis mysterium. *Henricus Aquensis: Wirtzeburgi,* 1588. 4°. 1568/8312;1489.bb.6(3)(impf.)
Dilbaum, Samuel. Bericht vnd kurtze Erzehlung dess heroischen gemüts, welche Sigismundus Batori bewisen hat. *Adam Berg: München,* 1596. 4°.
RB.23.a.3146.
Dinckel, Johann. Calendarium poeticum. *Iohannes Pistorius: Erfordiae,* 1580. 8°. RB.23.a.630
Dionysius, *of Halicarnassus.* Antiquitatum siue originum Romanarum libri X. *Tr.* Sigismundus Gelenius. (Lib. XI.) *Tr.* Lapo Birago. *Per Hier. Frobenium & Nic. Episcopium: Basileæ,* 1549. fol. Eve.b.24(impf.)
Dionysius, Nestor, *Novariensis.* Vocabula. *Ioannes Prüsz:* [*Strasburg,*] 1507. fol. 625.i.11
Distelmeier, Christianus. Nobilissimis sponsis Christiano Distelmeier & Catharinæ Luderitiæ γαμήλια Joannis Caselij [and others]. *Ex officina typographica Stephani Myliandri: Rostochij,* 1581. 4°. 1608/5542(1)
Dithmarus, Remigius. Lutherana veteris Catholicaeque litaniae correctio. *Henricus Aquensis: Herbipoli,* 1589. 4°. 1560/2685
Dobneck, Johann, *Cochlaeus.* De immensa Dei misericordia erga Germanos. *In officina Nicolai Vuolrab: Lipsiæ,* 1538. 4°. 1608/4412
— Erclerung der streittigen artickeln der Conuocation zu Marpurg. *Wolffgang Stöckel: Dressden,* 1530. 4°. C.117.ff.12
Dolearius, Johannes. Carmen de gloriosa Iesu Christi resurrectione. [*Georg Kote:*] *Halberstadij,* 1595. 4°. 1578/6079
Donatus, Aelius. [Ars minor.] *F. Kreusner: Nürnberge,* [14]93. 4°. IA.7699
Dorn, Gerardus. Lapis metaphysicus, aut philosophicus. *s.l.* 1570. 8°.
1400.a.35
Dorsprunner, Alexander. [A safe-conduct issued by A. Dorsprunner on behalf of Frederick, Margrave of Brandenburg; in three settings.] [*Anton Koberger: Nuremberg,* ca.1496.] *s.sh.* 4°. IA.7499
Driel, Godefridus. Rosarii hyperaspistes. *Ex officina Henrici Aquensis: Herbipoli,* 1588. 4°. Cup.403.s.15
Droet, Pierre. Consilium nouum de pestilentia. *Apud Bernhardum Iobinum: Argentorati,* 1576. 8°. 1166.b.12
Duerrenbacher, Johannes. Schlacht des Hohenpriesters mit dem Bapst. *s.l.* 1567. 8°. RB.23.a.3151(1)
— Ein schön Gesang, dardurch ein einfeltiger Christ der Caluiner lehr als ketzerisch vrtteln kann. *s.n.* [ca.1567.] 8°. RB.23.a.3151(2)
Dungersheym, Hieronymus. Examinatio libelli Lutherani de bonis operibus. [*Valentin Schumann: Leipzig,* ca.1530.] 4°. 1560/3072
Duranti, Jean Étienne. De ritibus Ecclesiae Catholicae libri tres. *Apud Ioannem Gymnicum: Coloniae Agrippinae,* 1592. 8°. 1489.aa.11
Dutch Cities. Newe Zeittung der niderlendischē Stette an die Kron auss Hispanien vbergeben. Verantwortung der Stette. *s.n.* 1567. 4°.
9073.de.2

Du Tillet, Jean. Commentariorum & disquisitionum de rebus Gallicis libri duo. *Tr.* Lotarius Philoponus. Vincentii Lupani De magistratibus Francorum lib. III. *Apud Andream Wechelum: Francofurti ad Moenum,* 1579. fol. 1565/15(1)

E

Eber, Paul. De uita et scriptis C. Plinii quædam. *Hæredes Georgii Rhauu: VVitebergæ,* 1556. 8°. 1568/8049
Eberbach, Adamus. In natalem Iesu Christi carmen heroicum. *Conradus Dreher: Erphordiae,* 1572. 8°. C.104.d.10
Eccard, Johann. Der erste (ander) Theil Geistlicher Lieder mit fünff Stimmen. Tenor. 2 pt. *Bey Georgen Osterbergern: Königsberg,* 1597. obl. 4°. A.186.c
Edmund [Campian], *Saint. See* Campian, E.
Eisengrein, Martin. Beschaydne erkläung dreyer Hauptarticul Christlicher lehr. *Alexander Weissenhorn: Ingolstatt,* 1568. 4°. C.104.d.8(1)
— Ein frey Concilium von dreyen strittigen Articul vnsers Christlichen glaubens. *Alexander & Samuel Weissenhorn: Ingolstatt,* 1567. 4°.
C.104.d.8(2)
Eisleben. — Synod. Acta des löblichen Synodi in der Stad zu Eisleben. *Jacob Berwalt: Eisleben,* 1554. 4°. 1578/2456
Elijah ben Asher, *hal-Lēvī.* ספר הדקדוק Grammatica Hebraica. *Tr.* S. Münster. *Heb. & Lat.* 2 pt. [*Apud Io. Frobenium: Basileae,* 1525.] 8°.
Davis II, 24(3)(impf.)
Elizabeth I., *Queen of England.* Gründliche vnd eigentliche warhaffte Beschreibung von der Königin in Engellandt, warum̃ sie dic Königin von Schottlandt hat enthaupten lassen. [A translation of "Mariae Stuartae in arce Fodringhaye interfectae supplicium & mors".] *Cöllen,* 1587. 4°. 597.d.28
Ellander, Blasius. Examen dessen allermaisten strittigen Artickels von der Communion. *Georg Widmanstetter: Grätz,* 1588. 4°. 4323.bb.14
Elogii, Caspar. Leichtpredig vber Maximiliani des andern Absterben. *Michael Peterle: Prag,* [1577.] 4°. 1578/393
Emser, Hieronymus. Missae Christianorum contra Lutheranam missandi formulā assertio. [*Emser's Press: Dresden,*] 1524. 4°. C.106.cc.33
Enchiridion. In hoc enchiridio haec insunt. Rubricae caesarei ac pontificij iuris [and other matter]. *Apud Ioannem Schoeffer: Moguntiæ,* 1529. 8°.
C.113.a.14(3)
England. — Elizabeth I., *Queen.* Elizabethae edictum. [18 Oct. 1591. With a reply by Robert Persons.] *Apud Ioannem Fabrum: Augustæ,* 1592. 8°. *The imprint is false; printed at Antwerp by Arnout Coninx.* 300.a.1; G.6097
— [Another edition.] pp. 361. *s.l.* 1593. 8°. 847.h.10
— [Another edition.] pp. 341. *s.l.* 1593. 8°. G.6096
— Elisabethen Edict. [18 Oct. 1591. With a reply by Robert Persons.] *Ger. Durch Dauid Sartorium: Ingolstatt,* 1593. 4°. 1368.d.6; 1570/1825
— **Church of England.** [*Articles of Religion.*] Artickel deren sich die Bischoff vnd Gleerten des Künigreychs Engelland vereiniget habēd. *Bey Andrea Gessner dem jüngeren: Zürych,* [1553.] 8°. C.142.a.4

— — [*Injunctions.*] Regiæ Maiest. Angliæ Mādatorum epitome. *s.n.* [1547?] 8°.
C.175.aa.32; G.11829(1)

— — [*Appendix.*] Verantwortung der Christenlichen Kirchen der Kron Engelland. [A translation of John Jewel's "Apologia Ecclesiae Anglicanae".] *s.l.* 1563. 8°. 1368.a.36

Eobanus, Helius. [Bonae valetudinis conservandae praecepta. With other works.] *Per Henricum Sybold: Argentorati,* 1530. 8°. C.112.a.8(1)(impf.)

— De non contemnendis studijs hūaniorib⁹ aliquot clarorū virorum epistolæ. *Ed.* H. Eobanus. *Mattheus Pictor: Erphurdię,* 1523. 4°. C.127.c.7

Ephemerides. [*Unnamed, anonymous Calendars.*] [Fragments of four different calendars for 1569.] 6 pt. *Christoffel Froschower: Zürych,* [1568.] *s.sh.* fol.
1881.a.4(134)

— [Two coloured woodcut Bauernkalender for 1585.] *Hans Hofers Erben: Augspurg,* [1584.] *s.sh.* fol. Tab.597.d.1(9, 10)

Epicurus, *King.* Epicurus der gottlose König mit seinem Hofgesind. *s.l.* [ca.1568?] 4°. 11517.ee.55(2)

Eppendorff, Heinrich von. Kriegsübung dess römischen Kaisers Julij, sampt anderer Fürsten vergleichung durch Franciscum Floridum [and works by other authors]. *Tr. & ed.* H. von Eppendorff. *In Hans Knoblouchs druckerey, durch Georgen Messerschmidt: Strassburg,* 1551. fol. 1605/709

— Türckischer Keyszer Ankunfft, Kryeg vnd Händlung gegen die Christen [and other matter]. *Tr.* H. von Eppendorff. *Bey Hans Schotten: Strasszburg,* 1540. fol. C.107.h.27

Erasmus, Desiderius. [*Two or more Works.*] Libellus nouus de pueris instituendis, cum alijs compluribus. *Per Hieronymum Frobenium, Ioannem Heruagium, & Nicolaum Episcopium: Basileæ,* 1529. 4°. C.189.bb.21

—[*Letters.* — *Single Letters.* — *Ad Fridericum Ducem Saxoniae.*] Epistola ad Ducē Saxoniæ. [With works by Johann von Eck, Martin Luther and Andreas Bodenstein.] [*Melchior Lotter the Elder: Leipzig,* 1519.] 4°. 1570/1936

— [*Adagia.*] Epitome adagiorum. *Apud Mart. Gymnicum: Coloniæ,* 1549. 8°.
1493.t.58

— [*Apophthegmata.*] Apophthegmatum opus. *In officina Hieron. Frobenij & Nicolai Episcopij: Basileæ,* 1532. fol. C.129.mm.3

— [*Colloquia.*] Familiarium colloquiorum opus. *Eucharius [Cervicornus:] [Cologne,*]1528. 8°. Davis II, 295

— — Colloquiorum familiarium opus. *Apud Mathiam Harscher: Basileæ,* 1554. 16°. 1606/914

— — Colloquia. Ger. *Tr.* Justus Alberti. *Haynrich Stayner: Augspurg,* 1545. fol.
C.186.c.15

— [*Concio de puero Jesu.*] De ineffabili Jesu puero concio. *Per Fridericum Peypus: Nurenberge,* [ca.1520?] 4°. C.104.cc.21

— [*De conscribendis epistolis.*] Opus de conscribendis epistolis. *Hæred. Gymnici: Coloniæ,* 1544. 8°. C.108.u.8(1)

— [*De copia verborum.*] De duplici copia uerborum ac rerum commentarij. *Ed.* Joannes Veltkirch. *Martinus Gym.: Coloniæ,* 1545. 8°. C.108.u.8(2)

— [*Enchiridion militis Christiani.*] A shorte recapitulation of Erasmus Enchiridion. Drawne out by M. Coverdale. *Adam Anonymus: Ausborch,* 1545. 8°. *The imprint is fictitious; printed at Antwerp by Steven Mierdman.*
C.37.a.33

Erbenius, Nicolaus. Vermanung zum Gebet. *Durch Georgium Bawman: Erffordt*, 1583. 4°. 1509/3835

Ernest, *Duke of Bavaria.* Hertzog Ernst christlich verendert. *See* Schnauss, Ciriacus.

Ertzberg, Heinrich. Gruntliche erklärung orthodoxischer Leer vom h. Abendmal. *s.n.* [1575.] 8°. 1568/8652

Estienne, Henri. Oratio ad Rodolphum II aduersus lucubrationem Vberti Folietæ. *Typis Wechelianis: Francofordii*, 1594. 8°. Davis II, 348
— Orationes II. I. Aduersus lib. Vberti Folietæ. II. Ad expeditionem in Turcas persequendam exhortatoria. *Typis Stephani Myliandri: Rostochii; sumptibus Laurentii Alberti:* [*Lübeck,*] 1595. 8°. 1090.c.18

Euclid. [*Elementa.*] Das sibend, acht vnd neünt bûch Euclidis. *Tr.* Johann Scheybl. *Valentin Ottmar: Augspurg*, 1555. 4°. C.107.bb.66

Euonymus, *Philiatrus, pseud.* [i.e. **Conrad Gesner.**] Thesaurus de remediis secretis. *Per Andream Gessner f.& Rodolphum Vuyssenbachium: Tiguri*, 1552. 8°. 1568/1362

Euripides. [*Single Plays.*] Tragœdia Hecaba. *Ed.* Joannes Posselius. *Gr. Typis Stephani Myliandri: Rostochii*, 1595. 8°. 1578/2377

Evagatorium. [Euagatoriū Benemy.] [With other works.] *Retro minores: Colonie*, 1499. 8°. IA.5157(impf.)

Evangelical Penitence. De poenitentia euangelica et confessione. [*Valentin Curio: Basle,* 1521.] 4°. C.111.c.23

Evangelical War. Summarium dess Euangelischen, das ist, Schmalkaldischen Kriegs. [*Ivo Schöffer: Mainz?,*] 1548. 4°. 1347.a.3

Evax, *King of Arabia.* Marbodaei De gemmarum formis opusculū. *Ed.* Alardus Amstelredamus. *Hero Alopecius: Coloniæ*, 1539. 8°. 987.b.28

Eyssvogel, Johann. Ein schön newes Lied, darinnen der Betrug der Hueterischen Widertauffer vor Augen gestellt wirdt. *Wolffgang Eder: Ingolstatt*, 1586. 8°. 11525.aa.61

Eytzinger, Michael von, *Baron.* Postrema relatio historica. (Appendix. — Appendicis appendix.) *Ger.* 3 pt. [*Gottfried von Kempen: Cologne,*] 1588, 89. 4°. C.127.d.3

F

Faber, Gellius. [Eine antwert vp einen breeff der Wedderdöper.] *By Ambrosio Kerckenher: Magdeburg*, [ca.1557.] 4°. C.53.d.9(frag.)

Faber, Henricus. Compendiolum musicæ pro incipientibus. *In officina typographica Georgij Hantzsch: Lipsiæ*, 1556. 8°. Hirsch I.164

Faber, Petrus, *Arvernus.* Ad Petri Carpenterii de retinendis armis consilium responsio. *Neustadii*, 1575. 8°. *The imprint is fictitious.* 8026.de.4

Fabri, Wenceslaus, *de Budweis.* [Aderlasstafel.] [*Johann Winterburg: Vienna,* 1513.] *s.sh.* fol. C.18.e.3(33)(frag.)

Fabricius, Andreas, *Leodius.* Religio patiens. Tragœdia. *Apud Maternum Cholinum: Coloniæ*, 1566. 8°. 1606/1413

Fabricius, Georgius, *Chemnicensis.* De metallicis rebus observationes. [*Jacob Gessner:*] *Tiguri*, 1566. 8°. *A separate issue of the sheets otherwise published as part of Conrad Gesner's "De omni rerum fossilium genere".* 1509/2218

Fachineus, Andreas. Controuersiarum iuris tomi tres. *Ex typographia Adami Sartorii: Ingolstadii,* 1600. fol. 1605/331

Falloppio, Gabriello. [*Collections.*] Opera omnia. *Hæredes Andreæ Wecheli: Francofurti,* 1584. fol. 1575/227

Farkas, Márton. Newe Zeittung: von grawsamen Morden, so von zweyen Vbelthetern (Martin Farkasch, Paul Wasansky) bekennet sind worden. *Bey Georgen Daschitsky: Prag,* [1570.] 4°. C.185.a.26(3)

Fasciculus. Fasciculus tēporum. [By W. Rolewinckius.] [*J. Prüss: Strasburg,* not before 1490.] fol. IB.1758

Faunteus, Laurentius Arturus. Apologia libri sui de inuocatione contra Danielis Tossani criminationes. *In officina Birckmannica sumptibus Arnoldi Mylij: Coloniæ Agrippinæ,* 1589. 8°. 1607/503(1)

Felman, Tyman. An den groszmechtigsten Fürsten Karolum ein Suplication. [*Martin Flach the Younger: Strasburg,* 1519.] 4°. 11521.ee.10

Fener von Weyl, Georg. Eyn sturm wyder eyn leymen thurm. *See* Roman Preacher.

Ferinarius, Joannes. Orationes duæ. *Iohannes Schuuertel: VVitebergæ,* 1567. 8°. 1651/319(4)

Ferrandus, Fulgentius. Ad reginum comitem paræneticus, qualis esse debeat dux religiosus in actibus militaribus. *Apud Iohannem Heruagium: Argentorati,* 1526. 8°. 1568/9046

Feyerabend, Sigmund. Kurtzweilige vnd lächerliche Geschicht vñ Historien. Ed. S. Feyerabend. *Gedruckt durch Christoff Raben, in verlegung Sigmund Feyerabendts: Franckfort am Mayn,* 1583. fol. C.107.h.28

Ficino, Marsiglio. De triplici vita. [*Johann Amerbach, Johann Petri & Johann Froben?: Basle,* ca.1507.] 4°. 1039.h.11; 1560/4460;1560/4465

Finck, Hermannus. Practica Musica. *Typis hæredum Georgii Rhauu: Vitebergæ,* 1556. 4°. *A different edition from that at* 1042.k.1. Hirsch I.173

Fischer, Bartholomaeus. Gratulatorii versus in celebritatem nuptiarum Bartholomæi, Francisci Fischeri filii. *Ex officina typographica Abrahami Lambergi: Lipsiæ,* [1594.] 4°. 1568/6707

Flacius, Mathias, *Illyricus.* Kurtze anwort [*sic*] auff der Schmach Zettel. [*Heinrich Geissler: Regensburg,* 1562.] 4°. 1509/3951

— Ein Sendbrieff an einen guten Freund, von der gedruckten Schmehezettel. [*Urban Gaubisch: Eisleben,*]1562. 4°. RB.23.a.3145

— Von der Disputation zwischen Matthia Flacio vnd den Jesuitischen Doctoren zu Fulda. *s.l.* 1573. 4°. 1608/1907

— Wider den Euangelisten des heiligen Chorrocks, D. Geitz Maior. *Basel,* 1552. 4°. *The imprint is false; printed by Michael Lotter at Magdeburg.* C.135.d.9

Flamand, Claude. La guide des fortifications. (Les mathematiques.) 2 pt. I. *Foillet: Montbéliard,* 1597. 8°. C.75.a.3

Flaschius, Sebastian. Professio Catholica. *Ex officina typographica Alexandri Uueyssenhorn & eius cohæredum: Ingolstadii,* 1576. 4°. 1578/390

Fleissner, Georg. Ritter Orden des podagrischen Fluss. *s.l.* 1594. 8°. 1568/8358

Foesius, Anutius. Oeconomia Hippocratis. *Apud Claudium Marnium & Io.Aubrium: Francofurdi,* 1588. fol. 539.i.9

Formula. Formula viuendi canonicorum. [By Werner Rolewinckius.] [*Arnold ther Hoernen: Cologne*, ca. 1475.] 4°. IA.3103

Formulare. [Formulare vnd Tütsch rethorica.] *Johannes prüss: Strassburg*, 1502. fol. 1562/263(2)(impf.)

Fornerus, Fridericus, *Bishop of Hebron*. Vom Ablass vnd Jubeljar orthodoxischer Bericht. *Durch Andream Angermayer: Ingolstatt*, 1599. 4°. 1609/5437

Fox, John. Locorum communium tituli & ordines centum quinquaginta. *Apud Ioannem Oporinum: Basileæ*, 1557. 8°. 1386.i.9

France. — **Henry III.,** *King*. Remonstrance au Roy sur le faict des deux edicts dōnez à Lyon [10 Sept. & 13 Oct. 1574]. [With the texts.] *Gabriel Iason: Aygenstain*, 1576. 8°. *The imprint is fictitious; printed in Basle?* 1193.c.4(1)

— [*Appendix.*] Kurtzer vnd warhafftiger Begriff newer zeitungen auss Franckreich, Italien. *Wilhelm Lützenkirchen: Cölln*, 1593. 4°. 1568/9001

— — Newe zeitung aus Franckreich. Warhafftige Erklerung was sich verlauffen in Kriegshandlung. *s.l.* 1576. 4°. 1508/650

— — Newe Zeyttung auss Franckreich. Sumarische anzeigung als dessen so sich zwischen dem Königischen vnd Hugenottischen Kriegsuolck zugetragen hat. *Durch Jacobum Weiss: Cöln*, [1570.] 4°. 1508/649

— — Ain schöner Dialogus zwischen ainem Priester vn̄ Ritter von einer steür über die gaistlichenn in Frāckreich. *Tr.* Joseph Pollinger. [*Augsburg?*, 1579.] 4°. 3907.bb.9

Francis, *of Assisi, Saint*. Alcoranus Franciscanorum [extracted by Erasmus Alberus from Bartholomaeus de' Rinonichi's "Liber conformitatum vitae Beati Francisci", *pref.* M. Luther]. (Alcoranus Dominicanorum e sermonibus Gabrielis Baraleti collectus.) *s.n.* [ca. 1544.] 8°. C.190.d.19

Francisci, Adamus. Margarita theologica. Źemcźuga theologischka. (Apie popieszischkaie missche. [By] Aegidius Hunnius.) *Tr.* Simonas Waischnors. *Per Jurgi Osterbergerą: Karaliaucziuie Prusu*, 1600. 8°. 3557.aaa.9

Franck, Caspar. Ein schön new geystlich Lied, vom schlaff vnd aufferstehung der Christen. *See* Christians.

— Ein Trostbüchlein wieder das Schrecken für der Sünde. *Ed.* Joachimus Francus. *Michael Wolrab: Budissin*, 1581. 8°. 1509/2041(3)

— Von dem ordentlichen beruff der Priester. *Alexander Weissenhorn, inn verwaltung vnnd kosten Annæ Weissenhornin: Ingolstatt*, 1571. 8°. 1578/6779

Franck, Sebastian. Paradoxa ducenta octoginta auss der H. Schrifft. *Johan Varnier: Vlm*, [1534.] 4°. C.186.e.9

Franck von Franckenstein, Valentinus. Tractatus de fideiussoribus. *Michael Lantzenberger, impensis Henningi Grosii: Lipsiæ*, 1594. 4°. 497.b.3(1)

Frankfort-on-the-Main. — **Ministers.** Entschuldigung der diener am Euangelio Jesu Christi zu Franckfurt vff einen Sendbrieff Martin Luthers. [By Martin Bucer.] [*Christian Egenolff: Frankfort*, 1533.] 4°. 3905.ee.126

Frantz, Wolffgang. Jar rechnung. *Jacob Kündig: Basel*, 1556. 8°. C.190.a.23(1)

— Treidt vnnd Zentner rechnung. *Jacob Kündig: Basel*, [1556.] 8°. C.190.a.23(2)

— Win Rechnung. *Jacob Kündig: Basel*, 1556. 8°. C.190.a.23(3)

21

Franzoesische Zeitung. *See* French News.

French Border. Gründlicher Bericht von dem gewaltigen Zorn Gottes, so er aus hat gehen lassen an der Frantzösischen Grentze. [In verse.] *Bey Samuel Apiario: Basel,* 1581. 8°. 11517.aaa.28

French News. Merckliche frantzösische Zeitung von den Ceremonien, so bei dem RitterOrden vom H.Geist gebraucht. [With texts by Johann Fischart.] [*Bernhard Jobin: Strasburg,*] 1579. 4°. 1608/3344

Frenzelius, Salomon. Ad Germaniam oratio de calamitate Turcicá. *Typis Georgij Mulleri: VVitebergae,* 1594. 8°. 1509/3173(2)

— Epigrammatum sylvula prima. *Typis Georgij Mulleri: VVitebergæ,* 1593. 8°.
1509/3173(1)

— Monomachia divi Georgii & draconis Libyci. *Typis Iacobi Lucii: Helmstadii,* 1595. 4°. 1568/8052

Frese, Rembertus. Carmen gratulatorium in honorem Edonis Hilderici. *Per Augustinum Colbium: Martisburgi Cattorum,* 1578. 4°. 837.h.3(32)

— Tragica historia de miseranda laniena. Per F.R.E.F.O.O. [i.e. R. Frese.] [*Eewardus Oostfreese: Emden,* 1584?] 8°. G.9859

— [A reissue.] Tragica historia de miseranda laniena. *Evvardus Frisius: Æmdæ,* 1584. 8°. G.9858

Friedrich, *Count.* Ein gar schön Lied von Graff Friderichen. *Friderich Gutknecht: Nürnberg,* [ca.1555?] 8°. 11517.aaa.29

Frischlin, Nicodemus. Epistolæ duæ. *Apud Alexandrum Hockium: Tubingæ,* 1575. 8°. 1509/3827

— Hildegardis magna. *Apud Georgium Gruppenbachium: Tubingæ,* 1579. 8°.
1509/3828

Frith, John. A boke answering unto M.Mores lettur. *Conrade Willems: Monster,* 1523. 16°. *The imprint is fictitious; printed at Antwerp by Henrick Peetersen?* C.12.b.9(3)

Froeschel, Vigilius, *Bishop.* [A mandamus dated Passau, 20 Dec.1508.] [*Erhard Ratdolt: Augsburg,* 1509?] fol. C.129.k.2(5);C.129.k.2(6)

Funck, Johann. Ein Sermon vber das Euangelion Matthei ix. *Hans Weinreych: Königsberg jn Preüssen,* 1548. 4°. 1578/6335

G

Gaius, *the Jurist.* Institutionum libri duo. *Per Ioannem Schæffer: Mogunt.,* 1529. 8°. C.113.a.14(2)

Galen. [*Two or more Works.*] Duo libri, vnus de plenitudine, alter de curatiua sanguinis missione. *Tr.* Christophorus Heyl. *Ex officina Francisci Rhodi: Dantisci,* 1558. 4°. C.117.ff.13

Gallus, Nicolaus. Confutationes etzlicher gegenwertiger Secten. *Jhena,* 1562. 8°. 1578/355

Gameren, Hannardus de. Via regia ad Musas. *Adamus Berg: Monachii,* 1567. 8°. 1509/2588

Garcaeus, Johann. Sterbbüchlein. (Tractetlein von den Seelen der verstorbenen. Durch Basilium Fabrum.) *Peter Seitz: Wittemberg,* 1568. 8°. RB.23.a.341(1)

— Eine vermanung von Schulen. *Witteberg,* 1571. 4°. 1578/4054

Gardiner, Stephen, *Bishop.* Ad Martinum Bucerum de impudenti eiusdem Pseudologia Conquestio. *Ex officina Melchioris Nouesiani: Coloniæ,* 1545. 4°. 1226.b.1; 3906.bb.76(6)
Gebhardt, Joannes. Lusus poeticus. *Typis Nicolai Voltzij: Francofurti,* 1600. 4°. 1481.aaa.43(2)
Gebrauch. Rechter Gebrauch d' Alchimei. [*Christian Egenolff: Frankfort on the Main,*] 1531. 4°. 8907.aa.2
Gechauf, Thomas. De uirtute Christiana libri III. *Fœdericus* [sic] *Peypus, impensis Leonardi de Aich: Norimbergae,* 1529. 8°. RB.23.a.609
— Ein kurtze vnterricht von beyden sacramenten. *Johann Stüchs: Nürnberg,* 1530. 8°. 1568/8031
Geiler, Johann, *von Kaisersberg.* [Der bawm der selen heil.] Arbor salutis anime. *Tr.* Johannes Schiplitz. *Per Martinum tretter: in vrbe Franckenfordensi cis Oderam,* 1502. 8°. C.145.e.12
— [Sermones de arbore humana.] Das buoch Arbore humana. *Getruckt vō Johanne grieninger: Strassburg,* 1521. fol. C.102.k.23
Geldenhaurius, Gerardus. Institutio scholæ Christianæ. *Apud Christianum Aegenolphum: Francofurti,* 1534. 8°. 1606/718
Gemma. Vocabularius Gemma vocabulorum. *Per me Mauritiū Brandiss: Magdeborch,* 1497. 4°. IA.10958
George, *Prince of Anhalt.* Conciones synodicæ. *Ed.* Joachimus Camerarius. *In officina Ualentini Papæ: Lipsiæ,* 1555. 8°. C.135.e.12
— Von dem hochwirdigen Sacrament des Leibs vnd Bluts Jhesu Christi vier Predigten. 2 pt. *Wolff Günter: Leipzig,* 1551. 4°. 1568/5403
— Zwo predigten über das Euangelium Matth.vij. von falschen Propheten. *Wolff Günter: Leipzig,* 1552. 4°. 1578/1812
George John, *Count of Pfalz-Veldenz.* Oratio de Scholæ Heydelbergensis instauratione. *Ex officina Ioannis Carbonis: Heydelbergae,* 1558. 4°.
1509/1711
Gerardus, Andreas, *Hyperius.* Elementa Christianæ religionis. *Per Thomam Guarinum: Basileæ,* 1563. 8°. 3559.aa.5
Gerardus, Arnoldus. De fide Catholica liber vnus. *Apud Maternum Cholinum: Coloniae,* 1556. 8°. 1607/4272
German Language. Eyn schone Lere, mit kortzen synnen begriffen Deutsch vnd Polnisch zu redenn. *Durch Jeronimum Vietorem: Krokaw,* 1544. 8°.
C.125.aaa.1
German Vigil. De düdesche Vigilie. [*Johann Balhorn: Lübeck,* ca.1535?] 8°.
11501.aa.3
Germany. — Charles V., *Emperor.* Romischer kayserlicher Maiestat Ordnungen, wie wider die vergweltiger, bschediger vnd landtfridens verprecher gehandelt werden sol. [10 Feb. 1522.] [*Silvan Otmar: Augsburg,* 1522.] fol. D.c.5/8
— — [Interim, 15 May 1548.] Bericht vom Interim der Theologen zu Meissen versamlet. [*Christian Rödinger: Magdeburg,* 1548.] 4°. 3906.b.15
— — — [Another edition.] [*Christian Rödinger; Magdeburg,* 1548.] 4°.
3905.g.21
— — Ordenung vnd Mandat vernewert im April Anno 1550. Zu aussrotten die Secten [and other matter]. *Ed.* Mathias Flacius. [*Christian Rödinger: Magdeburg,* 1550.] 4°. C.190.aaa.33

— **Ferdinand I.**, *King of the Romans.* [A proclamation enjoining preparation against a Turkish invasion. 23 Dec. 1536.] [*Johann Singriener: Vienna,* 1536.] *s.sh. obl.* fol.   KTC.7.b.5

— **Reichstag.** Abschiedt dess Reichsstags zu Regenspurg anno M.D.XLI. [*Ivo Schöffer:*] *Meyntz,* 1541. fol.   C.144.d.12

Gersonites, *Landavus,* pseud. [i.e. **Georg Witzel,** *the Elder.*] Causa tam diuturnæ calamitatis ecclesiastici status in Germania. *Ex officina Quenteliana: Coloniæ,* 1546. 8°.   3905.b.12

Gese, Johann. Christliche vermanung aus dem CXXVIII. Psalm. *Lorentz Schwenck: Witteberg,* 1565. 4°.   1509/1698

Gesicht. Ein wunderbarlich gesicht so von vielen am himel gesehen ist worden. *s.l.* [ca.1555?] 4°.   11517.dd.20(5)

Gesner, Conrad. Sanitatis tuendæ præcepta. *Per Iacobum Gesnerum: Tiguri,* [ca.1560.] 8°.   1651/319(2)

Gespraechbuechlein. Ein tröstlich gesprechbüchlein auff frag vnd antwort gestellet, den glawben vnd die lieb betreffend. *Hans Lufft: Wittemberg,* 1525. 8°.   C.190.d.20(2)

Gienger, Georg. New Christlich teutsch Betbuech. (Lectionbüch.) 2 pt. *Michael Zimmerman: Wien,* [ca.1562?] 8°.   1018.f.11

Gigas, Johann. Ein schön news tröstlichs Lied, in Sterbens läufften. *Durch Mattheum Francken: Augspurg,* [ca.1565?] 8°.   C.175.i.31(52)

Giovio, Paolo. Elogia virorum literis illustrium. *Industria & opera Petri Pernæ, sumptibus communibus cum Henrico Petri: Basileæ,* 1577. fol.   C.189.c.8

Glait, Oswald. Die zehen Gebott Gottes, zu singen. *Heinrich Geisler: Regenspurg,* 1561. 8°.   C.175.i.31(58)

Gletting, Benedikt. Der geystlich Joseph. *Durch Mattheum Francken: Augspurg,* [ca.1560?] 8°.   C.175.i.31(55)

— Die geystliche Bilgerfart. [*Matthäus Franck: Augsburg,* ca.1560?] 8°.   C.175.i.31(5)

Goedeman, Caspar. Drey Osterpredigten. *Durch Clemens Schleich & Antonium Schöne: Wittemberg,* 1577. 8°.   1568/6075(2)

Goetling, Caspar. Memorial der Summarien aller Bücher der Bibel. *Durch Nicolaum Schneider: Liegnitz,* 1593. 8°.   1214.a.17

Gogrevius, Mento. Bekentniss vnd Lehre, von wahrer gegenwertigkeit des Leibs vnd Bluts Christi im Abendtmal. *Cunrad Horn: HeinrichStadt,* 1571. 8°.   1568/9045

Goldwurm, Caspar. Kirchen Calender. *Christian Egenolffs Erben: Franckfurt am Mayn,* 1597. 8°.   1228.a.13

— Die schöne Historia von Joseph. *Georgen Rhawen Erben: Wittemberg,* 1551. 4°.   1578/5656(impf.)

Golius, Theophilus. Onomasticon latinogermanicum. *Iosias Rihelius: in libera Argentina,* 1590. 8°.   1578/5618

Goltz, Hubert. Lebendige Bilder gar nach allen Keysern. *Für Hubertum Gholtz; in Ægidij Copenij Truckerey: Anttorff,* 1557. fol.   816.m.26

Goniaeus, Joannes. Selectarum declamationum professorum Academiæ Ienensis tomus primus. *Ed. J. Goniaeus. Blasius Fabricius: Argentorati,* 1554. 8°.   1578/5654

Gordonio, Bernardus de. Tractatus de conseruatione vitæ humanæ. Imprimebat Iohannes Rhamba, curante Ernesto Vogelin: Lipsiæ, 1570. 8°.
1039.c.11

Gottingen. [Official Documents.] Christliche Kirchenordnung. Martin Lechler, in verlegung Simon Hüters: Franckfurt am Mayn, 1568. 4°. 1509/4707

Gra., The. See Graminaeus, D.

Graitz. See Greitz.

Graminaeus, Dietrich. Mysticus Aquilo. Epistola VVilhelmi Damasi Lindani. Apud Ludouicum Alectorium & hæredes Iacobi Soteris: Coloniæ, 1576. 8°. 1568/6071

— Trutina pacis. Hær. Sot.: Col., 1579. 4°. 1608/637

Gratianus, the Canonist. Decretum. Com. Bartholomaeus Brixiensis. Michael wenssler: in vrbe Basilea, 1481. fol. IC.37104

Greff, Wolffgangus. Eyn Gebet in Gesangsweise, vmb errettunge der Christlichen Kirchen. Durch Georgium Bawman: Erffurdt, 1559. 8°.
C.175.i.31(45)

Gregory III., Pope. Der Weiber Krieg wider den Bapst, darumb das er zehen tage aus dem Calender gestollen hat. s.l. 1590. 4°. 1347.a.16(4)

Greitz. — **Preachers.** Confessionschrifft etlicher Predicanten in Graitz, Geraw, Schönburg. [Andreas Petri: Eisleben?, 1567.] 4°. 1578/2381

Grimaldi Robio, Pelegro. [Discorsi.] Cordissiano. Tr. Matthias Leyman, rev. Petrus Colman. Ger. Durch Nicolaum Bassum, in verlegung Sigmund Feyerabendt: Franckfurt am Mayn, 1571. 8°. C.136.bb.32

Gropper, Johann, Cardinal. Wie bei haltung vnd reichung der sacramenten die Priester das volck vnderrichten mögen. Jaspar von Gennep: Cöllen, 1549. 8°. 1578/6029

Gruenfelt, Friderich. Antwortt auff Joannis Pollicarij schrifften wider den Bischoffen zur Nawmburgk. Durch die Erben Johan Quentels & Gerwinū Caleniū: Cöln, 1562. 4°. 1578/1817

Grunius, Joannes. Σκιαγραφία scholæ trivialis recte aperiendæ. Typis Simonis Gronenbergii: Vitebergæ, 1579. 8°. 1568/8843

Gueltlingen, Balthasar von. Newe zeitung vnd Relation, so Balthasar von Gültlingen an den Hälen hauffen der Landtsknecht gethan hat. s.n. [1546.] 4°. 4662.aa.15

Guentherus, Petrus. De arte rhetorica libri duo. ī officina libraria Ioannis Schæffer: Moguntiae, 1521. 4°. 1560/3507

Guethel, Caspar. Eyn selig New iar. [Matthes Maler:] Erffurdt, 1522. 4°.
1568/6154

— Von den straffen vnd plagen, die Gott vber die Jüden hat verhangen lassen. [Gabriel Kantz: Zwickau,] 1529. 4°. 4034.bbb.8

Guevara, Antonio de, Bishop. Lustgarten vnd Weckvhr. Tr. Aegidius Albertinus. Tl.1, 2. Durch Nicolaum Henricum: München, 1599. 8°.
1568/5457

Guido, de Monte Rocherii. Manipulus curatoɤ. Per Cōradum de hombourch: Colonie, 1478. fol. IB.4028

Gunarius, Halvardus. Ἀκροστιχις de inauguratione Christiani Quarti. Typis Myliandrinis: Rostochii, [1596.] 4°. 154.e.7(2)

Gundermann, Christoph, pseud. Ein klechlich Gesprech Christophori Gundermans. s.l. 1591. 4°. 1568/9244

Guntherus, *Cisterciensis.* Ligurinus. *Ed.* Conradus Rittershusius. 2 pt. *Apud Georgium Gruppenbachium: Tubingæ,* 1598,97. 8°. 1608/3543

Gustavus I. [Vasa], *King of Sweden.* Von der grausamen Mysshandlunge, so Künig Christiern von Deñmarck im Reich zů Sweden begangen hat. [*Peter Schöffer the Younger: Worms,* 1524.] 4°. 9435.cc.1

Guthel, Caspar. *See* Guethel.

H

H., A.S. Newe Zeitung von dem grossen Pültz. *s.l.* 1567. 8°. 11522.aaa.10(1)

H., C. Von gůten züchtigen sitten ein vast nutzlich büchlin. *Christoffel Froschouer: Zürich,* 1539. 8°. 11515.a.15

Habermann, Johann. Grammatices Ebraicæ linguæ tres partes. 3 pt. *Ex officina Cratoniana: Witebergæ,* 1597. 8°. 1607/5083

Haendl, Jacobus. Moralia quinque, sex et octo vocibus. 5 pt. *In officina typographica Alexandri Theodorici: Noribergæ,* 1596. *obl.*4°. K.3.f.19(impf.)

Haferitz, Simon. Ein Sermō vom Fest der heiligen drey Konig. [*Jakob Stöckel & Nikolaus Widemar: Eilenburg,*] 1524. 4°. 3906.d.32

Haich, Heinrich. [A copy of a will dated 4 July 1452.] [*Hermann Bumgart: Cologne,* ca.1510?] fol. KTC.23.a.2(1)

Hájek, Václav, *z Libocan.* Böhmische Chronica. *Tr.* Johannes Sandel. 2 Tl. *Gedruckt durch Nicolaum Straus: Prag; inn Verlegung Andreassen Weidlichs: Brüx,* 1596. fol. C.185.b.2

Hall, *Suabian.* [Syngramma clarissimorum qui Halæ Sueuorum conuenerunt virorum. Gegrundter beschlus etlicher Prediger zu Schwaben.] *See* Suabia.

Haller, Berthold, *Reformer.* Ein Christenlich gespräch gehalten zů Berñ zwüschen den Predicanten [B.Haller and others] vñ Hansen Pfyster Meyer von Arouw. [*Christoph Froschauer: Zürich,*] 1531. 8°. 3908.bbb.14

Handl, Jacobus. *See* Haendl.

Hanober, Georg. Seltzame vnerhörte newe zeytung, wz gestalt Georg Hanober ist hingerichtet worden. *Strassburg,* 1597. 4°. 1347.a.16(7)

Harmonius, Joannes, *Marsus.* Comoedia Stephanium. *Hieronymus Vietor: Vienñ,* 1515. 4°. 11712.c.71

Hartman, Georgius. [Woodcut designs for an astrolabe.] [*Nuremberg,*] 1551. *s.sh. obl.* fol. Tab.597.d.1(7)

— Compast oder Sonnen Vr. [*Nuremberg,*] 1551. *s.sh. obl.* fol. Tab.597.d.1(3)

Hatzger, Anton. Compendium artis notariatus. *Ger. Bernhardt Dalbin: Speyr,* 1596. 8°. 706.a.16(2)

Hebenstreit, Christoff. Ein new Lied, Ach Gott eyl mir zů helf. *s.n.* [ca.1552.] 8°. 11522.df.90

— Ein news Lied, Ach Gott wem soll ichs klagen. [*Matthäus Franck: Augsburg?,* ca.1560?] 8°. C.175.i.31(3)

Hebenstreit, Joannes. Wunderzeichen, so sich an Son vnnd Mond begeben. *Jeremias Portenbach: Erfordt,* [1564.] 4°. 1578/3114

Hebeysen, Valentin. Helden Lied von Doctor Luthern. *s.n.* [1590.] 8°. 11522.df.80

Heerbrand, Jacob. Ein Predig von dem Wunderzeichen am Himmel. *Georg Gruppenbach: Tübingen,* 1577. 4°. 1509/3956

Hefftrich, Martinus. De substitutionibus. *Praes.* Joannes Barterus. *Hæredes Iacobi Lucij: Helmaestadii,* 1598. 4°. 500.c.5(2)

Hegesippus, *Historical Writer.* De rebus à Iudæorum principibus in obsidione gestis libri V. *Tr. St.* Ambrose. *Iohannes Soter: apud sanctā Coloniam,* 1530. fol. 1602/150

Heidenreich, Esaias. Hauss liedlein zur zeit der Pestilentz zu singen. [*Crispin Scharffenberg:*] *Bresslaw,* [ca.1570?] 8°. 11517.b.39(3)

— Sechs vnd zwantzig Busspredigten vber den Propheten Joel. *Georg Defner: Leiptzig,* 1581. 8°. 1509/2041(1)

— Vierzehen Lehr vnd Trostpredigten vber das Gebet Mosis. *Georg Defner: Leiptzig,* 1581. 8°. 1509/2041(2)

Heidenstein, Reinhold. De bello Moscouitico commentariorum libri VI. *Per Conrad. Valdkirchium: Basileæ,* 1588. 4°. 1056.g.6; 150.a.6

Heilandus, Samuel. Aristotelis Ethicorum Nicomachum libri decem expositi. *Georgius Gruppenbachius: Tubingæ,* 1588. 8°. Cup.407.m.47

Heilbronn. [*Official Documents.*] Statuten, Satzung, Reformation vnd Ordnung burgerlicher Pollicey. [*Jobst Gutknecht: Nuremberg,* 1541.] fol. C.186.dd.7

Heilbrunner, Jacob. Synopsis doctrinæ Caluinianæ. *Ger.* 2 vol. *Leonhard Reinmichel: Laugingen,* 1591, 95. 4°. 1609/2708

Helding, Michael, *Bishop.* Predig auff den grienen donnerstag von der heyligisten Eucharistia. *Alexander Weissenhorn: Ingolstat,* 1548. 4°. 3906.c.5

Helias, Petrus. Tractatus nominū diminutiuorū. [*Martin Landsberg: Leipzig,* ca.1494.] 4°. IA.11946

Helmreich, Andreas. Ein gründlichs kunstbüchlein, wie man etzen soll. *Vrban Gaubisch: Eisleben,* [1563.] 8°. 1560/4188(2)

Hendschele, Tobias. Disputatio theologica de theologiæ necessitate. *Praes.* Gregorius de Valentia. *Ex officina typographica Dauidis Sartorii: Ingolstadii,* [1589.] 4°. 3559.aaa.24

Henricpetri, Jacobus. [Pro solemni inauguratione doctorali Iacobus Henricpetri de pactis positio. disput. tueb.] [*Typis Leonh. Ostenij: Basileæ,* 1592.] 4°. 1508/1593(impf.)

Henricus, *de Wrimaria.* Preceptoriū. [*Nicolaus Gotz: Cologne,* ca.1475.] fol. IB.3842

Henry I. [de Lorraine], *Duke de Guise.* Kurtze beschreibung des Lottringischen vnd Guisischen einfals in die Graueschafft Mümpelgart. *Ed.* Johann Fischart. [*Bernhard Jobin: Strasburg,*]1588. 4°. 1609/3307

Henry VIII., *King of England.* Ad Saxoniç principes de coercenda abigendaq̃ Lutherana factione & Luthero ipso epistola. [With other matter.] *Ed.* Hieronymus Emser. *Vvolffgangus Monacensis: Lipsie,* [1523.] 4°. C.175.c.4

Henry IV., *King of France.* Erklärung vnd Protestation des Königs von Nauarra vnnd des Printzē von Conde vnd des Hertzogen zu Mommerantz. [10 Aug.1585.] *Bergerach,* 1585. 4°. *The imprint is false; printed at Strasburg by Bernhard Jobin.* 1609/3308

Henry Julius, *Duke of Brunswick-Wolfenbüttel.* Comœdia von einem Edelmann, welcher einem Abt drey Fragen auffgegeben. *See* A., H.I.B.A.L.D.E.H.

Herbarius. Herbarius. [*Johann Petri:*] *Patauie,* [14]86. 4°. IA.11329

Herbst, Georg. Notwendige vnd grundliche verantwortung auff zwey falsche Zeugnuss Christophori Irenæi. *Durch Johannem Burger: Regenspurg,* 1575. 4°. C.107.bb.84(6)

Herdesianus, Christoph. *See* also Pacificus, Hermanus, *pseud.*

Hermann, Nicolaus. Ein geystliches Lied, von der Aufferstehung der Todten. *See* Lied.

Heshusius, Tilemannus, *Bishop.* [*Letters.*] De exorcismo in actione baptismi epistolæ tres, quarum duæ à Tilemano Heshusio, tertia à Philippo Melanchthone scripta. *Ex officina typographica Achatij Liscani: Halae Saxonum,* 1591. 4°. 1568/1047

— Das Jesu Christi Leib vnd Blut im heiligen Abendmal gegenwertig sey. *Wolff Kirchener: Magdeburg,* 1560. 4°. 1608/2882

— Oratio de synodis Ecclesiæ. *Guntherus Huttichius: Ienæ,* 1571. 8°. 1578/4048

— Oratio in qua refutatur calumnia Osiandri. *Ex officina Cratoniana: VVittebergæ,* 1553. 8°. 1568/8851

— [*Appendix.*] Von enturlaubung Tilemanni Hesshusij erzelung der geschicht. *Durch Joachim Walden: Magdeburgk,* 1564. 4°. 1509/3094

Hesiod. [*Works.*] Opera. Gr. & Lat. Iohannes Steinman typis Voegelinianis: *Lipsiæ,* 1572. 8°. C.189.d.24

Hess, Ernst Ferdinand. Flagellum Iudeorum. Juden Geissel. *Bey Martin: Wittel: Erffurdt,* 1600. 8°. 4033.de.7(3)

Heupoldus, Bernhardus. Ein künstlich Lossbüchlin. [*Heirs of Christian Egenolff?:*] *Franckfurt,* 1595. 8°. C.106.a.14

Heydeck, Friedrich von. An Herrn Walthern vonn Blettenbergk, eyn Christlich Ermanung czu der leer Christi. [*Hans Weinreich:*] *Königssberg ynn Preussen,* [1526.] 4°. 3908.d.25

Heyden, Sebaldus. Die Einsetzung vnd brauch des heyligen Abentmals. *Hermañ Hamsing: Nüremberg,* 1553. 8°. 11517.aa.36

— Pædonomia scholastica. *In officina Ioannis Montani & Vlrici Neuber: Noribergæ,* 1550. 8°. RB.23.a.1808

— Puerilium colloquiorum formulæ. Lat., Czech & Ger. *Skrze Jana Hada Kantora: w Starém Miestie Pražském,* 1557. 8°. C.114.r.26(4)

Hildebrand, *Hero of Romance.* Das lied von dem alten Hiltebrant. *Christoff Gutknecht: Nürnberg,* [ca.1545.] 8°. 11517.aa.26

Hiller, Matheus. Vonn geferlichen verenderungen in dieser Welt. *Leipzig,* 1586. 4°. 11517.ee.50(9)

Hiltstein, Johannes. Geistliche vnd christliche Gesenge. *Görg Bawman: Erffurdt,* 1557. 8°. C.175.i.31(1)

Hippocrates. [*Two or more Works.*] Francisci Vallesii in Aphorismos [and other works] commentarij VII. [With the text.] *Coloniæ; Ioannis Baptistæ Ciotti ære:* [*Venice,*] 1589. fol. *The Cologne imprint is false; printed by Johann Feyerabend at Frankfort on the Main.* 539.h.14

Hoefer, Michael. Wes man sich inn disen gefährlichen zeyten halten soll. *s.l.* 1546. 4°. 3906.h.9

28

Hoffman, Christophorus, *of Ansbach.* De Christiana religione et de regno Antichristi. *Ex officina Petri Brubachij: Francofurti,* 1545. 8°.   4375.aa.26

Hoffmeister, Johann. Articuli conciliati inter nouos ministros. *Ed.* J. Hoffmeister. *Alexander Uueissenhorn: Ingolstadii,* 1546. 8°.   1606/1194

Hofmann, Daniel. Piæ exequiæ, quas ad cohonestandum funus D. Iulii Ducis Brunsuicensium ac Lunæburgensium Academia Iulia orationibus prosecuta est. *Typis Iacobi Lucij: Helmestadii,* 1589. 4°.   1568/8317

Holandrinus, Joannes. Obligationū & insolubiliū tractatul[9] in cōpendiu₃ redact[9] [by Martinus Edlinger]. *Impensis & opera Joannis Winterburger:* [*Vienna,*] 1509. 4°.   C.104.dd.17(4)

Hollen, Gotschalcus. Sermonum opus. 2 pt. *Per industriū Henricū Gran: Hagenaw; expēsis Joannis Rynman:* [*Augsburg,*] 1519, 20. fol.   C.106.f.20

Holthusius, Joannes. Syntaxis. *In officina typographica Michaëlis Mangeri: Augustæ Vindelicorum,* 1582. 8°.   1568/8802

Holtorpius, Bernardus. De peregrinatione Stanislai a Lasco liber primus. *Ioannes VVeinreich: in Academia Regii Montis,* 1548. 4°.   1509/1712

Holtzhausen, *in Thuringia.* Etliche gesichte so zu Holtzhausen gesehen worden. [*Peter Schmidt: Arnstadt?*] 1548. 4°.   1315.c.4(8)

Homer. [*Odyssey.*] Ex Odyssea libri quatuor carmine redditi per Ioannem Prassinum. [Books 9–12.] *Apud Ioannem Lufft: Vitebergae,* 1539. 8°.
1509/2168(2)

Hooper, John, *Bishop.* An answer vnto my lord of wynchesters booke. *Augustyne Fries: Zurych,* 1547. 4°.   C.25.e.32

Hoppenrod, Andreas. Wider den Huren Teufel. *Vrban Gaubisch: Eisleben,* 1566. 8°.   1578/2380

Hortulus. Ortulus anime. The garden of the soule. *Tr.* George Joye. *Francis Foxe: Argentine,* 1530. 16°. *The imprint is false; printed at Antwerp by Martin de Keyser.*   C.107.a.30

Hovaeus, Antonius. De arte amandi Christum libri. Liber præcum. 2 pt. *Apud Maternum Cholinum: Coloniæ,* 1566. 8°.   1509/2168(1)

Huetwol, Johann. Vom churfürstlichen pfaltzischen Bergwerck zu Dhaumbach. *s.l.* 1575. 4°.   1196.f.43(13)

Huguccio, *Bishop.* Tractatulus intricationes nūeralium uocabulorum exponens. [*Martin Landsberg: Leipzig,* ca.1495.] 4°.   IA.11892

Hund, Wigulejus. Bayrisch Stammen Buch. 2 Tl. *Durch Adam Sartorium: Ingolstadt,* 1598. fol.   136.b.7

— Metropolis Salisburgensis. *Ex officina typographica Dauidis Sartorii: Ingolstadii,* 1582. fol.   4660.h.4; C.74.e.9(2)

Hungarian Disease. Artzney vnnd ordnung wider die Vngerische Kranckheyt. *Michael Manger: Augspurg,* 1572. 4°.   7306.de.14(5)

Hunnius, Egidius, *the Elder.* [*Collections.*] Catechismus. Christlicher Hausstaffel nützlicher Erklärung. *Johann Spiess: Franckfort am Mayn,* 1596. 8°.   1578/6008

— Articulus de Trinitate. *Ioannes Spies: Francofurdi ad Mœnum,* 1592. 8°.
1568/6526

— Calvinus iudaizans. *Vidua Matthæi VVelaci: VVitebergæ,* 1593. 8°.
1578/4666(2)

— Catechismus von den Häuptpuncten Christlicher Religion. [*Johann Spiess:*] *Franckfurt am Mayn,* 1592. 4°. C.104.d.7(1)
— Christliche Hausstafel. *Johann Spiess: Franckfurt am Mayn,* 1591. 4°.
C.104.d.7(2)
Huth, Johann. Ein sendbrieff. *Com.* Urbanus Rhegius. *Alexander Weyssenhorn: Augspurg,* 1528. 4°. 3906.aaa.78; 3906.aaa.83
Hyeble, Christoff. Tractat von der aller fürtrefflichsten Artzney wider allerley Gifft. *Bey Nicolao Kalt: Costantz,* 1598. 8°. RB.23.a.3122
Hymnals. [*German.*] Schöne Christliche Gesenge, zum Begrebnus der Todten. [By Michael Weisse.] *Valentin Newber: Nürnberg,* [ca.1555?] 8°.
C.175.i.31(13)

I

Ignatius, *Saint, Bishop of Antioch.* Epistolæ undecim. Beati Polycarpi epistola. *Ioannes Knoblouchus: Argentorati,* 1527. 8°. 1607/2502
Ilferus, Lazarus. Poemation de creatione primorum parentum. *Lat. & Ger. Per Ioachimum VValden: Magdeburgi,* [ca.1570.] 8°. 11521.ee.5
Ingolstetterus, Joannes. De natura occultorum dissertatio. *Abraham Lamberg: Lipsiæ,* 1597. 8°. 1170.b.7
Innocent III., *Pope.* Opera. *Ioannes Nouesianus: Coloniæ,* 1552. fol.
1602/48; 1605/744(1)
Insulanus Menapius, Gulielmus. Diuinatio extremorum mūdi tēporū. *Iaspar Gennepæus: Coloniæ,* 1549. 8°. 1509/3321
Irenaeus, *Saint, Bishop of Lyons.* Irenæi Opus eruditissimum. *Ed.* Desiderius Erasmus & Johann Jacob Grynaeus. *Per Eusebium Episcopium & Nicolai fratris hæredes: Basileæ,* 1571. 8°. Eve.a.91(1)
Irenaeus, Christoph. Censuren vnd Vrtheil der heiligen Propheten, Christi vnd Aposteln. 2 Tl. [*Andreas Petri:*] *Mansfelt,* 1574. 4°. 1568/8829
Isaac, *Monachus.* Scholia in Euclidis Elementorum geometriæ sex priores libros. *Tr. & ed.* Conradus Dasypodius. *Nicolaus Vuyriot: Argentorati,* 1579. 8°. 1578/8070
Isocrates. [*Extracts.*] Ἰσοκρατης γνωμολογηθεις. Sententiæ græcolatinæ. *Ed.* Hieronymus Wolfius. *Ex officina Heruagiana, per Eusebium Episcopium: Basileæ,* 1572. 8°. Davis II, 341
— Φρασεολογία ἰσοκρατικὴ ἑλληνικολατίνη. *Ed.* Michael Neander. *Ex officina Oporiniana: Basileae,* [ca.1580?] 8°. 1608/3402

J

Jābir ibn Ḥaiyān, *al-Ṭarasūsī.* De alchimia libri tres. *Arte & impensa Iohannis Grieninger: Argentoragi,* 1529. fol. 1652/37(1)
Jacob, *the Patriarch.* Drey gaistliche Jacobs Lieder. *Durch Mattheum Francken: Augspurg,* [ca.1560?] 8°. C.175.i.31(27)
Jacob, Nickel. Gründtlicher vnterricht von Wartunge der Bienen. *Durch Ambrosium Fritsch: Görlitz,* 1586. 8°. 1152.a.22
Jacobus [Arrigoni], *Bishop.* Oratio de condemnatione Hieronymi cuiusdam Bragensis [*sic*]. [*Closterdruckerei:*] *Tegernsee,* 1573. 8°. 1568/6079

Jacobus, *de Clusa.* Tractatus saluberrimus in se doctrinas continens. [*Gregorius Boettiger: Leipzig,* ca.1495.] 4°. IA.11848
Jacobus, *de Voragine.* [Legenda aurea.] *J. Koelhoff: Colonie,* 1479. fol. IB.3529
— Legenda sanctoru3 [*Georg Husner:*] *Argentine,* 1479. fol. IB.1041
Jaeger. Ein schön new Lied, Der geistlich Jäger genant. *Bey Hansen Burger: Straubing,* [ca.1562.] 8°. C.175.i.31(30)
Jagenteufel, Andreas. De iustificatione hominis coram Deo assertiones. Praes.Polycarp Leyser. *In officina typographica Simonis Gronenbergii: Vitebergæ,* [1581.] 4°. 3905.d. 84(11)
Jansonius, P. A., *pseud.* [i.e. **Michael ab Isselt?**] Mundi furiosi continuatio. [Dec. 1596–Aug. 1597.] *Apud Gerhardum Greuenbruch: Coloniæ,* 1600. 8°. 582.a. 8
Jena. — **Academia Ienensis.** Bekentnis von der Rechtfertigung für Gott den Theologen in der Vniversitet Jhena. [Signed by Johann Wigand and others.] *Christian Rödinger: Jhena,* 1569. 4°. 1560/2687
Jerome, *Saint.* De essencia diuinitatis. (Summa edita a thoma de aquino de articulis fidei.) [*Günther Zainer: Augsburg,* before 5 June 1473.] fol. IB.5538; IB.5538a(frag.)
Jesus Christ. Ein prophetische Buspredigt für die jenigen, so Christum mit dem Antichrist verfolget haben. See B., G., *Probst zu Berlin.*
— Ein schön geistlich Lied, vom Leiden Jesu Christi. [By Michael Weisse.] *Friderich Gntknecht* [sic]: *Nürnberg,* [ca.1555?] 8°. C.175.i.31(36)
— The true beliefe in Christ and his sacraments. [By Wolfgang Capito.] *Tr.* William Roye. [*Steven Mierdman: Antwerp;*] *for Gwalter Lynne: London,* 1550. 8°. *The body of the text is a reissue of sheets printed by Johann Schott at Strasburg in* 1527. C.38.a.57; C.46.a.7
Jewel, John, *Bishop.* Verantwortung der Christenlichen Kirchen der Kron Engelland. See **England.** — **Church of England.**
Johann, *von Eck.* Explanatio Psalmi vigesimi. *Alexander Vueyssenhorn: Augustæ Vindelicorum,* 1538. 8°. 1509/3822
— Schutz red kindtlicher vnschuld wider Andre Hosander. [*Alexander Weissenhorn: Ingolstadt,*] 1540. 4°. Cup. 408.zzz.61
John, *Chrysostom.* [*De sacerdotio.*] Dialogus de episcopatu & sacerdotio. *Tr.* Germanus Brixius. *Apud Eucharium Ceruicornum: Marpurgi,* 1537. 8°. 1607/2555
John, *of Damascus, Saint.* Omnia opera. *Tr.* Jacques Lefèvre d'Etaples and others. 2 pt. *Henricus Petrus: Basileæ,* 1535. fol. IB.51309(2)
John VI., *Patriarch of Jerusalem.* Ioannis Damasceni uita. *Tr.* Joannes Oecolampadius. [*Sigmund Grimm & Marcus Wirsung;*] παρα τῶ Βερναρδω ἀδελμαννω: ἐν τῇ ἀυγυστα, [1522.] 4°. 4825.c.26
John Frederick, *Elector of Saxony.* Zwey schöne newe Lieder. [In fact, the first by Ambrosius Blaurer, the second anonymous.] *s.n.* [ca.1548.] 8°. 11515.a.17
— Wahrhafftiger Bericht wie Johans Friderich Hertzog zu Sachsen abgeschieden. *s.l.* 1554. 4°. 1578/6523
John William, *Duke of Saxony.* Abdruck: auff vnnd abforderung des Schlosses Grimmenstein vnd Stadt Gotha. *s.l.* 1567. 4°. 1608/3346
Jonas, Justus. The true hystorie of the departynge of Martyne Luther. [*Derick van der Straten: Wesel,* 1546.] 8°. C.115.d.17

— [*Appendix.*] Zwei geistliche schöne newe Lieder, das erste, Herrn Doctor Justus Jonas seeliger Abschied genant. *Hans Kholer: Nürmberg,* [ca. 1565?] 8°. C.175.i.31(66)
Joseph, *the Patriarch.* Ein hüpsch new Lied, von dem Gottesförchtigen Joseph. *Durch Mattheum Francken: Augspurg,* [ca.1565?] 8°. C.175.i.31(71)
Josephus, Flavius. [*Works.*] Josephus Teütsch. *Tr.* Caspar Hedio. 2 pt. *Michael Meyer & Balthassar Beck: Strassburg,* 1531. fol. 1605/768
Joye, George. George Joye confuteth Winchesters false articles. *Wesill,* 1543. 8°. *The imprint is false; printed at Atwerp by the widow of Christoffel van Ruremunde.* C.122.b.30
— The subuersiō of Moris false foundacion. *Jacob Aurik: Emdon,* 1534. 8°. *The imprint is fictitious; printed at Antwerp by Govaert Dumaeus.* C.53.aa.3
Julius, *Duke of Brunswick-Wolfenbüttel.* Beschreibung der Verordnung, wie es mit Herrn Julij Begrebnus gehalten worden. *Conrad Horn: Juliusfriedenstedt,* 1589. 4°. 1608/3368
Juncker, Matthias. Beweiss, das die fünff Heuptstück vnserer Christlichen Lehr in der Heiligen Schrifft gegründet. *Gedruckt durch Georgium Hoffman; in verlegung Georgij Stümpffeldts: Freybergk,* 1583. 4°. 1578/2503
Juvenalis, Decimus Junius. Liber satyrarum. *Diligentia Jacobi Thanners:* [*Leipzig,*] 1507. fol. C.186.d.5(2)

K

Kempe, Zacharias. Newe Zeitung. Erinnerung vnd was Deuschlande vor ein abschied gegeben worden *Conrad Horn: Heinrichstad,* 1597. 4°. 11521.ee.29(8)
Kerssenbrock, Hermann. Catalogus episcoporum Padibornensium. *Bartholomæus Schlottenius: Lemgouiæ,* 1578. 8°. 1578/8903
Kettner, Leonhard. Ein schön geystlich lied von der heyligen Dryfeltigkeyt. *Valentin Neuber: Nürnberg,* [ca.1555?] 8°. C.175.i.31(8)
Khirchmarius, Blasius. Epicedium in obitum Alberti Bauariæ Ducis. *Adamus Berg: Monachii,* 1580. 4°. 1568/178
Kimedoncius, Jacobus, *the Elder.* De redemtione generis humani libri tres. Tractatio de prædestinatione. *Typis Abrahami Smesmanni: Heidelbergæ,* 1592. 8°. 1509/3829
Kittelman, Christian. Apologia in welcher er sein Büchlein vom Exorcismo rettet. [*Achatius Lieskau: Halle,*] 1592. 4°. C.104.e.34(2)
Klein Leupsch. Ein wunderbarliche, vnerhörte vnd warhafftige geschicht von einer Junckfrawen, geschehen zu Klein Leupsch. *Wolffgang Meyerpeck: Zwickaw,* 1544. 4°. 1570/3573
Kling, Melchior. Tractatus matrimonialium causarum. *Ex officina hæredum Christiani Egenolphi; impensis Adami Loniceri, Ioannis Cnipij, & Pauli Steinmeyers: Francoforti ad Mœnum,* 1577. 8°. 700.b.4(1)
Klostermair, Martinus. Chronographia particularis. *Adamus Berg: Monachij,* 1567. 4°. 1481.aaa.43(1)
Knaust, Heinrich. In geometriam et sphæram introductio. *Per Ioannem VVeiss: Berlini,* 1541. 8°. C.117.ff.9
Koch, Conrad, *Wimpina.* Præcepta coaugmentande rhetoricae orationis. *See* Praecepta.

Koebel, Jacob. Jacobs Stab künstlich vñ gerecht zumachen vnd gebrauchen. *Christian Egenolph: Franckfurt am Meyn,* 1531. 4°. *Precedes the other 1531 edition entitled "Den Stab Iacob . . . zemachen", STC p. 475.* 1651/295

Kokoschkius, Matthaeus. Lobgesprech neunerley Tugenden von Erwehlung Rodolphi secundi. *s.l.* 1577. 4°. 11521.ee.29(7)

Kolbenschlag, Sixt. Ein tröstliche Ordnung wider die Kranckhait der vergifften Lufft vnd Pestilentz. *Leonhart Milchtaler: Nürmberg,* 1540. 4°.
RB.23.a.333

Kollekten. Collecten edder Gebede der hilligen Kercken dorch dat gantze Jar. *Dorch Ambrosium Kerckener: Magdeborch,* [1558.] 8°. C.106.e.12

Koythar, Johann. Thesaurus pauperum. Hauszapoteck. *Lorentz Seuberlich: Wittemberg,* 1600. 4°. 1039.g.11(4)

Krage, Tilomann. Von dem Bilde Gottes in den ersten Menschen. *Georgen Rhawen Erben: Wittemberg,* 1550. 4°. 1509/2917

Kratwol, Henricus. Oracio habita in consecratioñ Georgy Eр̄i Babenbergeñ. [*Johann Pfeil: Bamberg,* 1504.] 4°. C.127.bb.7

Kreitman, Martinus. Histori von S. Castl. *Adam Berg: München,* 1584. 8°.
4827.aa.34

Kromer, Marcin, *Bishop.* Polonia. *Apud Maternum Cholinum: Coloniæ,* 1577. 8°. 1490.c.39

Krueger, Bartholomaeus. Hans Clawerts werckliche Historien. *s.n.* [1588?] 8°. 12330.c.18

— Eine schöne Action von dem Anfang vnd Ende der Welt. *s.l.* 1580. 8°.
1343.a.5

Kuchenmeister, Adamus. Elenchus quaestionum sacrorum ordinum candidatis apud Moguntiacū proponendarum. *Franciscus Behem: Moguntiae,* 1544. 8°. RB.23.a.735

Kuehn, Johann. Zodiaci medicinæ tomus primus. *Apud Gerhardum Greuenbruch: Coloniæ,* 1588. 8°. 1168.b.2

Kuenste. Artliche kunste mancherley weise Dinten zubereiten. *Wolff Meyerpeck: Zwickaw,* 1532. 8°. 1560/4189

— [Another edition.] Begin Dinten zū machen. *Hans Zimmerman: Augspurg,* [ca.1550.] 8°. 1036.a.48(impf.)

— [Another edition.] Kunstbüchlein. [A]uff mancherley weyss Din[ten] zu bereiten. *Michael Manger: Augspurg,* 1588. 8°. 1578/3231

Kunstbuechlein. Künstbüchlin, gerechtten gründtlichen gebrauchs aller kunstbaren Werckleüt. *Heinrich Steyner: Augspurg,* 1535. 4°. 1651/1735

— Kunstbüchlin, gerechten gründtlichen gebrauchs aller kunstbaren Werckleut. *Christian Egenolph: Franckfurt am Meyn,* [1535.] 4°.
C.104.cc.22

Kymeus, Johann. Ein klag Liedt vom Fall Adams vnd Heua. *See* Adam.

L

Laetus, Erasmus. Rerum Danicarum libri vndecim. *Per Georgium Coruinum: Francoforti ad Mœnum,* 1573 (1574★). 4°. 1489.w.7

Lampadius, Auctor. Oratio de conciliatione ueteris & noui Adami. *Per Mathiam Apiarium: Bernæ Heluet.,* 1543. 8°. 1578/8043

Lang, Andreas. Der hohe Eydt Gottes in sechs Busspredigten erkleret. *s.l.*
1571. 8°. 1578/1418

Langenwalde, Hans von, called *Magnus,* and **Schwenckfeld, Caspar.** Ain
Christliche ermanung zů fürdern das wort Gottes. [*Philip Ulhart:
Augsburg,* 1524,] 4°. 3906.e.69

La Ramée, Pierre de. Arithmetices libri duo, et Algebræ totidem. *Ed.*
Lazarus Schonerus. [With works by Schonerus.] *Apud heredes Andreæ
Wecheli, Claudium Marnium & Ioan. Aubrium: Francofurti,* 1592. 8°.
1607/702(3)

— Dialecticæ libri duo. *Ed.* Rollo MacIlmaine. *Apud Andream Wechelum:
Francofurti,* 1581. 8°. 1607/702(1)

Lasius, Christoph. Fundament warer Bekerung wider die flacianische
Klotzbus. *Johan Eichorn: Franckfurt an der Oder,* 1568. 8°.
RB.23.a.3151(5)

Lasso, Orlando di. Laudent Deum cithara, chori. [*Johann Sadeler: Munich,.*
ca.1590.] *s.sh.* fol. K.9.b.13

Laurus, Guilielmus. Harmonia laurea. *Apud Petrum Keschedt: Coloniae,* 1595.
8°. 11408.b.25

Laymannus, Matthaeus. Defensio nobilis causæ Honoldinæ. *Apud Dauidem
Sartorium: Ingolstadii,* 1580. 4°. Davis II, 345

Lazarus, *Saint, the Beggar.* Ein schön geistlich new Lied: von dem reichen
Mann, vnd armen Lazaro. *Durch Mattheum Francken: Augspurg,*
[ca.1560?] 8°. C.175.i.31(40)

— Zwey schöne newe geistliche Lieder. Das erste, vom reichen Man vnd
armen Lazaro. *Valentin Newber: Nürnberg,* [ca.1555?] 8°. C.175.i.31(41)

Lazius, Wolfgang. Commentariorum Reipub. Romanæ in exteris prouincijs
constitutæ libri duodecim. *Per Ioannem Oporinum: Basileæ,* [1551.] fol.
Cup.1261.aa.13

— Tituli ac catalogi cum operum magnorum tum veterum autorum. *Ex officina
Egidij Aquilæ: Viennæ Austriæ,* [1552?] fol. C.186.d.7

Leipsic. — **Rat.** Der Stad Leipzig allerley Ordnunge. *Valentin Bapst: Leipzig,*
1544. 4°. 1578/8849

— — Ordenung von der Tracht der Einwohner. *Valentin Bapst: Leipzig,*
1550. 4°. 1578/8850

— — Ordenung vom lohn der Dienstboten. *Valentin Bapst: Leipzig,* 1551. 4°.
C.186.bb.24

— — Vornewerte Ordnung vnnd Reformation wegen der Tracht [and other
matters]. *Johan Beyer: Leipzig,* 1595. 4°. 1234.a.1

— — Vornewerte Ordnung vnd Reformation wegen der Tracht [and other
matters]. *In Vorlegung Henningi Grossen: Leipzig,* 1596. 4°. 1234.a.3

— **Academia Lipsiensis.** Endlicher Bericht der Theologen beider
Vniuersiteten, Leipzig vnd Wittemberg, belangend die Lere, so gemelte
Vniuersiteten gefüret haben. *Hans Lufft: Wittemberg,* 1570. 4°. 1578/6328

Leisentrit, Johann. Cursus piarum Euangelicarum precum. *Iohan. UUolrab:
Budissinæ,* 1571. 8°. 1607/3290

Lentz, Johannes. Augustochristianeis. *Per Hieronymum Schütz: Dresdæ,* 1595.
4°. 1608/5303

Leucht, Valentin. Ein christliche catholische Predigt von dem
Jüngstengericht. *Durch Casparum Beheṃ: Meintz,* 1583. 4°. 1509/3416

— Zwo Christliche Catholische Predigten vber das acht vnd zwantzigste Capitel Ezechielis. *Durch Casparum Behem: Meintz*, 1583. 4°.
RB.23.a.3118

Leutinger, Balthasar. Kurtzer vnd historischer Bericht, aus was vrsachen Balthasar Lewtinger in Gefengnis kommen. *s.l.* 1591. 4°. 1570/3295

Leuwis, Dionysius de, *de Rickel.* [Contra Alchoranum.] Alchoran. [Extracts from "Contra Alchoranum".] *Tr.* Heinrich von Eppendorff? *Bey Hans Schotten: Strasszburg*, 1540. fol. C.103.i.16

Leyser, Polycarp. Rettung der Ehren Martini Chemnitii. Gestellet von den Predigern der Stadt Braunschweig (Polycarp Leyser [and others]). *Durch Thobiam Steinman: Jhena*, 1592. 4°. 1578/2395

Lied. Ein geistlich Lied, Es ist ein Schaffstal vnd ein Hirt. *Valentin Newber: Nürmberg*, [ca.1555?] 8°. C.175.i.31(42)

— Ein geystliches Lied, von der Aufferstehung der Todten. [By Nicolaus Hermann.] *Durch Mattheum Francken: Augspurg*, [ca.1560?] 8°.
C.175.i.31(25)

— Ein Lied von einer fawlen Diernen. *Michaël Manger: Augspurg*, [ca.1590?] 8°. 11517.aa.17

— Ain new geystlich Lied, Ewiger Vatter im Himmelreich. [By Adam Reissner.] *Durch Hannsen Burger: Straubing*, [ca.1562.] 8°. C.175.i.31(20)

— Ein schön geistlich Lied, in dem Thon, Nach willen dein. *Durch Hannsen Burger: Straubing*, [ca.1562.] 8°. C.175.i.31(10)

— Ein schön geistlichs Lied, von beschaffenem Glück. [*Augsburg?*, ca.1560?] 8°. C.175.i.31(7)

— Ein schön new Lied von dem Engelischen Gruss. *Hans Kholer: Nürnberg*, [ca.1565?] 8°. C.175.i.31(31)

— Ein schön news Lied, Die Ehebrecher Bruck [by Hans Sachs]. Ein ander schön Lied. [*Michael Manger: Augsburg*, ca.1590?] 8°. 11515.a.55(16)

— Ein schöns Lied, von Götlicher Maiestat [by Jörg Breining, adapted by Johann Böschenstein]. Ein ander Lied [by J. Böschenstein]. *Matthe⁹ Franck: Augspurg*, [ca.1560?] 8°. C.175.i.31(59)

Lieder. Drey geistliche Lieder, das Erste, Bewar mich Herr. *Valentin Nnwber* [sic]: *Nürnberg*, [ca.1560?] 8°. C.175.i.31(14)

— Drey geistliche Lieder. Das erste, Von den sieben worten. *s.n.*[ca.1580?] 8°.
C.104.dd.68(3)(impf.)

— Drey geystliche Lieder, das erste: Wer Gott nicht mit vnns dise zeit. *Valentin Newber: Nürnberg*, [ca.1560?] 8°. C.175.i.31(67)

— Drey schöne geystliche Lieder, das erste von der gedult. *Valentin Newber: Nürnberg*, [ca.1560?] 8°. C.175.i.31(65)

— Vier newe Lieder. Das erst, Von der Vntrew. *s.n.* [ca.1560?] 8°.
C.175.i.31(21)

— Zwey schöne geistliche Lieder, das erste, Elend hat mich vmbfangen [by Johannes Hiltstein]. *Friderich Gutknecht: Nürnberg*, [ca.1555?] 8°.
C.175.i.31(49)

— Zwey schöne geistliche Lieder, das erste, Von Gott wil ich nicht lassen. *Durch Crispinum Scharffenberg: Bresslaw*, [ca.1575?] 8°. 11515.a.58(8)

— Zwey schöne newe geystliche lieder, das erst, Ach Got mich thut bezwingen. *Valentin Newber: Nürnberg*, [ca.1560?] 8°. C.175.i.31(15)

— Zwey schöne, newe, geystliche Lieder. Das erst: Ich rüff dich hymlischer Vatter an. [By Joannes Botzhemius Abstemius.] *Durch Mattheum Francken: Augspurg,* [ca. 1560?] 8°. C.175.i.31(18)

Linacre, Thomas. De emendata structura Latini sermonis libri VI. *Ed.* Joachimus Camerarius and others. *In officina Valentini Papæ: Lipsiæ,* 1555. 8°. 1507/247

Linck, Johannes. Cunæ Christi. *Antonius Bertramus: Argentorati,* 1586. 4°.
1568/1548

Linguae. Sex linguarum dictionarius. *Philippus Vlhardus: Augustæ Vindelicorum,* [ca. 1550?] 8°. C.54.g.8

Listenius, Nicolaus. [Rudimenta musicae.] *Apud Georgium Rhau: Vitebergæ,* 1534. 8°. Hirsch I. 321 (impf.)

Liturgies. — Greek Rite. — Leitourgikon. Divina liturgia Sancti Ioannis Chrysostomi. *Tr.* Ambrosius Pelargus. *Sebastianus Vuagner: Vormatiæ,* 1541. 4°. 1509/2925

— **Latin Rite. — Antiphoners.** Liber canticorum. *Apud Ioannem Montanum & Vlricum Neuberum: Noribergæ,* 1550. 8°. Hirsch III.894

— — — [Another edition.] *In officina Vlrici Neuberi & hæredum Ioannis Montani: Noribergæ,* 1565. 8°. Hirsch III.895

— — **Hymnals.** Vslegunge der hymbs. [*Johann Grüninger: Strasburg,*] 1494. 4°.
IA.1421

— — **Missals.** Alle Kirchen Gesäng vnd Gebeet des gantzen Jars. *Tr.* Christophorus Flurheym. 2 pt. *Philipp Vlhart: Augspurg,* 1563. 8°.
1568/8849

— — — [*Extracts.*] Lectura super canone misse. [By Gabriel Biel. With the text.] *Impensis & cura Iohãnis otmar: [Reutlingen,]* 1488. fol. IB.10720

— — — **Lübeck.** *Begin.* KL Januarius habet dies xxxj. [*Peter Drach the Younger: Speyer,* 1505?] fol. C.110.k.5

— — — **Meissen.** Codices librorum missaliũ ecclesie Misneñ. p *Conradũ Kachelofen: Freiberg,* 1495. fol. IC.14503

— — — [*Appendix.*] Expositio misteriorum misse christi passionẽ figurantiũ. [By Balthasar, Provisor Collegii S. Bernardi Lipsiae.] p *Johannẽ Froschaüer: Auguste,* 1501. 4°. 1568/6081

— — **Rituals. — Basle.** Sacerdotale Basiliense. 2 pt. *Per Ioannem Fabrum: Brunntruti,* 1595. 4°. Legg 268

— — — **Mainz.** Agẽda Magũtiñ. *Per Johannem Schöffer: in vrbe Maguntina,* 1513. 4°. C.133.dd.15

— — — **Munster.** Agenda Ecclesiastica. *Typis Lamberti Rasfeldt: Monasterii VVestph.,* 1592 (1591*). 4°. 1608/4796

— — — **Treves.** Libri officialis siue Agendae Treuerensis Ecclesiæ pars posterior. *Ex officina Zachariæ Brittellmanni: Augustæ Treuerorum,* 1576. fol. C.143.dd.5(2)

— — **Occasional Prayers.** Piae aliquot precationes contra aereas tempestates. [*Closterdruckerei:*] *Tegernsee,* 1576. 8°. 1606/2045

— — [*Appendix.*] Defensio Ecclesiasticæ liturgiæ. [By Georg Witzel.] *See* V., S.G.

— **Church of England. — Common Prayer.** Ordinatio Ecclesiae. *Tr.* Alexander Alesius. *In officina VVolfgangi Gunteri: Lipsiae,* 1551. 4°.
221.c.5

— **Lutheran Churches.** Missale, hoc est Cantica, preces, et lectiones sacræ, collectæ a Matthæo Ludeco. 2 pt. *Zacharias Lehman, impensis Samuelis Seelfischij: Witebergæ,* 1589. fol. C.131.h.13

Liubichts, Joannes. Oratio de venerabili sacrificio altaris. *Ioannes Cruciger: Nissæ,* 1563. 4°. 1608/3369

— Oratio in electione novi episcopi. *Ioannes Cruciger: Nissæ,* 1574. 4°.
1608/5930

Livius, Titus. Libri omnes. [Books 1–10, with the epitomes of Florus of books 1–20.] *Impressum apud Georgium Coruinum, impensis Sigismundi & Iohannis Feyerabendinorum: Francofurti ad Mœnum,* 1578. 8°.
C.143.b.4(impf.)

— Romische historien mit etlichen newē Translation. *Tr.* Bernhard Schöferlin, Johann Wittig & Nicolaus Carbach. *Durch Johanñ Schoeffer: Mentz,* 1523. fol. C.186.dd.8

— [*Selections.*] Orationes. [With other matter.] *Ed.*Reinhardus Lorichius. *In officina Christiani Egenolphi: Marpurgi,* 1541. 8°. 1506/128

Llwyd, Humphrey. Commentarioli Britannicæ descriptionis fragmentum. *Apud Ioannem Birckmannum: Coloniae Agrippinae,* 1572. 8°.
598.a.35; G.3257(2)

Lobera de Avila, Luis. Vanquete de nobles cauaIleros. *Per Henricum Stainerū: in vrbe Augusta,* [1530.] 4°. RB.23.a.219

Lobgesang. Ein schön news gaistlich Lobgesang. Iñ Thon: Es fleügt ein Vögelein leyse. *Durch Mattheum Francken: Augspurg,* [ca.1560?] 8°.
C.175.i.31(32)

— Ein schön news geystlich Lobgesang. Ein ander Lied. *Michael Manger: Augspurg,* [ca.1575?] 8°. 11522.de.47

Locher, Jacob. De cometa sub septentrionibus viso carmen. [*Hans Froschauer: Augsburg,* 1506?] 4°. C.106.d.13

— Threnodia in laudem Heduigis cantata. [*Hans Froschauer: Augsburg,* 1502.] 4°. C.171.bb.15

Lochner, Zacharias. Probier Büchlein. *Durch Mattheum Francken: Augspurg,* 1565. 4°. C.106.d.25

— Tractätlein, darinnen etliche schöne Exempel auss der Geometria. *Valentin Newber: Nürnberg,* 1583. 4°. 1570/869

Loewe, Simson. Türckenbüchlein. *s.n.* [1595.] 8°. 706.a.16(4)

Lonicer, Johann. Contra Romanistam fratrem Augustinū Aluelden̄. *Apud Collegium Nouum: VVittenbergae,* 1520. 4°. 1570/1937

Loosaeus, Cornelius. Thuribulum aureum sanctarum precationum. *Apud Franciscum Behem: Moguntiae,* 1581. 16°. 1568/9043

Lord's Prayer. [*Appendix.*] Zwey schöne geystliche Lieder, im Thon des Vater vnsers zu singen. *Valentin Neuber: Nürnberg,* [ca.1555?] 8°.
C.175.i.31(35)

Lorich, Jodocus. Kurtzer begriff dern rechten eigenschafften der Kirchen Gottes. *Steffen Graff: Freyburg,* 1579. 8°. 1568/9250

Losow, Clemens. Sermones Rosarij. *Per Martinū de werdena: Colonie,* 1508. 8°. RB.23.a.73

Loss, Lucas. Annotationes in Grammaticen Philippi Melanthonis latinam. *Apud hæred. Chr. Egenolphi: Franc.,* 1557. 8°. C.127.bb.12

— Arithmetices erotemata puerilia. *Andreas Eichorn: Francofurti March.*,
  [ca. 1600.] 8°.   1578/4902
Louis, *Prince de Condé.* Bericht von der Handlung zu Schürmegg, zwischen
  den Condischen vnd Aumalischen. *s.n.* [1568.] 4°.   1568/1119
Lucerne. — Rat. Nutzlicher bericht, Regiment vnd Ordnung in
  pestilentzischen zytten zugebruchen. *Abraham Gemperlin: Freyburg in
  Vchtland*, 1594. 4°.   1167.f.23
Lucian, *of Samosata.[Works.]* Opera. *Tr.* Jacobus Micyllus and others. *Apud
  Christianum Egenolphum: Francoforti,* 1538. fol.   C.109.i.10
— [*Dialogues.*] Dialogi aliquot. *Tr.* Desiderius Erasmus & Thomas More. *In
  officina Frobeniana: Basileae,* 1534. 8°.   1607/1773(impf.)
Lucius, Cyriacus. Breuis de lithosophistica doctrina obseruatio. *Ex
  typographia Dauidis Sartorii: Ingolstadii,* 1582. 4°.   1568/176
— De variis medicorum sectis doctrina. pt.1. *Ex officina typographica
  VVolfgangi Ederi: Ingolstadii,* 1583. 4°.   1185.k.21(11)
Luis, *de Granada.* Introductionis ad symbolum fidei libri quatuor. *Tr.* Giovanni
  Paolo Gallucci. *Apud Geruinum Calenium & hæredes Ioannis Quentelij:
  Coloniæ,* 1588. 4°.   1489.a.62
— Introductionis ad symbolum fidei compendium. *Tr.* Michael ab Isselt. *Apud
  Arnoldum Quentelium: Coloniæ,* 1595. 8°.   1507/540
Luther, Martin. [*Works.*] Der achte Teil der Bücher Martini Lutheri. *Durch
  Antonium Schön: Wittemberg,* 1583. fol.   1505/151
— [*Smaller Collections.*] Lucubrationum pars una. *Adam Petri: Basileæ,* 1520.
  fol.   C.110.g.19; C.127.i.6
— [*Biblical Commentaries.*] Summarien vber die Psalmen. *Friderich Peypus:
  Nürnberg,* 1533. 8°.   1568/4742
  [*Disputations.*] Acta Lipsiae. Resolutiones Lutherianæ. Epitome Philippi
  Melanchthonis. Inuectio Eccii. [*Andreas Cratander: Basle,* 1519.] 4°.
                                                                C.135.b.19(1)
— — [Disputatio de operibus legis et gratiae.] Eine Disputation von den gůten
  Wercken. *Tr.* Mathias Flacius. *Ed.* Albertus Christianus. *Jacob Frölich:
  Strassburg,* 1557. 8°.   1578/3695
— [*Auf das Schreien etlicher Papisten.*] Auff das schreien etlicher Papisten
  Antwort. [*Hans Bär: Coburg,*] 1530. 4°.   C.175.m.6
— [*Auf des Königs zu England Lästerschrift Antwort.*] Auff des konigs zu
  Engelland lester schrifft Antwort. [*Gabriel Kantz: Zwickau,*] 1527. 4°.
                                                                Cup.408.zzz.62
— [*Auslegung des Glaubens.*] Auslegung des Glaubens. *Ed.* Georgius Rorarius.
  Vrban Gaubisch: Eisleben, 1563. 4°.   1568/9189
— [*Bekenntnis zu Augsburg einzulegen.*] De bekentenisse vp den Rykesdage tho
  Augsburg. *Hans Wolther: Magdeborch,* 1530. 8°.   1509/3093
— [*Brief an die Christen im Niederland.*] Ayn Sendbrieff an die Christē im
  Niderlande. [*Hieronymus Höltzel: Nuremberg,* 1523.] 4°.   3905.bbb.38
— [*Brief an die Christen zu Antorf.*] Eyn brieff an die Christen zu Antorff. [*Josef
  Klug:*] *Wittemberg,* 1525. 4°.   C.127.c.8
— [*Catechismus, Kleiner.*] Catechismus für die gemeine Pfarrherr vnd Prediger.
  Durch Hermann Gülfferichen: Franckfurdt am Mayn, 1553. fol.   C.127.i.4
— — Enchiridion. Der kleine Catechismus. *Jacob Berwalds Erben: Leipzig,*
  1575. 8°.   1578/4889

— — Paruus catechismus. *Ed.*Leonhard Jacobi. *Ex officina Valentini Papae:
Lipsiae*, 1552. 8°. RB.23.a.734
— — Paruus catechismus. *Apud hæredes Christiani Mylij: Argentorati*, 1568. 8°.
1578/1520
— [*Eine schreckliche Geschichte.*] Ein schrecklich geschicht vnnd gericht Gottes über Thomas Müntzer. [*Friedrich Peypus: Nuremberg*, 1525.] 4°.
C.143.ff.11
— [*Tractatulus de his qui ad ecclesias confugiunt.*] Tractatulus dehis qui ad Ecclesias confugiunt. *Per Joannem Weyssenbuger: Landsshut*, 1520. 4°. C.143.ff.12
— [*Von den Juden.*] De Iudaeis et eorum mendaciis. *Tr.* Justus Jonas. *Ex officina Petri Brubachij: Francofurti*, 1544. fol. C.110.g.20
— [*Wider die mörderischen Rotten der Bauern.*] Aduersus latrocinantes cohortes rusticorum. Responsio Iohannis Cochlæi. [With other matter.] [*Servatius Kruffter:*] *Colonie*, 1525. 4°. 9365.a.5
Lycosthenes, Conradus. Theatrum uitæ humanæ. *Ed.* Theodor Zwinger. *Per Ioan. Oporinum, Ambrosium & Aurelium Frobenios: Basileæ*, 1565. fol.
C.108.aaa.9

M

Macchiavelli, Niccolò. [Discorsi.] Disputationum de republica libri III. *Tr.* Joannes Nicolaus Stupanus. *Per Iacobum Foilletum: Mompelgarti*, 1591. 8°.
8005.aa.27
— [Il principe.] Princeps. *Tr.* Sylvester Telius. [With texts by other authors.] 2 pt. *s.n.* 1589. 8°. 521.c.9
— — De officio viri principis. *Tr.* Sylvester Telius. [With texts by other authors.] [*Jakob Foillet:*] *Montisbelgardi*, 1599. 8°. 523.c.32
Maffeus, Raphael. Commentariorum urbanorum octo & triginta libri. Oeconomicus Xenophontis [*tr.* R. Maffeus]. *Apud Hieronymum Frobenium & Nicolaum Episcopium: Basileæ*, 1544. fol. Davis II, 332(2)
Magdeburg. — Bürgermeister und Rat. Ein warhafftiger Bericht dero von Magdeburgk, das ihennen was Mantags nach Matthei ergangen. *Michel Lotther: Magdeburgk*, 1550. 4°. 1578/6320
Magdeburg, Joachim. Ein Lobgesang. [*Urban Gaubisch: Eisleben*, 1563.] 8°.
C.175.i.31(6)
Magirus, Johannes. Artis musicæ libri duo. *Ex officina Paltheniana, sumtibus Iohannis Spiessij: Francofurti*, 1596. 8°. Hirsch IV.1514
Magnesius, Eleutherius. Gute Zeyttung von der Christlichen Armata eroberung Castello nouo vnd Rixana. [*Johann Petreius: Nuremberg,*] 1539. 4°. 1312.c.52
Mahediah. Die eroberung der sttat [*sic*] Affrica. Durch Melchiorn Kriegstein: Augspurg, [1550.] 4°. 1509/1700; G.7094
Mai. Der geistlich May. *Andre Schobsser: München*, [ca.1550?] 8°. 3257.bb.26(1)
Makowinus a Makowa, Vincentius. Dialogi pueriles. *Lat., Czech & Ger. In officina Georgij Melantrichi: Pragæ*, 1579. 8°. C.114.r.27(4)
Malaciola, T. Curtius, *pseud.* [i.e. **Joannes Caesarius?**] Dialogus, Bulla. *Excusum impensis & opera Iohannis Coticulæ; Callyrius Trulla excudebat: apud Burlassiam*, [1520.] 4°. *The imprint is fictitious; printed by Melchior Lotter at Wittenberg.* C.136.b.25

Malleus. Malleus maleficarum. 2 tom. *Apud Wolfgangum Richterum, impensis Nicolai Bassæi: Francofurti ad Mœnum,* 1600. 8°. *Tom.*2 *was printed by Johann Saur, and is an imperfect duplicate of that in the set in STC.*
                                                                                                719.b.3, 4(impf.)
Mancinellus, Antonius. Sermonum decas ad Angelum Colotium. *In libraria officina Matthiæ Schurerij: Strassburg,* 1510. 4°.   1608/2867
— Speculum de moribus & officijs. *Ioannes Gymnicus: Coloniæ,* 1537. 8°.
                                                                                                1509/2168(3)
Mancinus, Georgius. Honori Ioachimi a Bassevitz et Elissæ Smekers carmina. *Typis Stephani Myliandri: Rostochii,* 1597. 4°.   1213.k.17(2)
— In honorem ultimum Sigismundi Augusti carmina. *Typis Myliandrinis: Rostochii,* 1600. 4°.   1213.k.17(1)
Mandagotus, Gulielmus, *Cardinal.* Tractatus de electionibus nouorum prælatorum. *Ed.*Nicolaus Boerius. De permutatione beneficiorum Frederici de Senis tractatulus. *Apud Theodorum Baumium: Coloniæ Agrippinæ,* 1574. 8°.   1607/3483
Mansfeld, Carl von, *Count.* Manssfeldische History, Schlacht vnd Victoria in Vngern. *Prag,* 1595. 4°.   9325.aaa.34
Manuzio, Paolo. Apophthegmatum ex optimis scriptoribus libri VIII. *Ed.* P. Manuzio. *Coloniæ; impensis Lazari Zetzneri: [Strasburg,]* 1596. 16°.
                                                                                                12315.a.29
Marchtaler, Vitus. Rerum a Sigismundo contra Turcas gestarum breuis enarratio. [*Vienna?,*] 1595. 4°.   1312.c.41
Marcus, Joachim. Cantio gratulatoria ad Ernestum Ludouicum ducem Stetini. 4 pt. *Typis Augustini Ferberi: Gryphisuualdiæ,* 1585. *obl.* 4°.
                                                                                                K.5.a.25
Margaret, *Saint.* Senct Margrate Passie. *Durch Anthonium Keyser: [Cologne,* ca.1550?] 4°.   C.127.e.19
Marlianus, Joannes Bartholomaeus. Vrbis Romæ topographia. *Per Ioannem Oporinum: Basileæ,* 1550. fol.   1575/222
Martini, Lucas, *Pfarrer.* Der Christlichen Jungfrawen Ehrenkräntzlein. *Michael Peterle: Prag,* 1585. 12°.   847.b.5(1)
Mary, *the Blessed Virgin.* Determ̃iatio de īmaculata conceptione beate virginis. [By J. de Breitenbach.] [*Conrad Kachelofen: Leipzig,* 1490.] 4°.   IA.11542
— [Sermo de praesentatione virginis Mariae.] De magnificādo meritoīe festū presentacōis marie virginis in tēplū sermo. [*Ulrich Zel: Cologne,* ca 1470.] 4°.   IA.2858a
— **Congregatio Beatissimae Virginis Annunciatae, Ingolstadt.** Poematia sacra Christi Corpori dicata. *Ex officina typographica Wolfgangi Ederi: Ingolstadii,* 1583. 4°.   1568/494
Mary, *Queen of Scotland.* Proditionis ab aliquot Scotiæ perduellibus aduersus suam Reginam perpetratæ breuis narratio. [*Sebald Mayer: Dillingen,*] 1566. 4°.   G.4992
Matthaeus, Burcardus. Oratio de Anna Burgio. *Iohannes Schuuertelius: VVitebergæ,* 1573. 8°.   878.h.10(2)
Matthesius, Johann. Diluvium. *Durch Katharinam Gerlachin: Nürmberg,* 1587. 4°.   1570/863
— Zwo Trostpredigten. *Ed.* Caspar Franck. *Georg Hantzsch: Leipzig,* 1556. 8°.   1607/2925

Mattioli, Pietro Andrea. Kreutterbuch. *Tr.* Georgius Handsch. *Ed.*
Joachimus Camerarius. *Johan Feyrabendt, in verlegung Peter Fischers & Heinrich Dacken Erben: Franckfort am Mayn*, 1590. fol. L.35/145
Maurice, *Saint,* and **Mary Magdalen,** *Saint.* — **Collegiate Church at Halle.**
Glosse des hochgelarten Ablas der tzu Hall. [By Lignacius Stürll. With the text of the announcement by the Chapter of the Stiftskirche at Halle.] [*Nickel Schirlentz: Wittenberg,* 1521.] 4°. C.107.b.49
Meckhart, Georg. Zehen fürneme Jrthum Caspar Schwenckfelds widerlegt. *Philipp Vlhart: Laugingen*, 1575. 4°. 1509/2334
Meichsner, Johann Helias. Handtbüchlin grundtlichs berichts, recht vnd wolschreibens. [*Widow of Ulrich Morhart the Elder:*] *Tüwingen*, 1556. 8°.
1578/2372
— Hoch oder gemainer Teütscher Nation Formular. Sampt Handbüchlin gründlichs Berichts recht vnd wol Schreibens. *Ed.* Sebastian Meichsner. 4 pt. *Georg Raben & Weygand Hanen Erben: Franckfurt am Mayn*, 1563. fol. 1505/8
Meier, Georg, *Professor at Wittenberg.* Commonefactio historica de statu temporis, quod Euangelii lucem præcessit. *Ex officina Iohannis Lufft: Vuitebergæ,* 1567. 8°. 1506/154
— Eine Predig von der Himelfart Jhesu Christi. *Hans Lufft: Wittemberg*, 1550. 4°. 1578/1811
Melanchthon, Philipp. [*Letters.*] Epistolæ selectiores aliquot. *Ed.* Caspar Peucer. *Iohannes Crato: VVitebergæ,* 1565. 8°. C.106.e.15
— Annotationes [in epistolas Pauli ad Romanos et Corinthios]. Verzaichnung des rechten verstands der Epistel, die S. Paulus zů den Rhömern geschribē hat. [*Sigmund Grimm:*] *Augspurg*, 1523. 4°. 1578/4316
— Catechesis puerilis. *Apud Christianum Egenolphum: Francoforti*, 1544. 8°.
C.190.a.31
— Commentarius de anima. *In officina Crato Myliana: Argentorati*, 1548. 8°.
C.127.dd.21(2)
— [De officio principum.] Das die Fürsten schuldig sind, bey iren vnterthanen abgötterey abzuthun. *Tr.* Georg Meier. *Joseph Klug: Wittemberg,* 1540. 4°. 1568/4319
— [De oppido Torga.] Von vrsprung der Stat Torgaw. *Christian Rödinger: Magdeburg,* 1552. 4°. *Signed* E. C.143.f.7
— Disputatio de inuocatione. [*Veit Kreutzer?:*] *Vuitebergæ,* [1549.] 8°.
1578/1347
— Enarratio aliquot librorum ethicorum Aristotelis. *Per Iosephi* [sic] *Klug: Vitebergae,* 1545. 8°. 1607/3473(2)
— Erotemata dialectices. *Chr. Egen.: Franc.,* 1550. 8°. C.133.e.23
— [Grammatica graeca.] Integræ græcæ grammatices institutiones. *In ædibus Thomæ Anshelmi: Haganoæ,* 1520. 8°. C.190.a.28
— In obscuriora aliquot capita Geneseos annotationes. (Discrimen legis et Euangelii.) [*Johann Schöffer:*] *Mainz,* 1524. 8°. Davis II, 326(2)
— Initia doctrinæ physicæ. *Apud Christianum Egenolphum: Francoforti,* 1550. 8°.
C.127.dd.21(1)
— Loci communes theologici. [*Peter Braubach:*] *Halæ Sueuorum,* 1539. 8°.
1606/1867

— [Loci communes.] Gemeine anweissung ynn die heilige schrifft. *Tr.*
Georg Burckard. *Wittemberg; gedruckt zu Hall ynn Sachsen,* 1525. 8°.
C.125.dd.10

— Philosophiæ moralis epitomes libri duo. [With other matter.] *Apud Cratonem Mylium: Argentorati,* 1544. 8°. 1607/3473(1)

Melemius, Andreas. Disputatio theologica, de speciebus eucharisticis. *Ex officina typographica VVolfgangi Ederi:* [Ingolstadt, 1594.] 4°. 1578/1215

Menochius, Jacobus. De adipiscenda retinenda et recuperanda possessione commentaria. *Apud Ioannem Gymnicum: Coloniæ Agrippinæ,* 1577. fol.
1605/318

Mensch. Das der Mensch in der Bekerung zu Gott gerecht werde durch Glauben. [With] Eine Predigt Jacobi Rungij. *Peter Seitzen Erben: Wittemberg,* 1555. 4°. 1608/2880

Menzel, Hieronymus. Postilla. *See* Bible. — *Liturgical Epistles and Gospels.* [*German.*]

Merus, Pasquillus, *Germanus, pseud.* [i.e. **Conradus Zutphanius.**] De mirifica Dei uirtute. [*Cologne?,*] 1561. 8°. 11409.aa.45(5)

Metius, Adriaan. Doctrinæ sphæricæ lib.V. *Ex officina Zachariæ Palthenij: Francofurti,* 1598. 8°. C.74.a.12(2)

Metri, Nicolaus de. Artzney bůch. *Ed.* Jeremias Martius. *Michael Manger, in verlegung Georgen Willers: Augspurg,* 1572. 8°. C.106.e.14(2)

Mexia, Pedro. Historia imperial y cesarea. *En casa de Ioan Oporino: Basilea,* 1547. fol. 587.i.1

Michaelis, Petrus. Christliche Entdeckung vieler Irrthumben, so von Johan von Münster fürgetragen. *Lambert Rassfeldt: Münster in Westphalen,* 1591. 4°. 1609/4764

Micyllus, Jacobus, *pseud.* [i.e. **Jacob Moltzer.**] Arithmeticæ logisticæ libri duo. *Per Ioannem Oporinum: Basileæ,* 1555. 8°. 1578/159

— Ratio examinandorum uersuum. *Apud Christianum Egenolphum: Francofurti,* 1539. 8°. RB.23.a.602

— Syluarum libri quinque. Apelles aegyptius. *Ed.* Julius Micyllus. *Ex officina Petri Brubachij:* [Frankfort on the Main,] 1564. 8°. 1568/4320

Mikropresbutikon. Μικροπρεσβυτικον ueterum theologorum. *Apud Henrichum Petri: Basileae,* 1550. fol. 3832.f.26

Milichius, Jacobus, *a Falckenburg.* Carmina de triumphali ascensu Christi Iesu. *s.l.* 1568. 4°. 1608/2559

Milis, Joannes de. Repertorium. *Ed.* Ludovicus Romanus Mathesilanus & Henricus Ferrendat. *Expensis Sigismundi Feyerabendt: Francofurti ad Moenum,* 1572. 8°. 1608/358

Milis, Nicolaus de. *See* Milis, Joannes de.

Milius, Erasmus, *pseud.* [i.e. **Jacob Gretser.**] Bona noua de Historia Ordinis Jesuitici. *Typis Georgii Gruppenbachii: Tubingæ;* [*David Sartorius:*] *Ingolstadii,* 1593. 4°. *The Tübingen imprint is false.* T.731(11)

Mirakel. Erschrecklichen, wunderbarliche vnnd warhafftige mirakel vnnd zeychen. *Erffurt,* [1555.] 4°. *The imprint is false.* Cup.403.y.19

Mirus, Martin. Sieben Christliche Predigten auff dem Reichstage zu Regenspurg gethan. *Esaias Mechler: Erffurd,* 1590. 4°. 1578/5985

Mizauld, Antoine. Alexikepus. *Apud Ioannem Gymnicum: Coloniæ,* 1576. 8°.
1509/2215

Model, Georgius. Ein new Lied. Das heylige Vater vnser gesangsweiss. *Durch Niclaus Knorren: Nürnberg,* [ca.1565?] 8°. C.175.i.31(29)

Modus. [Modus intellectus orationum et contemplationum.] [*Nicolaus Gotz: Cologne,* ca.1475.] fol. IB.3843

— Modus practicandi. [By Thomas Murner. Appendix to "Logica memorativa".] [*Johann Grüninger: Strasburg,* 1509?] 4°. 1134.e.38(1)

Molina, Ludovicus, *Jurist.* De Hispanorum primogeniorum origine libri quatuor. *Coloniæ; expensis Ioannis Baptistæ Ciotti:* [*Venice,*]1588. fol. *The Cologne imprint is false; printed by Johann Feyerabend at Frankfort on the Main.* C.79.g.1

Molitor, Joannes, *S. J.* Disputatio theologica de vera Christi Ecclesia. *Praes.* Sebastianus Heissius. *Ex officina Nicolai Henrici junioris: Monachii,* [1600.] 4°. 1490.m.88

Moltherus, Menradus. Lucta Christiana. Psalmi quinquagesimi deprecatoria. *Per Iohan. Secerium: Haganoæ,* 1527. 8°. 1568/6489

Montanus, Jacobus, *Spirensis.* Collectaneorum latinæ locutionis opus secūdum. *In ædibus Eucharij Ceruicorni: Coloniæ,* 1517. 4°. 1578/8592

Montboissier, Petrus de, *Abbot.* Contra Heinricianorum & Petrobrusianorum hæreses epistolæ duæ. S. Bernardi tres sermones ac nouem epistolæ. *In officina Alexandri Vueissenhorn: Ingolstadii,* 1546. 4°.
1609/4349

Montenay, Georgette de. Emblematum Christianorum centuria. *French & Lat. Apud Christophorum Froschouerum: Tiguri,* 1584. 4°. MS.Add.15841

Most, Wolff. Ordenliche Beschreibung, wie von den Herrn Burgermeister vnnd Rath der Hauptstatt Amberg ein Hauptschiessen gehalten. *Alexander Philip Dieterich: Nürnberg,* [1596.] 4°. 11517.ee.51(6)

Muehlenlied. Das alte gedicht, welchs man nennet das Mülenlied. *Com.* Johann Winnigstedt. *s.n.* [1552.] 8°. RB.23.a.280

Mueller, Johann, *Regiomontanus.* [Calendar for 1521.] [*Hans Dorn: Brunswick,* 1520.] *s.sh.* fol. C.52.h.4(2)(frag.)

Mueller, Johann, *Rhellicanus.* In C. Iulii Caesaris et Auli Hirtij Commentaria annotationes. *Per Hieronimum Curionem: Basileæ,* 1543. 8°. RB.23.a.719

Muenster, Sebastian. קיצור של חדקדוק Compendium hebraicæ grammaticæ ex Eliæ Iudæi libris. [*Hieronymus Froben, J. Herwagen & N. Episcopius:*] *Basileae,* 1529. 8°. Davis II, 24(1)

— Germaniae atque aliarum regionum descriptio. [*Andreas Cratander: Basle,* 1530.] 4°. C.190.aaa.11

Muentzer, M. R. Zwey schöne newe geistliche Lieder, auss Göttlicher schrifft. *See* Bible. — Appendix. [*Miscellaneous.*]

Muntz, Georgius. Ein wunigkliche, schöne predig. [*Closterdruckerei:*] *Thierhaupten,* 1592. 8°. 1607/5507(2)

Murer, Joss. Absolom. *Christoffel Froschower: Zürych,* 1565. 8°. 1606/1770

Muret, Marc Antoine. Variarum lectionum libri IV. et Obseruationum juris lib. singularis. *Ad insigne pinus: Augustæ Vindelicorum,* 1600. 8°.
C.109.p.12(2)

— Iuvenilia. *Ex officina Principis: Bardi Pomeraniæ,* 1590. 8°. 1578/6331

Murmelius, Joannes. Pappa. Uariaɥ rerū dictiones [and other matter]. *Lat. & Low Ger. In officina Quentell.: Colonie,* 1514. 4°. 1609/2812

Murner, Thomas. Modus practicandi. *See* Modus.

Musculus, Andreas. Leichpredig inn der Sepultur des Herrn Joachim Marggraffen zu Brandenburg. *Johann Eichorn: Franckfurt an der Oder*, 1571. 4°. 1608/3296(2)

— Sepultur des Herrn Joachim Marggraffen zu Brandenburgk. *Johann Eichorn: Franckfurt an der Oder*, 1571. 4°. 1608/3296(1)

— Vom Missbrauch des Sacraments, Vnterrichtung. *Durch Georgium Bawman: Erffurdt*, 1561. 8°. 1578/2222

Musler, Georg. Laudatio funebris in Leonardi à Fels obitum. *Matthæus Syngrenius: Viennæ Austriæ*, 1545. 4°. 10704.cc.12

Musler, Johann. De scholis et præceptoribus deligendis consilium. *Apud Georgium Vuachter: Norimbergæ*, 1529. 8°. 8307.aa.24

Mylius, Georg. Eilff Christliche Predigten. *Gedruckt durch Esaiam Mechlern: Erffurd; in Vorlegung Lenhard Wiprechts: Jehna*, 1590. 4°. 1568/1648

— Zehen Predigten vom Türcken. *Durch Tobiam Steinman, in verlegung Salomon Gruners: Jena*, 1595. 4°. C.104.e.34(1)

N

N., H. Comoedia. A worke in ryme set forth by HN [Hendrick Niclas]. [*Nikolaus Bohmberg: Cologne*, 1574?] 8°. C.34.a.5(2)

— Terra pacis. A true testification of the lande of peace set-foorth by HN [Hendrick Niclas]. [*Nikolaus Bohmberg: Cologne*, 1580?] 8°. C.34.a.5(1)

N., Joannes, *Pfarrherr zu N.* Auff die vnterredung, so die newe Kirchen ordenung belangend zu Torgaw geschehen. *s.n.* [1549.] 8°. 1607/3527

Nabod, Alexius. Ein schöner Trost den betrübten Christen. [*Veit Kreutzer?:*] *Wittemberg*, 1546. 4°. 1578/1625

Nachenmoser, Adam, *pseud.?* Prognosticon theologicum. Ger. 2 pt. *Werner Jobsson: Leiden*, 1588. fol. *The imprint is fictitious; printed by Bernhard Jobin at Strasburg.* 1505/355

— [Another edition.] 2 pt. *Hiob Warnfast: Leyden*, 1595. fol. *The imprint is fictitious; printed by the Heirs of Bernhard Jobin at Strasburg.* C.150.i.7

Naegelin, Mattheus. Ein kurtze Anleytung, zůbegegnen dem jrrthum̄ der Steinbachischen Secten. *Christian Müller: Strassburg*, [1566.] 4°. C.135.b.19(2)

Nannus Mirabellius, Dominicus. Polyanthea. *Apud Matthiam Schurerium: in libera Argentina; ductu Leonardi & Lucæ Alantsee:* [*Vienna,*] 1517. fol. 1605/744(2)

Nase, Johann, *Bishop*. Angelus parǽneticus contra solam fidem delegatus. Ger. *Wolffgang Eder: Ingolstatt*, 1588. 4°. 1560/573(1)

— Leuita catholicus contra Exodum pseudeuangelicum. Ger. *Wolffgang Eder: Ingolstatt*, 1589. 4°. 1608/5579

— Præludium in Centurias hominum sola fide perditorum. Ger. *Wolffgang Eder: Ingolstatt*, 1588. 4°. 1560/573(2)

— Widereinwarnung an alle frome Teutsche. *Alexander Weyssenhorn & Miterben: Ingolstatt*, 1577. 8°. 1568/867

Nauntelius, Rhemiginus, *pseud.?* Rationale Iesuiticorum. *Gerardus Pessus: Dantisci*, 1595. 8°. *The imprint is false.* 1509/2320

Nausea, Fridericus, *Bishop.* Pro sacrosancta missa adversum hæreticos miscellaneæ. *Apud Ioannem Schœffer: Moguntiæ,* 1527. 4°. 1608/3150

Neander, Michael, *of Joachimsthal.* Methodorum in omni genere artium breuis ὑφήγησις. *Per Ioannem Oporinum: Basileæ,* 1556. 8°. 1651/285

Neander, Michael, *of Sorau.* Theologia megalandri Lutheri. Theologia Bernhardi & Tauleri. 2 pt. *Vrban Gaubisch: Eisleben,* 1581. 8°. 1578/300

Neander, Valentin. [Sacræ cantiones quatuor, quinque et sex vocum.] 5 pt. [*Typis Matthæi VVelaci:*] *VVitebergæ,* 1584. *obl.* 4°. K.7.c.16(impf.)

Neanisci. *See* S., I.

Negligentiae. Negligentie et defectus in missa. [*Printer of Hundorn:*] *Erffordie,* 1494. 4°. IA.12636

Nestor, *Novariensis. See* Dionysius, N.

Netherlands.[Before 1581.] — **Staten Generaal.** [*Appendix.*] Summari Verclærung der billichen Ursachen, welche die Stend bezwungen haben, vmb sich wider Don Johann von Oesterreich zuuersehen. 2 pt. *Durch Wilhelm Silvium: Antorff,* 1578. 4°. 9415.a.24; 9325.c.53(impf.)

Neusidler, Melchior. Teütsch Lautenbuch. *Bernhart Jobin: Strassburg,* 1574. fol. K.2.i.28(impf.)

Nicephorus [Xanthopulus], *Callisti filius.* Kirchen Histori. *Tr.* Marx Fugger. 2 Tl. *Durch Dauid Sartorium: Ingolstadt,* 1588. fol. 1565/57

Nider, Johann. Manuale confessorum. [*Printer of Historia S. Albani: Cologne,* ca.1472.] 4°. IA.3415

Niderlendische Stette. *See* Dutch Cities.

Noguera, Jacobus. De Ecclesia Christi ab haereticorum conciliabulis dinoscenda libri duo. *Ed.* Stephanus Agricola. *Apud Sebaldum Mayer: Dilingæ,* 1560. fol. 4520.f.8(1)

Nomenclatura. Nomenclatura rerum. Vocabula mensurarum autore Philippo Melanthone. *Apud Nicolaum Bassee: Francofurti,* 1573. 8°. 623.a.5

Nostredame, Michel de. Zwey Bücher, darinn warhafftiger bericht, wie man einen vngestalten leib zieren soll. *Tr.* Jeremias Martius. *Michael Manger, in verlegung Georgen Willers: Augsburg,* 1572. 8°. C.106.e.14(1)

Nuber, Veit. Ein kurtze leer vom gehorsam der kinder. *Durch Hanssen Khol: Regenspurg,* 1545. 8°. C.142.dd.20

Nuremberg. — **Rat.** New ordenung der betthler halben. *Wolffgang Stöckel: Leypssgk,* [1552.] 4°. 1560/3611

— — [A decree forbidding poaching, 3 Jan.1579.] [*Nuremberg,*]1579. *s.sh. obl.* fol. MS. Egerton 1942, fol.520

— **Appendix.** Ein gründtliche vnd richtige Vnderweysung wie ferr der Stedt eine von Nürnberg einer zu raysen hat. *Margaretha Kreydlin: Nürnberg,* [ca.1565.] *s.sh.* fol. Cup.651.e(78)

Nymann, Hieronymus. Theses medicæ de variolis et morbillis. *Praes.*Andreas Schato. *Resp.* H. Nymann and others. *Typis Zachariæ Lehmanni: VVitebergæ,* 1593. 4°. T.577(8)

O

O., F.R.E.F.O. Tragica historia de miseranda laniena. *See* Frese, Rembertus.

Ochino, Bernardino. Prediche. 4 pt. [*Peter Perna?: Basle,* 1562?] 8°. 846.f.8–11

Octavian, *Emperor, Hero of Romance.* Ein schöne vnd kurtzweylige Histori von Keiser Octauiano. *Tr.* Wilhelm Saltzman. *Michael Manger: Augspurg,* [ca. 1590?] 8°. 12555.aa.6

Oderbornius, Paulus. Reges Poloni. *Typis Georgij Osterbergeri: Regiomonti Borussicæ,* 1579. 4°. 11408.aaa.37

Odrobornius, Paulus. *See* Oderbornius.

Oecolampadius.Joannes. Vrta[y]l vñ mainūg, auch andere reden. [*Erhard Oeglin: Augspurg,* 1520.] 4°. 3906.c.68

Ornithoparchus, Andreas [i.e. **A. Vogelsang**]. De arte cantandi micrologus. *Apud Ioannem Gymnicum: Coloniæ,* 1533. *obl.* 12°. Hirsch I.443

Ortelius, Abraham. Theatrum oder Schawplatz des erdbodems. *G. van Diest: Antorff,* 1572. fol. Maps C.2.c.6

— [Another edition.] *G. van Diest: Antorff,* 1573. fol. Maps C.2.c.10

— [Another edition.] *C. Plantin: Antorff,* 1580 [–84]. fol. Maps C.2.c.15

Orth, Zacharias. Oratio de arte poetica. *Iohannes Crato: VVitebergæ,* 1558. 8°. 1606/1098

Osiander, Andreas. Disputatio de iustificatione. *Ex officina hæredum Ioannis Lufftij:* [*Königsberg,* 1550.] 4°. C.117.ff.15(1)

— Ein Disputation von der Rechtfertigung des Glaubens. [*Hans Lufft:*] *Königsberg in Preussen,* 1551. 4°. C.117.ff.15(2)

Osiander, Lucas. [Ein Predig von dem Widertauff. Sampt Historien welcher Gestalt sich die Widertäuffer zu Münster gehalten. By Heinrich Dorpius.] [*Alexander Hock: Tübingen,* 1582.] 4°. 3906.b.16(impf.)

Osterreicher, Ambrosius. Ein new christlich Lied, zur zeyt der Pestlenz zu singen. *Durch Nicolaum Knorrn: Nürnberg,* 1562. 8°. C.175.i.31(12)

— Ein schön news geystlich lied von der Heymsuchung Gottes. [*Michael Manger: Augspurg,* ca. 1590?] 8°. 11515.i.58(1)

Otho, M. A., *von Hertzberg.* Antwort auff Christoff Lasij rechte Klotzbusse. *s.l.* 1568. 8°. RB.23.a.3151(6)

Otthe, Johann. Der Planet Vhr in ein ewigs Vhrwerck gebracht. *Leonhard Heussler: Nürnberg,* 1587. *s.sh.* fol. Tab.597.d.1(11)

Ovelius, Johannes. Ἐλεγεῖων κατα πολεμούντων συγγεγραμμένον. *Apud Iohan. Oridryum & Alb. Buysium: Dusseldorpii,* 1563. 8°. C.117.ff.10

Overyssel. Landtrecht van Auerissel. *Ed.* Melchior Winhoff. *Simon Steenberch: Deuenter,* 1559. 8°. 1568/2103

Ovidius Naso, Publius. De Ponto libri quattuor. *Ex ædibus Schurerianis: Argentorati,* 1515. 4°. 1609/2793

— Metamorphoseon libri XV. *Apud Nicolaum Brylingerum: Basileæ,* 1546. 16°. C.131.a.6

— Metamorphoseon libri XV. *Ed.* Jacobus Micyllus & Gregorius Bersmanus. *Ioannes Steinman: Lipsiæ,* 1582. 8°. C.189.a.16

— De tristibus libri V. *In officina typographica Michaëlis Mangeri: Augustæ Vindelicorum,* 1587. 8°. 1568/8035

P

Pachymeres, Georgius. In uniuersam fere Aristotelis philosophiam epitome. *Tr.* Philippus Bechius. [With the works of Synesius of Cyrene, *tr.* Janus

Cornarius.] 2 pt. *Ex officina Frobeniana, per Hieron.Frobenium & Nic. Episcopium: Basileae,* 1560. fol.   C.78.e.2

Pacificus, Hermanus, *pseud.* [i.e. **Christoph Herdesianus.**] Simplex et dilucida expositio, qua ratione controversia de Cœna Domini cognosci possit. [*Jean Barsages:*] *Francktaliæ,* 1578. 8°.   1578/4087

Paganus, Petrus. In Quinti Horatii Flacci poematum odas, satyras & epistolas argumenta. *Hæredes Christiani Egenolphi: Francofordiæ,* 1567. 8°.
                     11409.bbb.19(1)

Paleotti, Gabriele, *Cardinal.* De nothis spuriisque filiis liber. *Apud Nicolaum Bassæum & Ioannem Bellerum: Francoforti ad Moenum,* 1573. 8°. 1607/4010

Papa, Ambrosius. Bettel vnd Garteteuffel. *Paul Donat, inn vorlegung Ambrosij Kirchners: Magdeburgk,* 1586 (1587★). 8°.   1578/2419

Papa, Fridericus. Piis manibus Valentini Ritteri. *Typis Ambrosij Fritschij: Gorlicii,* 1587. 4°.   1578/389

Papenburgerus, Henricus. Themata περι των μετεωρων. *Andreas Eichorn: Francoford. Marchionum,* 1580. 4°.   531.l.1(1)

Pappus, Johann. Bericht vnd Warnung belangendt der Kirchen zu Strassburg Confession. *Georg Gruppenbach: Tübingen,* 1581. 4°.   RB.23.a.1723

Pastoris, Heinrich. Practica teütsch auf das 1524. Jar. [*Jörg Gastel: Zwickau,* 1523.] 4°.   4401.n.34

Patrizi, Francesco, *Bishop.* [*Selections.*] Compendiosa epitome commentariorum. [With other matter.] *Apud Ioannem Gymnicum: Coloniæ,* 1591. 24°.   1606/1446

Paul IV., *Pope.* Epistola consolatoria ad suos dilectos filios. *s.l.* 1556. 8°.
                     RB.23.a.3147

Peckhem, Joannes, *Archbishop.* Perspectiua communis. *Ed.* Georg Hartmann. *Apud Iohan. Petreium: Norimbergæ,* 1542. 4°.   537.f.26(1)

Peerus, Henricus. De gratia Dei theses theologicæ. *Praes.*Amandus Polanus. *Typis Conradi Waldkirchii: Basileæ,* 1597. 4°.   4372.bb.5

Pelargus, Christophorus. Hypomnemata in aliquot locos communes theologicos dn. Philippi. *Typis & impensis Friderici Hartmanni: Francof.ad Oderam,* 1597. 8°.   1578/4851

— Lusus poeticus anagrammatum. *Impensis Iohannis & Friderici Hartmannorum: Francoforti ad Oderam,* 1595. 4°.   1481.aaa.43(12)

Perault, Raymond, *Cardinal.* Aliqua extracta a iure diuino, canonico & ciuili. *s.n.* [1502 or 1503.] 4°.   C.125.cc.25

Peristerus, Wolffgang. Kurtze Bekentnus von der Rechtfertigung vnd heiligem Abendmal des Herrn. *s.l.* 1577. 4°.   1568/8800

Perottus, Nicolaus, *Archbishop.* [Grammatica nova.] *Ed.* Bernhard Perger. p *Albertum Kunne: Mēmingen,* 1485. 4°.   IA.11034

Perpinianus, Petrus Joannes. Orationes quinque. [With other matter.] *Sebaldus Mayer: Dilingae,* 1572. 8°.   1607/1377(1)

Persius Flaccus, Aulus. Vnicus satyrarū liber. [*Per*] *Melchiorē Lotter: Liptzk,* 1507. fol.   C.186.d.5(4)

Peter [Canisius], *Saint.* Notæ in euangelicas lectiones. *Excudebat Martinus Bocklerus: Friburgi Brisgoiæ; impensis Abrahami Gemperlini:* [*Fribourg,*]1595. 4°.   1488.cc.20

Petrarca, Francesco. De vita solitaria. *Ioannes le Preux: [Berne,]* 1600. 16°.
8411.a.37(3)

— [Secretum.] De contemptu mundi. *Ioannes le Preux: [Berne,]* 1600. 16°.
8411.a.37(2)

Petrus, *Anspach.* Antithesis der Lutherischen Bekenthniss. *J.H.* [*Johann Jamer*]: *Franckfurt an der Oder,* [1533.] 4°. 1568/8820

Petrus, *Lombardus, Bishop of Paris.* [Sententiae.] Tertia (Quarta) pars huius operis cū disputatis sancti Bonauēture. *Ed.* Stephanus Brulefer. 2 pt. *Industria Iacobi sacon: in lugduneñ. ciuitate; sumptibus & impensis Antonij Kobergis: [Nuremberg,]* 1510. fol. 1505/47

— Von dem hochwirdigen Sacramēt vnder beder gestalt: aus dem vierden bůch Sententiarum. *s.n.* [ca.1510?] 4°. 1560/3350

Pezel, Christoph. Examen theologicum Philippi Melanthonis. 2 pt. *Matthæus Harnisch: Neostadii,* 1587. 8°. C.131.ff.9

— Kurtze Resolution vnd Antwort auff zehen Fragen Tilemāni Heshusii. *s.l.* 1588. 8°. 1607/3119

— Der LXVII. Psalm, der CIIII. Psalm, der CXXXIX. Psalm aussgelegt. *Johann Meyers Erben: Newstatt an der Hart,* 1579. 8°. 1568/4351(1)

— Der 107. Psalm zusampt dem 92. Psalm. Mit kurtzer Ausslegunge. *Durch Mattheum Harnisch: Newstatt an der Hardt,* 1580. 8°. 1568/4351(2)

Pfafrad, Caspar. Theses de noticiis Dei. *Praes.*Daniel Hofmann. *Iacobus Lucius: Helmaestadii,* 1593. 4°. 480.a.6(9)

Pflug, Julius, *Bishop.* Oratio funebris in mortem Pet. Mosell. [*Melchior Lotter: Wittenberg,* 1524.] 4°. 1608/5537

Pfruendenmarkt. Von dem pfründtmarckt der Curtisanen vnd Tempelknechten. [*Adam Petri: Basle,* 1521.] 4°. 1226.a.82

Philadelphus, Eusebius, *pseud.* [i.e. **Georg Zigli.**] Libertatis Germanicæ querela. *s.l.* 1586. 4°. 1315.b.38

Philalethes, *Hyperboraeus, pseud.* [i.e. **Joannes Ludovicus Vives.**] In Anticatoptrum suū parasceue. *Per Sebastianum Golsenum: Lunenburgi,* 1533. 8°. *The imprint is fictitious; printed by Michiel Hillen at Antwerp.*
G.1238

Philip, *Landgrave of Hesse.* Ein Christlich schreyben an den Gardian zu Margburg. *Gabriel Kantz: Aldenburgk,* 1525. 4°. C.141.cc.25

— Tertia aduersus Ducis Henrici scriptum responsio. *s.n.* [1541.] 4°.
1568/8798

Picciolus, Antonius, *the Elder.* De manus inspectione libri tres. *Bergomi; expensis Ioannis Baptistæ Ciotti: [Venice,*]1587. 8°. *The Bergamo imprint is false; printed by Johann Wechel at Frankfort on the Main.* C.79.a.2(1)

Picolomineus, Dominicus. De laudibus liberalium disciplinarū oratio. *Per Jacobum Thanner: Lyptzgk,* 1511. 4°. Hirsch IV.1524

Pinu, Josephus a. Carmina cæsarum, regum et archiducum ex familia Austriaca natales indicantia. *s.l.* 1572. 8°. 11409.e.58

Pirckheimer, Bilibaldus. De uera Christi carne & uero eius sanguine responsio secunda. [*Johann Petrejus;*] *Norembergæ,* 1527. 8°. 1607/615

Pistorius, Johann, *of Nidda.* Badische Disputation. *Durch Gerwinum Calenium & die Erben Johan Quentels: Cöln,* 1590. 4°. 1578/2394

— De vita et morte Iacobi, Marchionis Badensis, orationes duæ. *Apud Geruinum Calenium & hæredes Ioannis Quentelij: Coloniæ*, 1591. 4°.
10703.bb.5

— Thesium D. Iacobi Herbrandi de visibili Christi analysis. [With other matter.] *Ex officina typographica Dauidis Sartorii: Ingolstadii*, 1589. 4°.
1609/2811(2)

Plautus, Titus Maccius. Comedia prima cui Amphitryo nomen inditum est. *Per Melchiarem* [sic] *Lotterū: Lypsi*, 1511. fol. C.186.d.5(3)

Plinius Secundus, Caius. Bücher von Natur, Art vnd Eygenschafft aller Creaturen Gottes. [Books 7–11.] *Tr.* Johann Heyden. *Durch Johañ Saurn, in Verlegung Eliæ Willers: Franckfort am Mayn*, 1600. fol. L.35/127

— Ad Titum Vespasianū in libros naturalis hystorie epistola. Cū Johānis Aesticāpiani epistolio. *Per Vuolfgangū monacensem: Liptzk*, 1508. 4°.
RB.23.a.736

Plonick. Ein hübsches Lied wie zu Plonig ein Christen eynes Juden Tochter schwanger macht. *Valentin Neuber: Nürnberg*, [ca.1560?] 8°. 11521.a.46

Plunderus, Heinricus. Eyns aussgangen Kartheusers Vntherricht sso er vrsach seyns aussgangs antzeigt. *W[olfgang] S[türmer]: [Erfurt,]* 1523. 4°.
C.117.ff.14

Plutarch. [*De curiositate.*] De curiositate libellus. *Tr.* Joannes Caselius. *Iacobus Lucius: Helmaestadii*, 1595. 4°. 1578/348

— [*Moralia.*] Opera moralia quæ latiné extant uniuersa. *Ed.* Hieronymus Gemusaeus. *Apud Mich.Isingrinium: Basileæ*, 1541. fol. 1505/54(1)

— — Guoter Sytten xxj Bücher. Syttliche Hoff Sprüch der alten Künigen. *Tr.* Heinrich von Eppendorff. 2 pt. *Bey Hans Schotten: Strassburg*, 1554 [1544?]. fol. *The date has been tampered with.* C.130.i.11

— [*Vitae parallelae.*] Las vidas de los varones Griegos y Romanos. *Tr.* Juan Castro de Salinas. *À costas de los herederos de Arnoldo Bircman: Colonia; Anuers*, 1562. fol. 10605.i.5; 135.b.7

— — Las vidas de dos illustres varones, Cimon y Lucio Lucullo. [*Johann Oporinus: Basle,*] 1547. 4°. 277.f.15

Poenitentia. Poenitentia evangelica. *See* Evangelical Penitence.

Poeta. Poeta salutaris. *Per Hermannū Būgart: Colonie*, 1502. 4°. 11409.c.18

— [Another edition.] *Per Martinū de Werdena: Colonie*, 1510. 4°. 11405.e.30

Pol., S. *See* Pollio, Simphorianus.

Pole, Reginald, *Cardinal.* Testamentum vere Christianum. [*Sebald Mayer: Dillingen,*] 1559. 4°. G.11708

Polichius, Martinus. Compendium quindecim propositionum in astrologiā. [*Bartholomaeus Ghotan: Magdeburg*, ca.1483.] 4°. IA.10910

Pollicarius, Johannes. Ein Sendbrieff von der Schlacht, vnd abschied aus diesem leben des Churfürsten zu Sachsen. *George Hantzsch: Leipzig*, 1553. 4°. 1609/3335

— Trostspiegel der armen Sünder. *Durch Jacobum Berwald: Leipzig*, 1556. fol.
RB.23.c.30

Pollio, Simphorianus. Göttlicher vñ Bäpstlicher Recht gleich förmige zůsag. [*Johann Schott: Strasburg,*] 1529. 8°. 1578/8423

— [Another edition.] Göttlicher vnnd Bäpstlicher Recht gleich förmige zůsag. [*Hans Gruener: Ulm,*] 1529. 8°. 846.b.15

Polybius. Römische Historien. *Tr.* Gulielmus Xylander. *Sebastian Henricpetri: Basel,* 1574. fol. C.103.i.17

Pomarius, Johann. Christlicher junger Herren Ehrenschild. *Wilhelm Ross, in verlegung Johann Francken: Magdeburgk,* 1582. 12°. 1578/8162

Pomponius Laetus, Julius. De antiquitatibus urbis Romæ libellus. [With other matter.] *Per Thomam Platterum: Basileæ,* 1538. 8°. 1578/5068

Pope. Non esse iure prohibitum, quin Summus Pontifex dispensare possit, vt frater demortui fratris vxorem legitimo matrimonio sibi possit adiungere. [By Joannes Ludovicus Vives.] *Lunemburgæ,* 1532. 4°. The imprint is false; printed by Martinus de Keyser at Antwerp.
G.1234; C.24.e.1(impf.)

Porcia, Bartolomeo di, *Count.* Oratio de cinerum habita. *Sebaldus Mayer: Dilingæ,* [1562?] 4°. 1609/5726

Porrentruy. [*Official Publications.*] Offentlicher widerouff der Johannetten Geste Hausfrawen des Nicolai Febur. [Report by Reinhard Schmit.] [*Johann Schmidt: Porrentruy?,* 1600.] *s.sh.* fol. Cup.645.a.5(4)

Porta, Conrad. Jungfrawen Spiegel. *Vrban Gaubisch: Eisleben,* 1580. 8°.
1578/6021

Porta, Giovanni Battista della. De occultis literarum notis libri. *Apud Iacobum Foillet: Montisbeligardi; expensis Lazari Zetzneri:* [Strasburg,] 1593. 8°. 8707.aaa.14

— Magiæ naturalis libri viginti. *Apud Andreæ Wecheli heredes: Francofurti,* 1591. 8°. 1651/83

Posselius, Joannes. Οἰκειῶν διαλογῶν βιβλίον ἑλληνιστὶ καὶ ῥωμαιστὶ. *Zacharias Lehman: VVitebergæ,* 1590. 8°. 1568/8850(impf.)

Possevino, Antonio. [Responsio regi septentrionali.] Fragstuck von der Kirchen Gottes. *Tr.* Joachimus Landolt. *Martin Böckler: Freyburg im Breissgaw,* 1593. 8°. 1607/5507(1)

Posthius, Joannes. Tetrasticha in Ouidii Metam. *Lat. & Ger. Ill.* V. Solis. *Apud Georgium Coruinum, Sigismundum Feyrabent, & hæredes VVigandi Galli: Francofurti,* 1569. obl. 8°. MS.Egerton 1194(3)

Potho, *Benedictine, of Prüffling.* De statu domus Dei libri. De magna domo sapientiæ liber. *Ed.* Joannes Alexander Brassicanus. *Per Ioan.Secerium: Haganoæ,* 1532. 8°. 1578/1521

Poynet, John, *Bishop.* The humble and unfained confession. *See* Confession.

Poyssel, Eustachius. Etliche Tractetlein. *Apud Rupertum Fluuium H.: ann der Oder,* 1595. 4°. *The imprint is fictitious.* 1607/740

Praecepta. Precepta coaugmētāde Rethorice oracōnis. [By Conrad Wimpina.] [*Printer of Capotius: Leipzig,* ca.1488.] 4°. IA.11780

Praetorius, Zacharias. De dicto Pauli, saluetur mulier per filiorum generationem. Scriptum epithalamion. *VVitebergæ,* 1555. 4°. 1568/1048

Prague. Newe zeytung vonn dem erschrockenlichen fewr, so newlich in der klainern statt Prag geschehen ist. *Heynrich Steyner: Augspurg,* [1541.] 4°.
8716.bb.19

Primasius, *Bishop of Adramyttium.* In omnes D.Pauli epistolas commentarii. *See* Bible. — Epistles.

Proles, Andreas. Sermones vff die Sōtagē. *Ed.* Peter Sylvius. *Valten Schuman: Leypsigk,* 1530. 4°. 1570/2618

Pulmannus, Jacobus. Ritus agni paschalis. *Clemens Schleich & Antonius Schöne: VVitebergæ,* 1578. 4°. 1578/2643

Purvey, John. A compendious olde treatyse. *See* Bible. — *Appendix.* [*English.*]

Q

Quadrivium. Quadruuij practici epitōata. *Apud p̄dicatores: Colonie,* [1510?] 4°.
Hirsch IV.1490

Quercu, Simon de. Opusculū musices. *Joañ. Weyssenburger: Landsshut,* 1516. 4°. Hirsch I.479

Quichelbergus, Samuel. Inscriptiones vel tituli theatri amplissimi. *Ex officina Adami Berg: Monachii,* 1565. 4°. RB.23.a.2776

Quinos, Bruno. Disce mori oder Sterbe Kunst. Tl.1. *Durch Nicolaum Schneider: Zittaw,* 1586. 8°. 1607/5514

R

R., L. The boke Reade me frynde and be not wrothe. [By William Barlow.] *Henry Nycolson: Wesell,* 1546. 8°. *The imprint is fictitious; printed at Antwerp by Steven Mierdman?* C.53.aa.24

Rabe, Johann Jacob. Ad Ludouicum patrem pro fide Catholica epistola. *Apud Maternum Cholinum: Coloniæ,* 1570. 8°. 1578/1419

Rabshakeh. Ein rechter lesteriger Rabsakes brieff. *Ed.* Mathias Flacius. [*Christian Rödinger: Magdeburg,*] 1549. 4°. 1608/3178

Radtmann, Bartholomaeus. [Introductio in linguam arabicam.] [*Andreas Eichorn: Frankfurt a.d.O.,* 1592.] 4°. 622.h.2(2★)(impf.)

Raedt, Hieronymus Arnoldus de. Assertionum matrimonialium pars prima (altera). *Resp.* H. A. de Raedt & Leonardus Treytwein. *Praes.* Henricus Canisius. 2 pt. *Ex officina Davidis Sartorii: Ingolstadii,* 1590, 91. 4°.
1568/5239

Randenburgh, Rutgerus. Disputationis de potestate Ecclesiastica pars prima, secunda & tertia. *Praes.* Petrus Thyraeus. *Casparus Behem: Moguntiæ,* 1586. 4°. 4051.bb.35

Ransanus, Petrus, Bishop. Epitome rerum Vngaricarum. *Ed.* Joannes Sambucus. 2 pt. *Raphaël Hofhalter: Viennæ Austriæ,* 1558. fol.
C.114.h.7(1)

Raphael, *Volateranus. See* Maffeus, R.

Raphelt, Martinus. Einfeltiger Vnterricht von den Brandschäden. *Typis Beyeri, in verlegung Johan. Börners des ältern: Leipzig,* [1592.] 4°. 1578/7194

Raspergerus, Christophorus. Verantwortung, die Communion einer gstalt betreffend. *Adam Berg: München,* 1567. 4°. 1578/2803

— Von dem Nachtmal dess Herrn einhellige Lehr der Theologen, so sich zu der Augspurgischen Confession bekennen. *Alexander Weyssenhorn & Miterben: Ingolstadt,* 1577. 4°. 1568/5091

Ratisbon, *Diocese of.* — **Johann,** *Count Palatine.* Statuta Diocesana. *Per Johannem Pfeil: in ciuitate Babenbergeñ.,* 1512. fol. C.131.g.17

Rausch, *Bruder.* Bruder Rausch. *Valentin Fuhrman: Nürnberg,* [ca. 1580.] 8°.
11517.de.24(6)

Raut, Georgius. Die siebenzehen hewbtartickel der gantzen schrifft. [*Johannes Rhau-Grunenberg:*] *Wittemberg,* 1525. 8°. 3559.a.1

Rebhun, Paul. Hausfried. *Veit Creutzer: Wittemberg,* 1552. 8°. 1578/3606

Regebrand, Georg. Elegia de vera nobilitate. *Per Martinum de Dolgen: Erphurdiæ,* 1571. 4°. 1608/2487

Regula. [Regula D]Ominus que pars. [By Remigius the Grammarian.] [*Friedrich Creussner: Nuremberg,* ca. 1493.] 4°. IA.7700

Regulae. Regule ɔgruitatū. *Per Fridericū Creusner:* [*Nuremberg,*]1493. 4°.
IA.7698

Reihen Lieder. Vier geistliche Reyen lieder. *Valentin Newber: Nürnberg,* [ca. 1555?] 8°. C.175.i.31(19)

Reineck, Reinerus. Familia Arsacidarum. *Lipsiæ,* 1571. 4°. 1568/5192

Reissner, Adam. Ain new geystlich Lied, Ewiger Vatter im Himmelreich. *See* Lied.

Rennecherus, Hermannus. Aurea salutis catena. *Apud Nicolaum Erbenium: Lichæ,* 1597. 8°. 4410.bb.48

Reuschius, Joannes. Propositiones aliquot de Spyrensis puellę inedia. *Per Anastasium Noltium: Spyrę,* 1542. 4°. 1165.e.11(1)

Reusner, Nicolaus. Icones sive imagines impp., regum, principum, electorum et ducum Saxoniæ. *Typis Tobiæ Steinmanni: Ienæ; impensis Henningi Grosij:* [*Leipzig,*] 1597. fol. 1605/812(2)

Reuss, Martin. Ein schön news Lied: von dem laster so von der Zungen kompt. *Durch Michaelem Manger: Augspurg,* [ca. 1570.] 8°. 11522.df.112

Reychart, Petter. Ain Christenlich gesprech Büchlin vonn zwayen Weybern. [*Heinrich Steiner: Augsburg,*]1523. 4°. 1568/5434

Reyna, Cassiodoro de. Declaracion o confession de fe. *See* Spaniards.

Reysacher, Barptolomaeus. Almanach zu Wienn calculiert. M.D.LVI. (Practica auff das M.D.Lvj.Jar.) 2 pt. *Michel Zimmerman: Wień,* [1555, 56.] 4°. 1609/1574

Reyssersperg, Johannes. *See* Geiler, Johann.

Rhegius, Urbanus. Erklerung der Zwelff Artickel Christlichs glawbens. *Hans Lufft: Wittemberg,* 1525. 8°. C.190.d.20(1)

Rhodes. Miracula que tempe obsidionis ciuitatis Rhodi contigerunt. [*Michael Greyff: Reutlingen,* 1480.] *s.sh. obl.* 4°. IA.10656

Rhomanus, Johannes. Das ist der hoch thuren Babel. [*Heirs of Matthias Schürer: Strasburg,* 1521.] 4°. 1226.b.2

Richter, Matthaeus. Einfeltiger vnterricht für die Christen in Magdeburgk. *s.l.* 1563. 4°. 1578/1437

Rigelius, Stephanus. Pythagoræ et Phocylidis carmina Latine reddita, authore S. Rigelio. Eiusdem epigrammatum libellus. *Ioannes Cruciger: Nissæ,* 1561. 8°. 1607/5475

Rigeman, Paulus. Exequiæ D. Iulio Duci Brunouicensi et Lunæburgensi. [*Konrad Horn:*] *Henricopoli,* 1589. 4°. 1509/2602

Riolan, Jean, *the Elder.* In libros Fernelij commentarij. *Per Iacobum Foyllet: Mompelgarti,* 1588. 8°. C.107.c.27

Rivius, Joannes. De erroribus pontificiorum. [*Johann Oporinus?:*] *Basileæ,*
[1546.] 8°. Davis II, 32(1)

— De perpetuo in terris gaudio piorū libellus. *Per Ioannem Oporinum: Basileæ,*
1550. 8°. 1568/6431

— De stultitia mortalium in procrastinanda correctione uitæ liber. [*Johann Oporinus?:*] *Basileæ,* [1547.] 8°. Davis II, 32(2)

Rodler, Hieronymus. Perspectiua. *Cyriacus Jacob: Franckfort,* 1546. fol.
C.189.bb.10

Roggius, Nicolaus. Musicæ practicæ elementa. *In officina Ulrici Neuberi & Theodorici Gerlatzeni: Noribergæ,* 1566. 8°. Hirsch IV.1539

Roman Preacher. Eyn sturm wyder eyn leymen thurm eins Romischen predigers. [By Georg Fener von Weyl.] [*Wolfgang Stürmer: Erfurt,* 1521.] 4°. C.119.dd.12

Rome. — **Emperors.** — **Theodosius II.** Codicis Theodosiani libri XVI.
Henricus Petrus: Basileæ, 1528. fol. C.188.c.8

— — **Justinian I.** [*Institutiones.*] Institutionum libri quatuor. Caij Institutionū lib. II. 2 pt. *Per Ioannem Schoeffer: Moguntiæ,* 1529. 8°. C.113.a.14(1, 2)

— — — Institutionum libri quatuor. *Ed.* Gregorius Haloander. *Apud Io. Petreium: Norembergae,* 1529. 8°. C.186.b.28

Rome, *the City.* [*Appendix.*] Eyn Sendbrieff so eyner von Venedig herauss geschickt hat, darynn begriffen wie es zu Rom ergangen ist. [*Melchior Sachse: Erfurt,*]1527. 4°. 1318.c.20

— — Warhafftige Anzaygung des grossen Gewessers so sich zu Rhom begeben. [*Philip Ulhart: Augsburg,* 1530.] 4°. 1608/5471

— — Warhafftige newe Zeittung vnd Wunderzeichen, so sich zu Rom vnnd zu Paris geschehen. *s.n.* [1584.] 4°. 1607/5686

Rome. — **Church of Rome.** — **Curia Romana.** Termini causarum in romana Curia. (Festa palacii Apostolici.) [*Heinrich Knoblochtzer: Heidelberg,* ca.1491.] 4°. IA.12988

— — **Nicholas V.,** *Pope.* Bulla cōcordatorū: inter sanctā sedē & nationē germanicā. [1 April 1447.] [*Johann Winterburg: Vienna,* ca.1510.] fol.
C.129.k.2(4)

— — **Paul II.,** *Pope.* Copia litterarū de publicatione anni jobilei. [19 April 1470.] [*Printer of Dares: Cologne,* 1470?] 4°. IA.3351

— — **Sixtus IV.,** *Pope.* [Indulgence to contributors to the war-fund against the Turks. Singular issue. Block-printed.] *s.n.* [1482.] *s.sh.* fol. IB.38

— — **Gregory XIII.,** *Pope.* Bann Bapst Gregorij, wasser gestalt er Gebhard Truchses, Ertzbischoff zu Cölln degradirt. [1583.] *Lugduni Batauorum,* 1584. 4°. *The imprint is false.* 1226.a.71

Rosignoli, Bernardino. De disciplina Christianæ perfectionis libri quinque.
Ex typographia Adami Sartorii: Ingolstadii, 1600. 4°. 1609/524

Rota, Petrus de. In illustrissimæ dominæ Reginæ Annæ obitum carmen.
[*Nuremberg,* 1547.] 8°. 1568/6651

Roth, Simon. Dialogi pueriles. Lat. & Ger. *Matthæus Francus: Augustæ Vindelicorum,* 1568. 8°. 1568/186

Rothenburg. Ein hüpsch lied von der vertreybung der Juden zů Rotenburg.
[*Heirs of Matthias Schürer: Strasburg,* 1521.] 8°. 11522.de.46

— Eyn Sermon wyder die vnzymliche Tragung đ zypffelbiredt zu Rottenburgk. [*Friedrich Peypus: Nuremberg,* 1521.] 4°. 3906.c.78

53

Roth von Schreckenstein, Hieronymus. Libellus de principalitate Romanæ Ecclesiæ. *Ex officina Alexandri Vueissenhorn: Ingolstadii*, 1550. 4°.
1578/3852

Rotmarus, Valentinus. Justa Alberto Bauariæ Duci exhibita autoribus Valentino Rotmaro et Ioanne Engerdo. *Ex officina Weissenhorniana apud Wolfgangum Ederum: Ingolstadii*, 1579. 4°. 1568/177

Rottingus, Michael. Testimonium contra falsam Andreæ Osiandri de iustificatione sententiam. *s.n.* [ca. 1551.] 4°. 1578/1445

Ruef, Thomas. Oratio funebris in exequiarum solennitate Ernesti Archiducis Austriæ. *Typis Leonhardi Formicæ: Viennæ Austriæ*, 1595. 4°. 10705.b.44

Rutland, Johann Caspar. Loci communes theologici. *Sebaldus Mayer: Dilingæ*, 1559. 8°. 849.e.22

Ruysbroeck, Jan van. Opera omnia. *Tr.* Laurentius Surius. *Ex officina hæredum Ioannis Quentel: Coloniæ*, 1552. fol. 494.i.4

Ryff, Walther Hermann. Bawkunst. *Sebastian Henricpetri: Basel*, 1582. fol.
C.127.k.10

S

S., C. Ein Gebet zum Herrn Christo in Kriegssnöten. C. S. [Caspar Schwenckfeld.] *Hans Zimmerman: Augspurg*, 1552. 4°. 1578/3850

— Die zehen gebott Gottes inn gesang weiss verfasset. C. S. *Georg Steinmetz: S. Annabergk*, [ca. 1560.] 8°. C.104.a.15

S., F. K. Kurtzer bericht welcher gestalt Kaiser Carl der fünfft Hertzog Moritzen zu Sachsen mit andern Herrschafften auff dem Reichsstage zu Auspurg belehenet hat. [Signed: F.K.S.] *Durch Crispinum Scharffenbergk: Görlitz*, 1548. 4°. C.107.d.34

S., I. Neanisci. 2 pt. [*Josias Rihel:*] *Argentorati*, 1565, 66. 8°. 1080.h.19(3, 4)

Sachs, Hans. Disputatio zwischen eynem Chorherren vnd Schumacher. [*Jakob Schmidt:*] *Spyer*, 1524. 4°. C.135.b.19(4)

— Der gantz Haussrat. [*Georg Merkel: Nuremberg*, 1550?] 4°. 1568/6449

— Eyn gesprech von den Scheinwercken der Geystlichen. *s.l.* 1524. 4°.
C.135.b.19(3)

— Ein schön Meister Lied, von der Gottsförchtigen Frawen Judit. *Valentin Newber: Nürmberg*, [ca. 1555?] 8°. C.175.i.31(43)

— Ein schön news Lied, Die Ehebrecher Bruck. *See* Lied.

— Die Zerstörung Jherusalem. *Valentin Newber: Nürmberg*, 1560. 8°.
C.175.i.31(38)

Sachs, Michael. Kurtzer ausszug dass getreweñ Eckards, seiner Vermahnung an alle Menschenkinder. *Bey & in verlegung Nicol Nerlichs: Leipzig*, [ca. 1595?] 8°. 11515.a.58(5)(impf.)

— Vier lehr vnd trostreiche Predigten von den Wunden Jhesu Christi. *Gedruckt durch Andream Hantzsch, impensis Hieronymi Reinhardi: Mühlhausen*, 1587. 8°. 1568/4340

Sacrobosco, Joannes de. Libellus de sphæra. Computus ecclesiasticus. [With other matter.] *Apud Vitum Creutzer: Vitebergæ*, 1545. 8°.
1606/1621(impf.)

Salfeld, Basilius. Zwo predigten vom Wucher. *Durch Wolffgangum Günter: Leipzig*, 1550. 4°. 3906.cc.96

Saltzman, Gregor. Ain new gar schön Büchlin von allen Wildbeder Natur. *Philipp Vlhart: Augspurg*, 1538. 4°. 1568/6479

Sampson, Thomas. A letter to the trew professors of Christes Gospell. *Strasburgh*, 1554. 8°. The imprint is false; printed by Josse Lamprecht at Wesel? G.5920

Santbech, Daniel. Problematum astronomicorum et geometricorum sectiones septem. *Per Henrichum Petri & Petrum Pernam: Basileæ*, 1561. fol. A separate issue of the edition also found as pt.2 of Johann Mueller: *De triangulis planis*. L.35/98

Sarcephalus, Christophorus. Duodecim domiciliorum cœlestium tabula nova. *Ex officina typographica Georgij Bawmanni: Wratislaviæ*, 1600. 4°. 1578/5988

Sarcerius, Erasmus. Creutzbüchlein. *Georgen Rhawen Erben: Wittemberg*, 1549. 8°. C.106.cc.25

— Hausbuch fur die Haus veter von den vornemsten Artickeln der Christlichen Religion. *Durch Jacobum Berwald: Leiptzig*, 1553. fol. C.175.dd.22

Sartorius, Joannes, *of Burckersdorf.* Eine christliche Trost vnd Leichpredigt. Bey dem Leichbegengnis Johan: Friderichen, Hertzogen zu Sachsen. *Gedruckt bey Martin: Wittel, in verlegung Ottonis von Risswick: Erffurd*, 1596. 4°. 1609/6300

Satler, Basilius. Eine christliche Predigt bey der Begrebnus der Frewlein Sabina Catharina, Hertzogin zu Sachsen. *Durch Jacobum Lucium: Helmstadt*, 1593. 4°. 1578/2536

— Zwo Predigten gehalten vber der Leich der Frawen Dorothea, Hertzogin zu Braunschweig vnd Lüneburg. *Conrad Horn: Juliusfriedenstedt*, 1587. 4°. 1568/5437

Saum, Conradt. Ein erzwügne antwurt vff das büchlin Hansen Schradins. [*Hans Grüner:*] *vlm*, [15]27. 4°. 3906.aaa.106

Savonarola, Girolamo. [*Expositio in Psal. XXX, L.*] Meditatio super Psalmos Miserere mei, et In te Domine speraui. [*Johannes Rhau-Grunenberg:*] *Vuittembergæ*, 1523. 4°. C.110.d.18

— [*Expositio in Psal. L.*] Auslegung des psalmē Miserere mei deus. *Peter wagner: nürmberg*, [ca.1499.] 8°. IA.8010

Saxony, *the Duchy.* —**Frederick** and **John,** *Dukes.* [An edict on coinage.] [*Martin Landsberg: Leipzig*, after 28 Sept. 1490.] *s.sh.* fol. IB.11850

Saxony, *the Electorate.* —**Maurice,** *Elector.* Ausschreiben, die Pollicey belangende. [18 Dec. 1549.] [*Matthes Stoeckel: Dresden?,*]1550. 4°. 1578/2375

Scalichius, Paulus, *Count.* Oration von der Genealogia der Scalichern. *Christian Müller: Strassburg*, 1561. 4°. 1578/3539

Schardius, Simon. Hypomnema de fide Pontificum Romanorum erga Imperatores Germanicos. *Per Ioannem Oporinum: Basileæ*, 1566. 8°. 1489.p.45

Scharschmied, Franciscus. Historia vom Christlichen wandel Martini Lutheri in Reim gestellet. *Veit Creutzer: Wittemberg*, 1546. 4°. 11517.d.32

Schechsius, Johannes. Christliche Predigt auss dem Euangelio Johan. 6. *Johan Spies: Heydelberg*, 1583. 4°. 1560/2682

Scheidt, Caspar. Ein kurtzweilige Lobrede von wegen des Meyen. *Durch Gregorium Hofman: Wormbs*, [1551.] 4°. 1578/8591

Schelchinus, Walthazarus. Die zehen gebot Gottes in gesang verfast. *Grätz,* [ca. 1565?] 8°. C.175.i.31(57)

Scheldt. Contrafactur der festung vnd schantzen wie iets die Schelde besatst ist. *s.l.* 1585. *s.sh.* fol. C.18.e.2(68)

Schelling, Vendelinus. [Actionum & exceptionum forensium explanatio.] [*Apud Christianum Egenolphum: Francoforti,*] 1549. 4°. 1560/506(impf.)

Schenck, Jacob. Auslegung des spruchs S. Pauls, Ir Weiber seid vnterthan Ewren Mennern. *Joseph Klug: Wittemberg*, 1540. 4°. 1578/1825

Scherer, Georg. Ob es war sey, das ein Bapst schwanger gewesen, gründtlicher bericht. *Leonhard Nassinger: Wienn*, 1584. 4°. 4787.aa.18

Schielborg, Hans. Erzelung eines Burgers Son Hans Schielborg genandt. *Gregor Huber: Wien,* [1597.] 4°. 1312.c.4

Schiff. Das verdorben schiff der handtwercks leut. *Hans Hofer: Augspurg,* [ca. 1540?] *s.sh.* fol. 1870.d.1(172)

Schiphower, Johannes. Tractat[9] de beata maria Magdalena. [*Ludwig von Renchen: Cologne,* ca. 1502?] 4°. 4808.bb.25

Schirmeister, Stephanus, *of Naumburg.* Querela lugubris de obitu Philippi Melanthonis. *Vitebergæ*, 1560. 4°. 11408.bb.9

Schmalkaldic War. Summarium dess Euangelischen, das ist, Schmalkaldischen Kriegs. *See* Evangelical War.

Schmidenstedt, Heinrich. Ein schöne Oration vonn Keyser Otten dem Ersten. *Tr.* Georg Lauterbeck. *Durch Georgen Raben & Weygand Hanen Erben: Franckfurt am Mayn,* 1563. 8°. 10704.aaa.23

Schmidlap, Johannes. Künstliche Fewerwerck. *Johann vom Berg & Vlrich Newber: Nürnberg,* 1564. 8°. 1560/4188(4)

Schmit, Reinhard. Offentlicher widerouff der Johannetten Geste. *See* Porrentruy.

Schnaitpeckh, Johann. Oratio ad Carolū Cesarem que Antwarpij dicta est. *Per Joannem Erffordianum: Wurmacie,* [1521.] 4°. 1578/3381

Schnauss, Ciriacus. Hertzog Ernst christlich verendert. *Valentin Newber: Nürmberg,* [ca. 1560?] 8°. C.175.i.31(2)

Schoener, Andreas. Γνωμονικὴ μηχανική. Ein kurtzer bericht leichtlich aller art Sonnen vhren zu machen. *Johañ von Berg & Vlrich Newber: Nürnberg,* 1562. 8°. 1487.ee.11

Schopper, Jacob, *the Elder.* Comœdiæ et tragœdiæ sacræ et nouæ. *Apud Maternum Cholinum: Coloniæ,* 1562. 8°. C.99.a.42

— Monomachia Davidis et Goliae. *Melchoir Soter: Tremoniae,* 1550. 8°. C.117.ff.8(1)

— Ouis perdita. *Apud Maternum Cholinum: Colonæ* [sic]*,* 1562. 8°. C.117.ff.8(2)

— Voluptatis ac virtutis pugna. *Mart. Gymnicus: Coloniæ*, 1546. 8°. G.17405

— [Another edition.] *Typis Christophori Lochneri & Iohannis Hofmanni: Noribergæ*, 1590. 8°. 11712.aa.43

Schorkelius, Sigismundus. In tumulum Philippi Melanthonis elegia.
Laurentius Schuenck: VVitebergæ, 1560. 4°. 11409.c.17
Schosserus, Joannes. Marchiados liber primus. *Pref.* P. Melanchthon. *[Johann Eichorn:] Francofordiæ cis Viadrum,* 1562. 4°. Davis II, 337
Schott, Johann. Enchiridion poeticum. *See* Virgilius Maro, Publius. *[Appendix. — Concordances.]*
Schradin, Johann. Gründtliche vrsach der yetz schwebenden Kriegssleuff. *[Ulrich Morhart: Tübingen?,]* 1546. 8°. 11515.a.39
Schrick, Michael. Von allē gebranten wassern. *Joseph Klug: Wittemberg,* 1530. 8°. 1568/1367
Schueler, Gervasius. Ain vast kurtz Christenlich gespräch von dem Gebeet. *Durch Syluañ Othmar: Augspurg,* 1534. 8°. 3908.aa.31
Schuirphius, Hieronymus. Oratio recitata cum Ioannes à Borcken doctoratus insignia reciperet. *Per Ioannem Eichorn: Francoforti ad Viadrum,* 1553. 4°. 525.e.22
Schultes, Jacobus. Quæstio singularis, an rex Christianus datam hæretico fidem servare teneatur. *Sumtibus Grosianis: [Leipzig,]* 1599. 8°. 699.c.57
Schutz, Henricus. Conclusiones de appellationibus. *Ex officina Oporiniana: Basileæ,* [1591.] 4°. 1509/1502(impf.)
Schwarzenberg, Adolph von, *Count.* Warhaffter Bericht vnnd widersprechen auff das vnwarhafft gedicht. *Michael Manger: Augspurg,* 1598. 4°. RB.23.a.3148
Schwarzenberg, Johann von, *Baron.* Der zutrincker vnd Prasser Ordenung. *See* Zutrinker.
Schyphower, Johannes. *See* Schiphower.
Schyrlentz, Hieronymus. Ein Lobspruch zu Ehren Christiano dem IIII. Könige zu Dennemarck vnd Norwegen. *Augustin Ferber: Rostock,* 1596. 4°. 1578/5230
Scultetus, Abraham. Sphæricorum libri tres. De solutione triangulorum tractatus Bartholomæi Pitisci. *Typis Abrahami Smesmanni: Heidelbergæ; impensis Matthæi Harnisch: [Neustadt a.d. Haardt,]* 1595. 8°. 533.b.6(3)
Sebastus, Alphonsus Aemilius, *pseud.* Pasquillus, der vertriben von Rhom. *s.n.* [1546.] 4°. 8026.b.29
Seccervitius, Joannes. Hymnus de Spiritu Sancto. *s.n.* [1557?] 4°. 3437.ff.8
Sedelius, Wolfgang. De templo Salomonis mystico tractatus. *Franciscus Behem: apud S. Victorem prope Moguntiam,* 1548. 8°. 1507/543
— Ob der abgestorben Seelen ein ander erkennen, Catholische resolution. *Alexander & Samuel Weyssenhorn: Ingolstat,* 1551. 4°. 1608/2527
Seitz, Alexander. Ein nutzlicher tractat von der aderlass. *Johann Weyssenburger: [Landshut,]* 1527. 4°. 1508/651
Selneccer, Nicolaus. Summa der Lehre von dem heiligen Abendmal. *[Konrad Horn:] Heinrichszstadt,* 1571. 8°. 1578/1428
Sendler, Veltin. Ein schöne Frag von einem Bawren. *s.n.* [ca.1545?] 4°. 3906.f.98
Seneca, Lucius Annaeus. [*Letters.*] Epistolarum ad Lucilium flores. *Ed.* Johann Chrysostomus. *Franciscus Behem: Moguntiæ,* 1559. 8°. RB.23.a.1962

— [Supposititious Works.] [De moribus.] Ain kurtzer ausszuge den ich Dieterich von Pleningen gethon hab. *Johann Weyssenburger: Landsshüt*, 1515. 4°.
C.186.e.8

Sententiae. Centum et XIIII sententiæ patrum, de officio rectorum ecclesiæ Dei. *Ioannes Praël: Coloniæ*, 1531. 8°. 1607/2523

Sermones. Sermones quadragesimales Thesauri noui. [*Martin Flach:*] *Argentine*, 1494. fol. IB.2177

— Sermones Thesauri noui de tempore. [*Printer of Sermones Thesauri novi:*] *Argentine*, 1486. fol. IB.1316

— [Another edition.] *Per Martinum flach: Argentine*, 1493. fol. IB.2176

Seyn, Georg von, *Count zu Wittgenstein.* Aussschreiben Gorgē von Seyn, Hermañ Adolphē Graffen zu Solms, Johañsen Freyherrn zu Wiñenberg, Ernstē Graffen zu Manssfeld. *s.l.* 1585. 4°. 1560/4435(impf.)

Sheba, *Queen of.* Sybilla. Die dreyzehend Sybilla ein küngin von Sabba. *Hans Schönsperger: Augspurg,* [ca.1515?] 4°. 12431.c.2

Siberus, Adamus. In Dauidis Psalterium commentariorum libri quinque. Pt.1. *Hæredes Iohannis Cratonis: Vitebergæ*, 1580. 8°. 1578/3386

Sigismund, *Emperor of Germany.* Ein offenbarūg vnd Gesicht dz geschehen ist dē Fürsten Sigismūdo zū Pressburg. [*Jakob Schmidt: Speyer,*] 1527. 4°.
1570/3461

Signa. Erunt signa in sole [et luna. Ungewitter zu Hamburg.] [An engraving.] *s.l.* [1598.] *s.sh.* 4°. 1750.c.1(33)(impf.)

Sitten. Von gūten züchtigen sitten ein vast nutzlich büchlin. *See* H., C.

Sixtus IV., *Pope.* Tractatus de sanguine Christi. (De Dei potencia.) *Ed.* J. P. de Ligname. *Per Fridericum Creussner: Nurēberge,* 1474. fol. *A reissue of the* 1473 *sheets.* IB.7587

Smidenstet, Hartuicus. Oratio funebris de Iulio, Brunouicensium ac Lunæburgensium Duce. *Iacobus Lucius: Helmæstadii,* 1589.4°. 1578/2534

Solinus, Caius Julius. Polyhistor. *Per Ioannem Singreniū;* [for] *Lucas Alantse: Vienne Austrie*, 1520.4°. 1489.tt.62

Solis, Virgil. Biblische Figuren. 2 pt. *Durch Johannem Wolffium: Franckfurt am Mayn*, 1565. *obl.* 8°. MS. Egerton 1194(1, 2)

— Effigies regum francorum omnium [by V. Solis & Jost Amman]. Epitome χρονικῶν. *In officina typographica Katharinæ Theodorici Gerlachii viduæ & hæredum Iohannis Montani: Noribergæ,* 1576. 4°. C.175.n.13

Solme, Thomas. The Lordis flayle. *Theophyll Emlos: Basyl,* [1540?] 8°. *The imprint is fictitious; printed at Antwerp by the widow of Christoffel van Ruremunde.* C.25.d.24

Solomon, *King of Israel.* [Dialogus Salomonis et Marcolphi.] [*Printer of Aristeas: Erfurt,* ca.1483.] 4°. IA.12617

Spagnuoli, Baptista, *Mantuanus.* ɔtra poetas impudice loqētes carmē. *Ed.* J. H. Crispus. *Cura & īdustria Iacobi Thāner: in civitate liptzensi,* 1499. 4°.
IA.12257

— Parthenices prime liber primus (-tertius). *Per Wolfgangum monacensem: in oppido Wittemburgensi,* 1504. 4°. C.175.h.18

Spandugino, Theodore. Der Türcken heymligkeyt. *Tr.* Caspar von Aufsess. *Georg Erlinger: Bamberg,* 1523. 4°. 1578/3123

Spangenberg, Cyriacus. Apologia der sieben Predigten halben, von der Prædestination. *Durch Andream Petri: Eisleben,* 1568. 8°. RB.23.a.3151(3)

— Chronicon Corinthiacum. *Durch Vrbanum Gaubisch: Eisleben*, 1561. fol.
1575/536(1)
— Deutliche erklerung der Lere von der Erbsünde. Kurtze Bekentnus M. Fl. Illyrici. *s.l.* 1571. 4°. 1568/8799
— Von der geistlichen Hausshaltung Martin Luthers zwo Predigten. *Vrban Gaubisch: Eisleben*, 1563. 8°. 1568/6077
— Der weyse Knecht Gottes. *Samuel Emmel: Strassburg*, 1558. 8°. 1568/6075(1)

Spangenberg, Johann. Artificiosæ memoriæ libellus. *Per Michaelem Blum: Lipsiæ*, 1539. 8°. Davis II, 330(4)

Spaniards. Declaracion o confession de fe hecha por ciertos fieles Españoles. [By Cassiodoro de Reyna.] [*Heirs of Christian Egenolff:*] *Francford*, 1577. 16°. C.189.a.13

Specker, Melchior. Auszlegung des Euangelii Matthei am XXV. Capitel. *Durch Theodosium Rihel: Straszburg*, 1568. 8°. RB.23.a.341(2)

Speculum. Aureum speculum anime peccatricis. [By Jacobus de Gruitroede.] [*Heinrich Quentell: Colgne*, ca. 1494.] 4°. IA.4896

Spelt, Heinrich. Ain ware Declaration der Profession, Gelübten vñ leben, so die falschen Gaystlichenn wider alle Ewangelische freyhayt thun. [*Heinrich Steiner: Augsburg,*] 1523. 4°. 1568/8053

Spruch. Ein hübscher newer Spruch, wie sich der mensch gegen Got halten sol. *Valentin Neuber: Nürnberg*, [ca. 1555?] 8°. C.175.i.31(17)
— Ein neüwer spruch vñ warhaffts bericht wie es kompt das so vil münch seind priester worden. [*Johann Knobloch: Strasburg*, ca. 1520.] 4°.
1347.a.14(15)

Stabius, Joannes. Pronosticon ad annos domini M.D.iii & iiii. [With a woodcut by Dürer.] [*Johann Weissenburger:*] *Nurmberg*, [1503.] 4°.
11408.c.85

Stammbuch. Stam oder Gesellenbuch. *Peter Schmidt in verlegung Sigmund Feyrabends: Franckfurt am Mayn*, 1583. 8°. MS. Egerton 1216

Stanbius, Joannes. *See* Stabius.

Stapleton, Thomas. Promptuarium Catholicum super Euangelia ferialia per totam Quadragesimam. *In officina Birckmannica, sumptibus Arnoldi Mylij; typis Godefridi Kempensis: Coloniæ Agrippinæ*, 1594. 8°. 1507/706(1)
— Promptuarium Catholicum super omnia Euangelia totius anni tam Dominicali quam de festis. 2 pt. *In officina Birckmannica, sumptibus Arnoldi Mylij;* [*pr. Gottfried von Kempen:*] *Coloniae Agrippinae*, 1594. 8°.
1507/706(2)

Statius, Publius Papinius. Syluarum (Thebaidos, Achilleidos) libri. *Per Henricum Petrum: Basileæ*, 1541. 8°. 11385.a.27

Stauf, Hieronymus von. Ein hibsch lied newgem acht wen vonn dem stauffer. *s.n.* [1516?] *s.sh.* fol. C.651.e(14)

Steeghius, Godefridus. Descriptio fontis medicati Kissingensis. *Ex officina Georgij Fleischmanni: Wirtzburgi*, 1595. 8°. 1171.d.48(2)

Steinbach, Johann. Vnterrichtung welcher Gestaldt sich ein jeder von der Herrschafft in Kriegsleufften verhalten sol. *Johann Daubman: Königsberg in Preussen*, 1564. 4°. 1608/3382

Stenius, Simon. Duo dialogi græcè scripti. *Abrahamus Smesmannus: Heidelbergæ*, 1592. 4°. 491.b.19(28)(impf.)

Sternhals, Johann. Ritter Krieg. *Ed.* Johann Schaubert. *Martin:Wittel: Erffordt,*
1595. 8°. 1213.c.41
Stifel, Michael. Antwort vff Thoman Murnars phantasey. [*Johann Schott: Strasburg,* 1523.] 4°. 1560/3298
— Ein Rechen Büchlin vom EndChrist. See Antichrist.
Stigel, Johann. Ad inuictissimum Imperatorem Carolum Quintum epistola. *Per Ioh. Petreium: Norimbergæ,* 1541. 4°. 1608/5002
— Hymni aliquot. *In officina Valentini Papae: Lipsiae,* 1548. 8°. 1607/5104
Stoeckelius, Anselmus. Commentarius de expeditione in Peloponesum suscepta. *Adamus Berg: Monachij,* 1575. 4°. 1312.c.10
Stoltz, Johannes. Refutatio propositionum Pfeffingeri de libero arbitrio. Matth.Fla.Illyrici de eadem controuersia. *s.l.* 1558. 4°. 3905.g.46
Strasburg. — **Rat.** [Proclamation against usury.] [*Balthasar Beck: Strasburg,* 1539.] *s.sh.obl.* fol. 5510.ee.6(134)
— — [Proclamation against Anabaptists.] [*Balthasar Beck: Strasburg,* 1540.] *s.sh.obl.* fol. 5510.ee.6(276)
— **Academia Argentinensis.** Actus tres Academiæ Reipub. Argentoratensis habiti sub Melchiore Iunio. 3 pt. *Nicholaus Vvyriot: Argentorati,* 1578. 4°. 1570/2018
Strasburg, *Diocese of.* [*Appendix.*] Trewhertzige Erinnerung betreffend das jetzige Kriegswesen in dem Bistumb Strasburg. *s.l.* 1592. 4°. 1560/3117
Strawe, Cuntz. Gründlicher vnd eigentlicher Bericht einer Historien, so sich im Dorf Binnfert mit einem Jüngling (Cuntz Strawe) zugetragen hat. *Durch Nicolaum Bassee: Franckfurt am Mayn,* 1567. 4°. 1395.h.46
Streuber, Peter. Christliches Gutachten, wie der Streit, so in der Reformirten Kirchen gewesen, könte auffgehaben werden. *s.l.* 1591. 4°. 3906.c.8
— Die fünffte Leich-Predigt, anniuersaria. *Durch Nicolaum Schneider: Soraw,* 1589. 4°. 1568/6410
— Rechtmessige Andtwort auff die zwo Schmecharten. *Soraw,* 1593. 4°.
RB.23.a.1587
Strigelius, Victorinus. Arithmeticus libellus. *In officina Vœgeliana: Lipsiæ,* [1563.] 8°. RB.23.a.335
— In erotemata dialecticæ Philip. Melanchthonis ὑπομνηματα. *Apud Iohannem Mayerum: Neapoli in Palatinatu,* 1579. 8°. C.104.d.9
— Oratio de propheta Esaia. [*Ernst Vögelin: Leipzig,*] 1564. 8°. RB.23.a.3150
Strigenitz, Gregorius. Gedechtnis vnd Leichpredigt nach dem tödlichen abgang der Frawen Dorothea Susanna, Hertzogin zu Sachssen. *Donat Richtzenhan: Jhena,* 1592. 4°. 1578/1525
Stuck, Johann Wilhelm. Vita Iosiæ Simleri. *Frosch.* [*Christoph Froschauer*]: *Tiguri,* 1577. 4°. RB.23.a.628
Stuerll, Lignacius, *pseud.?* Glosse des hochgelarten Ablas der tzu Hall. See Maurice, *Saint,* and Mary Magdalen, *Saint.* — *Collegiate Church at Halle.*
Stuermer, Wolfgang. Vorzeichnus vnd Gepräge der groben vnd kleinen Müntzsorten. See Verzeichnis.
Sturcius, Christophorus. See Sturtzius.
Sturm, Caspar. Die vier namhafftsten königreich. *Christian Egenolff: Franckfurt,* 1538. 4°. C.117.ff.16
Sturmius, Hubertus. De æterna prædestinatione Dei diatribe. *Excudebat Bonauentura Faber, sumptibus Iacobi Zanachii: Seruestæ,* 1597. 8°.
4257.a.25

Sturmius, Joannes, *Sleidanus.* Commonitio. *Ger. Durch Matthęum Harnisch: Newstatt an der Hardt,* 1581. 4°. RB.23.a.1722
— Linguæ Latinæ resoluendæ ratio. *Ed.* Joannes Lobartus. *Nicolaus VVyriot: Argentorati,* 1581. 8°. 1578/8001
Sturtzius, Christophorus. Oratio de Sigismundo Augusto Duce Megapolitano defuncto. *Prælo Reusneriano: Rostochii,* [1600.] 4°. 1568/8051
— Oratio memoriæ Davidis Chytræi. *Typis Myliandrinis: Rostochii; impensis Laurentij Alberti:* [*Lübeck,*] 1600. 4°. 4887.aaa.57
Suabia. Gegrundter beschlus etlicher Prediger zu Schwaben vber die wort des Abentmals. *Tr.* Johann Agricola [from "Syngramma clarissimorum qui Halae suevorum convenerunt virorum"]. *Durch Johan Secerium: Hagenaw,* 1526. 4°. 1608/3973
Suarez, Franciscus. Varia opuscula theologica. *Apud Balthasarum Lippium: Moguntiæ; sumptibus Arnoldi Mylij:* [*Cologne,*] 1600. 4°. 1572/341
Suflon, Andreas. Carmen gratulatorium in natalem Ernesti Ludovvici ducis Stetini filij. 2 pt. *Apud Augustinum Ferberum: Gryphisvvaldiæ,* 1585. *obl.*4°. K.5.a.23
Sultzerus, Julius. Christliche newe Jarswünschung. *Nicklas Basse: Franckfort am Mayn,* [ca. 1590?] *s.sh.* fol. Tab.597.d.3(16)
Sulz, Maria Cleophe von, *Countess.* Ein schön new geystlichs Trostlied: Mein Gott du bist mein trost auff Erden. *Michaël Manger: Augspurg,* 1569. 8°. 11521.cc.42
Susanna, *Wife of Joachim.* Susanna lied. *Melchior Ramminger: Augsburg,* [ca. 1540?] 8°. 11521.bbb.39
Sylvanus, Johannes. Carmen elegiacum de natale Saluatoris nostri. *Henningus Rudenus: Hannoueræ,* 1548. 4°. 1608/4548
Sylvius, Peter. Summa vnd schutz der waren Euangelischen lere. Marti. Luth. Ecclesia. 2 pt. [(pt. 1)*Nickel Schmidt;* (pt.2)*Valentin Schumann: Leipzig,*] 1529. 4°. 1568/6486

T

T., W. The practyse of prelates. [By William Tyndale.] *Marborch,* 1530. 8°. The imprint is false; printed at Antwerp by Johannes Hillen (Hoochstraten). C.38.c.40; G.1229(impf.)
Tabulae. Tabulæ abcdariæ pueriles. [*Valentin Bapst: Leipzig,* ca.1550.] *s.sh.* fol. C.121.g.6(3)
Taeucher, David. Tractatulus de fide, spe, et charitate. *Andreas Reinheckel: Nissæ,* 1587. 8°. C.136.b.19
Tagweise. Ein schöne Tageweis, von der liebhabenten seel zü Gott. *Durch Hannsen Burger: Straubing,* 1564. 8°. C.175.i.31(39)
Talaeus, Audomarus. Rhetorica e P. Rami prælectionibus obseruata. *Apud heredes Andreæ Wecheli, Claudium Marnium & Ioann. Aubrium: Francofurdi,* 1599. 8°. 1607/702(2)
Taurellus, Nicolaus. Carmina funebria. *Typis Gerlachianis: Noribergæ,* 1592. 8°. MS. Egerton 1230(2); Egerton 1540(2)
— Emblemata physico-ethica. *Paulus Kaufmann: Noribergæ,* 1595. 8°. MS. Egerton 1230(1); Egerton 1540(1)(impf.)
— Philosophiæ triumphus. *Per Sebastianum Henricpetri: Basileæ,* 1573. 8°. C.190.a.21

Ten Commandments. Die zehen gebott Gottes inn gesang weiss verfasset.
See S., C.
Terentius, Publius. Sechs verteütschte Comedien. *Tr.* Valentinus Boltz.
Vlrich Morharts Witfraw: Tübingen, 1567. 8°. C.135.b.14
— Elegantissimæ colloquiorum formulæ ex Terentij comædijs selectæ. *Lat.,
Czech & Ger. Tr.* Paulus Aquilinus. *Ioannes Gunthærus: Prostannæ,* 1550.
8°. C.185.a.21(1)
Terminaeus, Petrus. Processus iuris scripti et consuetudinis per Germaniam
usitatus. *Apud Ioannem Gymnicum: Coloniæ,* 1570. 8°. 1578/3982
Tertullianus, Quintus Septimius Florens. Opera. *Ed.* B. Rhenanus. *Apud
Io. Frobenium: Basileæ,* 1521. fol. C.190.c.11
Thann, Eberhart von der. Mein warhafftiger gegenbericht auff den
Abdruck, so in der Sechsischen Cantzley namen ausgangen. *s.l.* 1566.
4°. 1509/2923
Themistius, *Euphrada.* Orationes octo. *Tr.* Girolamo Donzellini. *Apud Petrum
Pernam: Basileæ,* 1559. 8°. 1568/4239
Theodoret, *Bishop of Cyrus.* Διαλογος α. (–γ.) cum versione Victorini
Strigelii. *Ed.* Marcus Beumlerus. 3 pt. *Apud Ioannem Wolphium: Tiguri,*
1593, 94. 8°. 475.a.37
Theodoricus, Sebastianus. Canon sexagenarum et scrupulorum
sexagesimorum. *Ioannes Crato: VVittebergæ,* 1564. 8°. 1578/2659
Theognis. Sententiæ. *Tr. & ed.* Philipp Melanchthon. *Gr. & Lat.* Laurentius
Schuenck: VVitebergæ, 1561. 8°. 1568/8353
Theophylact, *Archbishop of Achrida.* In omnes D. Pauli epistolas enarrationes.
See Bible. — Epistles.
Theorian. Legatio Imp. Cæsaris Manuelis Comneni Aug. ad Armenios. [With
works by other authors.] *Ed.* Joannes Sambucus. *Tr.* Joannes
Leunclavius. *Gr. & Lat. Ex officina Petri Pernæ: Basileæ,* 1578. 8°.
1009.a.17; 1011.e.2
Thomas, *Aquinas, Saint.* [Quæstiones de veritate.] Tituli questionū de veritate
disputatarū. *p Iohannem Koelhoeff: Colonie,* 1475. fol. IB.3480
Thomas [More], *Saint.* Libellus vere aureus. *Ed.* Petrus Aegidius. *Ex officina
Cratoniana: VVitebergæ,* 1591. 8°. C.175.ff.20
Thomas, Hubertus, *Leodius.* De Tungris et Eburonibus commentarius. *Apud
Vendelinum Rihelium: Argentorati,* 1541. 8°. 1193.i.1; 9325.aaa.19
Thomingius, Jacobus. Decisiones quæstionum illustrium. [*Niclas Bock:*]
Lipsiæ, 1579. 4°. C.127.c.8
Thucydides. Historia de bello Peloponnesiaco libri. *Tr. & ed.* V. Ortelius.
[*Matthaeus Welack:*] *VVitebergæ,* 1580. 8°. Davis II, 346
Tiber. Warhafftige anzeygung der grausamen übergiessung der Tiber zu Rom.
[*Friedrich Peypus: Nuremberg,* 1530.] 4°. 1393.b.38(1); T.964(1)
Tibertus, Antiochus. De chyromantia libri III. *Ed.* J. Dryander. *Ivo Schoefer:
Moguntiæ,* 1538. 8°. Davis II, 330(3)
Tilisch, Eleasar. Ein Lobspruch des deudschen Fürsten vnd Adelstands. *Georg
Hoffman: Freybergk in Meissen,* 1588. 4°. 9917.d.15
Tockler, Conrad, *Noricus.* Aderlastaffel. [*Johann Weissenburger: Nuremberg,*
1507?] *s.sh.* fol. C.18.e.3(40)(frag.)
— Practica Lipsensis auff des jar Tausent funffhundt vñ funffzechen.
[*Nuremberg,* 1514.] 4°. C.71.h.14(13)

Tollat, Johann. Margarita medicine. [*Matthias Hupfuff:*] *Strassburg,* 1508. 4°.
IA.11941(10)
Toltz, Johann. Eyn kurtz handbuchlyn fur iunge Christen. [*Michael Blum: Leipzig,*] 1526. 8°. C.190.d.20(3)
Tractatus. Tractat[9] de verbo rei collectus ex doctore sancto. [*Marcus Brandis: Merseburg,* ca. 1479.] fol. IB.9610
Tramenus, Ludovicus. De vera medendi methodo commentarius. *Ex officina Dauidis Sartorii: Ingolstadii,* 1590. 4°. 543.b.22(2)
Treatise. A treatise of the cohabitacyon of the faithfull with the vnfaithfull [by Pietro Martire Vermigli]. A sermon [by Heinrich Bullinger]. [*Wendelin Rihel: Strasburg,* 1555.] 8°. 696.a.19; 695.a.29
Treflerus, Florianus. Sex et triginta declamationes. [*Philippus Vlhardus: Augustæ Rheticæ,* 1550.] 8°. 1607/3183(impf.)
— Declamationes theologicæ triginta tres. Ioachimi Perionij orationes duę. *Apud Maternum Cholinum: Coloniæ,* 1561. 8°. 1607/3176
Treves, *Council of.* Christianæ institutionis liber æditus in Concilio Prouinciali Treuerensi. *Iaspar Gennepæus: Coloniæ,* 1549. 4°. 1578/2383(2)
— Decreta Concilii Prouincialis Treuerensis celebrati anno M.D.XLIX. [With additional material.] *Iaspar Gennepæus: Coloniæ,* 1549. 4°. 1578/2383(1)
Tritheim, Johann. De origine gentis principumque Bauarorum commentarius. *Per Cyriacum Iacobum: Francofurti,* 1549. 4°. 1578/1815
— Institutio vite sacerdotalis. [*Peter von Friedberg: Mainz,* 1494?] 4°. IA.379
Trubius, Ludovicus. Epitaphia duo de obitu Iohannis Nopelii eiusdemque coniugis. *Iohannes Rhambau: Lipsiae,* 1560. 4°. 1509/1699
Truckl, Christofferus. Contemplationes ad horas canonicas. *s.n.* [1543.] 8°.
3455.aa.63
Trusted, Jacobus. Disputatio de nuptiis. *Praes.* Joannes Borcholten. *Typis Iacobi Lucij: Helmaestadii,* 1600. 4°. 498.b.20(1)
Tuberinus, Joannes. Ad Georgiū Saxoniae ducē Musithias de cælitibus. *Melchiar Lotherus: in vrbe Lipsica,* 1514. fol. C.141.dd.4
Tudeschis, Nicolaus de, *Cardinal, Archbishop of Palermo.* [Lectura super libros Decretalium.] vol. 3, 4. [*Bernhard Richel:*] *Basilee,* 1481, 80. fol. IC.37190
Turk. Newe Zeitung. Wie der Türck die Stadt Nicosiam eingenommen. *s.l.* 1571. 4°. 1609/2221
Turks. Rerum gestarum Turcarum et Sophi de anno M.D.XIIII. breuiarium. [*Johann Miller:*] *Augustæ,* [1514.] 4°. 1560/152
Turner, Robert. Orationes XIV [and other works]. 2 pt. *Ex officina typographica Dauidis Sartorii: Ingolstadii,* 1584. 8°. 1607/1377(2)
Turrecremata, Joannes de, *Cardinal.* [Flos theologiae.] [*Johann Amerbach: Basle,* not after 1484.] fol. IB.37284
Tyndale, William. The obediēce of a Christen man. *Hans luft: Marlborow,* 1528. 8°. *The imprint is fictitious; printed at Antwerp by Johannes Hillen (Hoochstraten).* C.53.b.1
— The obedience of a Christen man. *Hans luft: Marlborow,* 1535. 8°. *The imprint if fictitious; printed at Antwerp, by Henrick Peetersen?*
C.25.a.35; C.53.a.19(1)(impf.)
— [The parable of the wicked Mammon.] *Hans luft: Malborowe,* 1528. 8°. *The imprint is fictitious; printed at Antwerp by Johannes Hillen (Hoochstraten).*
C.37.a.23

— The parable of the wycked mammō. *Hans Luft: Malborowe,* 1528 [1537?] 4°.
  The imprint is fictitious; printed in London? C.37.e.21
— The practyse of prelates. *See* T., W.

U

Uffenbach, Philipp. Bericht vnd Erkläung zweyer Kupfferstücken. *Matthes Becker, in verlegung Paul Brachfeldt: Franckfurt am Mayn,* 1598. 4°.
C.125.bb.11

Ulmer, Johann Conrad. De horologiis sciotericis ratio. *In officina Ioannis Montani & Vlrici Neuberi: Noribergæ,* 1556. fol. 537.m.36

— New Jesuwitspiegel. [Works by Martinus Chemnitius, Donatus Gotvisus & Wilhelm Bidembach.] *Tr. & ed.*J. C. Ulmer. *Conrad Waldkirch: Basel,* 1586. 4°. 4091.cc.5

Ungarische Krankheit. *See* Hungarian Disease.

Upilio, Christophorus. Spygmilogia. *Georgius Fleischmann: Wirceburgi,* 1596. 4°. 1179.c.3(5)

Urban, *Bishop of Gurk.* Publicirung keyserlicher Erleubnus, von Entpfahung des heiligen Abendmals. *s.l.* 1564. 4°. 1607/4397

Ursache. Gründtliche vrsach der yetz schwebenden Kriegssleuff. *See* Schradin, Johann.

Ursinus, Gulielmus. Disputatio I. (— IX., XIII., XIV.) quæstionum illustrium philosophicarum. [*Jena,* 1600?] 4°. 536.e.9(4)(impf.)

Ursinus Velius, Caspar. Epistolarum & epigrammatum liber. *Ed.* Rodolphus Agricola. [*Per Ioannem Singreniū: Viennæ Austriæ,* 1517.] 4°.
C.175.b.8(impf.)

Utzinger, Alexander. Kurtze vnd richtige Antwort auff zwo Fragen von der Geuatterschafft. *Donat Richtzenhan: Jhena,* 1579. 4°. C.107.bb.84(4)

— Summarischer Begriff der Papistischen Relligions vbung. *Donat Richtzenhan: Jhena,* 1579. 4°. C.107.bb.84(5)

V

V., I.D.D.I. Oratio quotidiana. I.D.D.I.V. [i.e. Joannes Diemmairus?] [*Johann Burger: Regensburg?,*] 1588. 8°. C.107.e.65(1)

V., S.G. Defensio Ecclesiasticæ liturgiæ. [By Georg Witzel.] *Apud hæredes Arnoldi Birckmanni: Coloniæ,* 1564. 8°. 1507/1370

Valentia, Gregorius de. Examen et refutatio mysterii doctrinæ Caluinistarum de re eucharistica. *Ex officina Dauidis Sartorii: Ingolstadii,* 1589. 4°.
1609/2811(1)

Valentinus, *Licentiatus.* De arte moriendi. *Per Mauricium Brandiss: Liptzk,* 1489. 4°. IA.11757

Valerius, Cornelius. Physicæ institutiones. *Ed.* Hermannus Wolfius. *Com.* Rodolphus Goclenius. *Typis Pauli Egenolphi: Marpurgi,* 1593(1591*). 8°.
536.c.12(3)

Valla, Georgius. Compendiaria et facilis disserendi ratio. *Per Adamum Petri: Basileæ,* 1522. 8°. 1578/3080

Valla, Laurentius. De rebus gestis Ferdinandi Aragonum et Siculorum Regis libri tres. *Ed.* Joannes Lange. *In officina Andreę Vingleri: Vratislaviae,* 1546. 8°. 1578/6028

Vallés, Francisco. In aphorismos Hippocratis commentarij VII. *See* Hippocrates. [*Two or more Works.*]

Vallibus, Hieronymus de. Tractatus de passioni domini. [*Martin Landsberg: Leipzig,* ca. 1494.] 4°. IA. 11885

Varolius, Constantius. Anatomiæ libri IIII. *Ed.* Joannes Baptista Cortesius & Hieronymus Mercurialis. *Apud Ioannem Wechelum & Petrum Fischerum: Francofurti,* 1591. 8°. 548.e.12

Vázquez de Menchaca, Fernando. Controversiarum illustrium libri tres. *Impressum apud Georgium Corvinum, impensis Sigismundi Feyerabend: Francofurti ad Mœnum,* 1572. fol. 1605/352

Vegetius Renatus, Flavius. [De re militari.] [Woodcuts without text.] [*Hans Knappe: Erfurt,* 1512?] fol. C.175.dd.10(impf.)

Vegius, Mapheus. [Philalethes.] Ein schön gespräche von einem waldtmann. *Tr.* Jakob Frey. *In Knoblochs druckerei: Strassburg,* 1555. 4°. C.186.e.5

Venatorius, Daniel. Analysis methodica iuris Pontificii. *In officina typographica Henrici Breem: Moguntiæ,* 1596. 8°. 1607/4882

Venice. [*Appendix.*] Newe Zeyttungen: auss Venedig von der türckischen Nyderlag. *Durch Josiam Wörlin: Augspurg,* 1586. 4°. RB.23.a.1621

Vergilius, Polydorus. De rerum inuentoribus libri octo. *Apud Isingriniū: Basileæ,* 1546. 8°. *A reissue of the* 1545 *edition.* 1651/80

Vergleichung. Vergleichung der grossen vnnd clainen Vhre. *Durch Hansen Burger: Regenspurg,* [ca. 1575?] *s.sh.* fol. Tab. 597.d.1(22)

Verhaer, Franciscus. Vitæ Sanctorum. *Tr.* Valentin Leucht. *Ger. Durch Johannem Gymnicum: Cölln,* 1593. 4°. 1560/2645(2)

Vermahnung. Eine Vermanung an die Oberkeit zu gotseliger regierung. *Bey Thoma Retschen & Wiliwaldt Haberkle: Culmpach,* [1552?] 8°. 11517.bb.48

Vermigli, Pietro Martire. A treatise of the cohabitacyon of the faithfull with the vnfaithfull. *See* Treatise.

Versor, Joannes. Dicta sup donato mīori. *Per Conradū Kacheloffen: Liptzk,* 1494. 4°. IA. 11565

Verzeichnis. Vorzeichnus vnd Gepräge der groben vnd kleinen Müntzsorten. [By Wolfgang Stürmer.] [*W. Stürmer:*] *Leipzig,* 1575. 4°. 1608/3345

— [Another edition.] *Wolffgang Stürmer: Leipzig,* 1579. 4°. C.186.e.4

Vhessel, Hieronymus. Itinerarium oder Reisebüchlein. *Durch Zachariam Berwaldt: Leipzig,* 1589. 8°. 10003.aaaa.46

Vincent [Ferrer], *Saint.* Mirabile [opusculū] de fine mūdi. [*Fratres Ordinis Eremitarum Sancti Augustini: Nuremberg,* 1483?] 4°. IA.7926

— Ain wunderbarlich Büechlin von den letsten zeitten. [*Andreas Schobser: Munich,* ca. 1545?] 4°. C.127.dd.5

— Sermones de sanctis. (Pars hyemalis de tempore.) 2 pt. [*Georg Husner:*] *Argentine,* 1503. fol. Davis II, 324

Vincentius, *Bellovacensis.* [Speculum doctrinale.] [*Adolf Rusch: Strasburg,* ca. 1477.] fol. IC.679a(frag.)

65

Virgilius Maro, Publius. [*Bucolica and Georgica.*] Bucolica et Georgica paraphrasi exposita ab auctore N. Frischlino. [With the text.] *Ioannes Spies: Francofurti ad Mœnum,* 1596. 8°. C.143.f.3
— [*Bucolica.*] Bucolicum decem aeglogarū opus. *Com.* Hermannus Torrentinus. *Apud Melchiorem Lottherū: Lypsiæ,* 1519. 4°. 1609/3289
— [*Appendix.* — *Centos.*] Vergiliocētones veteris ʔ noui testamēti. [By V. Falconia Proba.] [*Jakob Thanner: Leipzig,* ca. 1500.] 4°. IA.12305
— — [*Concordances and Dictionaries.*] Enchiridion poeticum; haec habet epitheta Vergilij ac aliorū. *Ed.* Johann Schott. *Ioanne Schotto pressore laboratum:* [*Strasburg,*] 1513(1514*). 4°. 1608/453
Vischer, Christoph. Valetpredigt. *Durch Andream Petri: Eisleben,* 1584. 4°.
1509/2919
Vives, Joannes Ludovicus. See also Philalethes, *Hyperboraeus, pseud.*
— De anima & vita libri tres. [With works by other authors.] *Apud Iacobum Gesnerum: Tiguri,* [1563.] 8°. 1133.b.1
— De disciplinis libri XX. *Ioannes Gymnicus: Coloniæ,* 1532. 8°. C.190.d.10
— Non esse iure prohibitum, quin Summus Pontifex dispensare possit, vt frater demortui fratris legitimo matrimonio sibi possit adiungere. *See* Pope.
Vogel, Heinrich. Bachanalia, Fastnacht. *Jost Martin: Strassburg,* 1599. 8°.
4379.a.18
Vogel, Niclass. Ein schön news Lied: Von dem verlornen Son. *Durch Mattheum Francken: Augspurg,* [ca. 1560.] 8°. C.175.i.31(28)
Voitus, Albertus. Mauricius. *Fabiranæ,* 1595. 4°. 1490.d.77
Vorzeichnus. *See* Verzeichnis.
Vuelpius, Henricus. *See* Welpius.
Vulteius, Hermannus. De feudis eorundemque jure libri duo. *Typis Pauli Egenolphi: Marpurgi,* 1595. 8°. 1578/3986

W

W., B. Ein geistlich Lied dariñ, was zu einem waren Christlichen leben gehörig, begriffen. [*Matthäus Franck: Augsburg?,* ca. 1560?] 8°.
C.175.i.31(16)
W., J.E.M. Eyn new vnd das letzt auszschreyben der xv. bundtgenossen. [By Johann Eberlein.] [*Matthes Maler: Erfurt,* 1521.] 4°. 3908.f.34(16)
Wacker, Steffen. Eyn getruwe warnüg aller Christgleubiger menschen, als Meister Steffen wacker anzeigt hat. [*Arnt von Aych: Cologne,* ca. 1525.] 4°. *Sig. B only of an unidentified work.* 1609/725(impf.)
Wagener, Bartholomeus. Christliche Auslegung des spruchs Christi, Gebet dem Keiser, was des Keisers ist. *Wolff Günther: Leipzig,* 1554. 4°.
1568/4315
Wagner, Bartholomaeus. Apostelpredigen. *Wolffgang Eder: Ingolstatt,* 1593. 8°. 1607/5507(3)
— Heptaphoreta. [*Closterdruckerei:*] *Thierhaupten,* 1591. 8°. 1607/5515
Wagner, Georg. Eyn new warhafftig geschicht von Jörgen wagner zu München verbrandt. [*Hans Hergot: Nuremberg,* 1527.] 4°. 4888.e.25(1)

Walbeck, Dithmar von, *Bishop.* Chronici libri VII. *Ed.* Reinerus Reineck. *Ex officina typographica Andreæ Wecheli: Francofurti ad Moenum,* 1580. fol.
1565/15(2)

Waldner, Wolfgang. Enchiridion. Von Luthers anfechtung. *[Nikolaus Knorr: Nuremberg,]* 1566. 8°.
1606/1573

Walther, Georgius. Trostbüchlein für Krancke, Sterbende, vnd betrübte Menschen. *Bey Ernesto Vögelin: Leipzig,* 1567. 8°. RB.23.a.618

Walther, Rudolph. De Iesu Christi & Christianorum vita & officio homiliæ. *Ed.* Henricus Wolphius. *In officina Froschouiana: Tiguri,* 1588. fol.
1602/377

Warleids, Hartman, *pseud.* Der rechte Caluinische Bawren Catechismus. Gesprech eines Caluinischen vnd Lutherischen Bawren. *s.l.* 1597. 8°.
1568/6212

Weber, Johann, *of Nuremberg.* Ein Lobspruch dem Handwerck der Neberschmid zu Ehren gemacht. *[Nuremberg,* 1587.*] s.sh.* fol.
Tab.597.d.3(12)

Wecker, Hanss Jacob. De secretis libri XVII. *Ex officina Pernea: Basileae,* 1587. 8°.
1651/85

— Ein nutzliches Büchlein von mancherleyen künstlichen wassern, ölen vnd weinen. *Peter Perna: Basel,* 1573. 8°. RB.23.a.1963

Weinrich, Georg. Christliche Leichpredigt bey dem Begrebnis der Frawen Maria, Johan Bergers Haussfraw. *[Leipzig,]* 1594. 4°.
1578/2252

Weisse, Michael. Ein schön geistlich Lied, vom leiden Jesu Christi. *See* Jesus Christ.

— Schöne Christliche Gesenge, zum Begrebnus der Todten. *See* Hymnals. [*German.*]

Weller, Hieronymus. Trostbüchlein. *[Henning Grosse:] Leipzig,* 1585. 8°.
C.107.bb.95

Welpius, Henricus. Libellus de communibus arithmeticæ practicæ regulis. *Ioannes Gymnicus: Coloniæ,* 1544. 4°.
529.c.2

Wennemeyerus, Zacharias. Hypotyposis Ecclesiæ de statu suo conquerentis. *Typis Clementis Schleich & Antonij Schönen: VVitebergæ,* 1574. 4°.
1568/8008

Werdmueller, Otto. Das Christenlich Läben. *See* Christian Life.

— Erinnerung wes sich ein Christ by absterbung siner mitbrüder trösten soll. *See* Christian.

— Ein kleinot von trost vnd hilff in allerley trübsalen. *Jacob Gessner: Zürych,* 1564. 12°.
1509/2039(3)

— Der Tod. *Bey Andrea Gessner dem jüngeren: Zürich,* 1558. 12°. 1509/2039(4)

Werlich, Abraham. Elegia in lamentationem mortis Ihesu Christi. *[Erfurt?,]* 1566. 4°.
1608/2560

Wernerus, Abrahamus. Oratio de confectione eius potus, qui cereuisia vocatur. *Iohannes Schuuertel: VVitebergæ,* 1567. 8°. 1651/319(3)

— Oratio de vita Galeni. *Iohannes Schuuertelius: VVitebergæ,* 1570. 8°.
1607/3125

Wernerus, Sebastianus. Warer bericht auff Bartholomei Strelen schmehewort. *Durch Joachim Walden: Magdeburg,* 1565. 4°. 1568/8819

Wesenbecius, Matthaeus. Aenigma timorumenon. *See* Aenigma.

Westphal, Joachim. Recta fides de cœna Domini. *Apud Michaelem Lottherum: Magdeburgæ,* 1553. 8°. RB.23.a.1823
Weyse, Nicolaus. Prognosticon astrologicum von dem 1572. bis auff das 1588. Jhar. [*Wittenberg?*, 1571?] 4°. 1609/748(9)
Whitaker, William. Disputatio de sacra scriptura contra papistas. *Ex officina Christophori Corvini: Herbornæ Nassoviorum,* 1600. 8°. 860.f.2
Wicknerus, Abdias. Tabula ascensionum obliquarum. [*Ulrich Morhart's widow:*] *Tubingæ,* 1561. 4°. RB.23.a.641
Widmann, Achilles Jason, *pseud.* [i.e. **Georg Widmann.**] History Peter Lewen. *Weygandt Han: Franckfurdt am Mayn,* [ca.1558.] 8°. C.127.bb.4
Wigand, Johann. Definitiones personarum. *In officina typographica Andrei Burgeri: Ratisponæ,* 1593. 8°. RB.23.a.276(2)
— Epitome doctrinæ sanctæ. *Andreas Burger: Ratisponæ,* 1593. 8°.
RB.23.a.276(1)
— Leichpredigt bey der Begrebnis Erasmi Sarcerii. *Durch Ambrosium Kirchner: Magdeburg,* 1560. 4°. 1568/5438
Wild, Johann. Examen ordinandorum. *Franciscus Behem: apud S. Victorem prope Moguntiam,* 1550. 8°. 1509/2038
— Iobi historia aussgelegt. *Franciscus Behem: Meyntz,* 1558. fol. 1565/5
William I., *Prince of Orange.* [An engraving of the funeral procession of the Prince of Orange at Delft, 3 Aug. 1584, with verses in German. Without letterpress.] *s.n.* [1584.] *s.sh.* fol. 504.l.10(12)
Willich, Jodocus. Prosodia latina. *Michael Blum: Lipsiæ,* 1539. 8°.
Hirsch IV.1553
Wilsnack. Dyt ys dy Erfindunge des hilligē sacramentes tho der Wilsnagk. *Jacob Winter: Magdeborch,* 1509. 4°. C.190.aa.13
Wimpheling, Jacob. Isidoneus Germanicus. [*Conrad Hist: Speyer,* after 22 Aug. 1497.] 4°. IA.8806
Winckler, Hans. Ein warhafftige Geschicht von dem Wunderzeichen, welches im 1574. Jar geschehen. *s.n.* [1575?] 8°. 11517.bb.44
Winckler, Nicolaus. Bedencken von dem VII. grossen Jar. *Michael Manger: Augspurg,* 1584. 4°. 1578/1205
Wispeckius, Wilhelmus. Hierusalem. *Adam Berg: München,* 1585. 8°.
10077.a.24
Wittekindus, *Monachus Corbeiensis.* Annales. [With other matter.] *Ed.* Reinerus Reineck. *Ex officina typographica And. Wecheli: Francofurti ad Mœnum,* 1577. fol. 1605/599
Wittenberg. — Academia Vitembergensis. Scriptorum publice propositorum a gubernatoribus studiorum in Academia tomus secundus (-quartus). *Ab hæredibus Georgij Rhauu:* [tom.2, 3] *impensis Cunradi Ruelii: VVitebergæ,* 1562, 59, 61. 8°. 1578/3378(2-4)
— — — tom.5. *In officina Iohannis Lufft: VVitebergæ,* 1564. 8°. 1578/3378(5)
— — — tom.7. *Clemens Schleich & Antonius Schöne: VVitebergæ,* 1572. 8°.
1578/3378(7)
Witzel, Georg, *the Elder. See also* Gersonites, Landavus, *pseud.*
— Defensio Ecclesiasticæ liturgiæ. *See* V., S.G.

Wolphius, Thomas. Vita. M. Catonis (per Cornelium Nepotem). Sextus
   Aurelius de vitis Cæsarum [and other matter]. *Comp.* T. Wolphius. 2 pt.
   Iohannes Prüs: Argentinæ, 1505. 4°. C.135.d.15; 1308.d.9(impf.)

X

Xenophon. [*Anabasis.*] 'Αναβασεως βιβλια ξ. *Iosias Rihelius: Argentorati,*
   1561. 8°. 1607/3341

Z

Zasius, Joannes Udalricus. In usus feudorum epitome. Orationes aliquot.
   Ioannes Faber: Friburgi Brisgoiae, 1538. fol. C.183.b.11
Zeitung. Newe Zeitung von dem grossen Pültz. *See* H., A.S.
Zichenius, Franciscus. Orationis Hieremiæ enarratio. *Apud Ioannem
   Birckmannum: Coloniae,* 1559. 8°. RB.23.a.1622
Zrínyi, Miklós, *Count.* Aigentliche Contrafactur dess Grafen Niclas von
   Serin. [*Augsburg?,* 1566?] *s.sh.* fol. 1870.d.2(7)
Zutrinker. Der zutrincker vnd Prasser Ordenung. [By Johann von
   Schwarzenberg.] *Mathes Maler: Erffordt,* [1516?] 4°. 8435.c.64
Zymmermann, Anton. Ob auch die sele Christi yn der Hellen gelitten habe.
   Gabriel Kantz: [*Altenburg,*] 1525. 4°. 4374.e.38

AMENDMENTS TO THE 1962 CATALOGUE

p.3. **Adamo, Antonio di.** An anatomi, 1556. Printed by Paul & Philipp Köpfel, not W. Köpfel.

— **Adelphus, Joannes.** Keyser Friderichs geschichten. *Franckfurt,* [1550?] Date should read: [ca.1558].

p.5. **Adrian VI,** *Pope.* Wie der Hailig Vatter, [1522.] Add: [By Pamphilus Gengenbach].

— **Aepinus, Joannes.** Insert: Bekentnuss vnnd Erklerung auffs Interim. *See* Germany. — Charles V, Emperor. [Interim, 15 May 1548].

p.7. **Aesop.** Erneuerter Esopus, [1600?] 12304.b.15. Cancel this entry. A seventeenth-century book.

p.9. **Agricola, Johann,** *of Eisleben.* Fünfhundert Gemainer Newer Teütscher Sprüchwörter. [*Augsburg,*]1548. 8°. 1070.k.22. Printed by Philip Ulhart.

— — Sybenhundert vnd fünfftzig Teütscher Sprichwörter. *Hagenaw,* 1534. 8°. 3837.b.7. Printed not by the Heirs of J. Setzer, but by Peter Braubach.

p.16. **Albertus, Salomon.** This heading, comprising six entries, should be moved to precede the heading **Alberus, Erasmus.**

p.19. **Alexander,** *de Ales.* Summa, 1515, 17. Date should read: 1515–17. Pt.1 (1515) and 2–4 (1516) were printed by Jacques Sacon at Lyons for Koberger; Myt was responsible for the Clavis (1517).

p.20. **Alexander,** *of Metz.* Der Alexander von Metz, [1550?] 8°. 11517.bbb.31. Cancel this entry. A seventeenth-century book.

p.24. **Ambach, Melchior.** This heading should be moved back one entry to include also: Vom Ende der Welt, [1550?].

p.26. **Amman, Jost.** Kunst vnd Lehrbüchlein. 2 Tl. *Franckfurt,* 1578, 80. 4°. Print Room. The imprint given applies to Tl.2. Tl.1 was printed by Peter Schmidt.

— [Another edition.] 2.Tl. *Franckfurt,* 1580. 4°. 683.e.16. Tl.2, a duplicate of the preceding, was printed by Johann Spiess.

71

p. 27. **Amsdorff, Nicolaus von.** Die haubt artickel, 1522, and Another edition, 1523 (p.28). In fact by Lazarus Spengler, edited by N. von Amsdorff.

p. 32. **Angelo**[Fondi], *Anchorita di Vallombrosa.* The heading should read: **Fundius, Angelus,** where there is a later edition of the same work.

p. 35. **Antoninus,** *Saint.* Sūma ɔfessionū [Defecerunt]. [*U. Zel: Cologne,* 1469?] IA.2764. Date should read: [1468].

— — Prima (-quarta) pars totius summe. *Argentina,* 1490. Now complete (with index volume) in 5 pt. Pressmark IB.1404–07 & IB.1404a.

p. 39. **Argumentum.** Argumenti . . . examinatio, 1591. Cancel this entry. A work by Faustus Socinus printed in Cracow.

p. 43. **Aristotle.**[*Organon.*] Dialectica, 1516, 17. Perfect copy now acquired, pressmark C.186.d.4.

— — [*Supposititious Works.*] Physiognomonica, 1538. Perfect copy now acquired, pressmark Davis II, 330(2).

p. 48. **Ars.** Auriferæ artis, etc., 1572. Add: 2 vol. Pressmarks now: 1568/9051; 717.e.38(vol.1).

p. 51. **Augsburg.** [*Appendix.*] Bericht vnd anzeigen aller Herren Geschlacht, [1560?]. Date should read: [1538]. The work was compiled by Paul Hector Mair.

p. 52. **Augustine,** *Saint.* [*Works.*] Prima [*etc.*] pars librorum diui Augustini, [1506,] 1505. Pt.6 now added to those listed. Pressmark of the set should read: C.109.i.1(impf.).

p. 62. **Badweiler, Johann Baptista.** Heading should read: **Badweiler, Johann Baptista,** *pseud.* [i.e. **J. B. Fickler**].

p. 65. **Barbaro, Ermolao.** Compendium, 1547. The title should be replaced by the following: [Compendium in libros Aristotelis physicos].

p. 70. **Basle. — Universität.** Dauid Gorge of his Lyfe and Heresi, 1560. Pressmark is C.110.c.8.

p. 71. **Bavaria.** [*Constitutional Documents.*] Dy new erclerūg der landssfreyhait, [1535?]. Add the imprint: [*Andreas Schobser: Munich*].

— — — Das buech der gemeinen Landpot, [1535?]. Add the imprint: [*Andreas Schobser: Munich*].

p. 73. **Bebelius, Henricus.** Latiuñ Ideoma, 1509. Pressmark should read: C.33.b.46.

p. 80. **Bernhardi, Bartholomaeus.** Apologia pro Barptolomeo, 1521. Delete the author statement. The work is variously attributed to Bernhardi, A. Bodenstein, or Melanchthon.

p. 87. **Bible.** [*Latin.*] Bibliorum codex sacer, 1591. Imprint should read: *Impensis S. Selfischij & B. Rab:* [*Wittenberg;*] [*J. Wechel pr.?:*] *Francofurti,* 1591.

p. 107. — **New Testament.** [*Greek.*] Τῆς καινῆς Διαθήκης ἅπαντα. Cum scholijs. *Basileæ,* 1543. 8°. 1003.b.13. Delete "[*and J. Wattenschnee*]" from the imprint.

p. 108. — — [*Polyglott.*] Nouum Testamentum omne ab Erasmo recognitū, emēdatum ac translatum, 1519. A slightly imperfect copy of the volume of Annotationes has now been acquired. Add to the description: ([Annotationes.]) 3 pt.

p. 111. — — [*German.*] Das neū testament grüntlich vnd recht. *Strassburg*, 1532. The date in the colophon is 1527.

p. 124. — **Appendix.** [*Proverbs.*] Lere vñ vnderweysung, 1472. Texts are by Albertanus Judex and others.

p. 126. **Biel, Gabriel.** Sermones. *Tubingñ*, 1499, 1500. IA.14824. Now complete in 4 pt.

p. 128. **Blindenspiegel.** Blindenspiegel, [1530?]. Add imprint: [*Melchior Ramminger: Augsburg*].

p. 132. **Bodenstein, Andreas.** Eyn frage. [*H. Knappe: Erfurt,* 1524]. Printed by Wolfgang Stürmer, not Knappe.

p. 136. **Boissard, Jean Jacques.** I(–VI) pars Romanæ vrbis topographiæ et antiquitatum, 1597–1602. Pt. 1 was printed by Johann Feyerabend, pt. 2 by Johann Sauer, and pt. 3 by Abraham Faber (of Metz).

— **Bolovesus, Conradus.** Heading should read: **Bolovesus, Conradus,** *pseud.* [i.e. **Conrad Gesner**].

p. 143. **Bote.** Der Hinckende Both, 1589. Add: [By Georg Rollenhagen].

p. 146. **Brandenburg-Anspach and Baireuth.—Albert,** *Margrave.* Fernere Erclerung, [1556]. Add the imprint: [*Hans Kohl: Adlersberg bei Pettendorf*].

p. 148. **Braun, Georgius.** Ein gründlicher bericht. Date should read: [1588].

p. 153. **Briessmann, Johann.** Vnterricht vnd ermanung, 1523. Imprint should read: [*Wolfgang Stürmer: Erfurt*].

p. 155. **Brubacchius, Petrus.** Catalogus librorum, [1550?]. Date should read: [1555].

p. 165. **Bugenhagen, Johann.** Etlich Christliche bedencken. [Another edition, 1525], is wrongly ascribed to the press of J. Prüss: it was printed by the Heirs of Matthias Schürer.

p. 166. — Wie man Christum ynn der schrifft sol süchen, 1530. In fact, by Michael Coelius, edited by Bugenhagen.

p. 175. **Calvinistic Cruelty.** Crudelitas Caluinianæ exempla, 1585. Printed by Gottfried von Kempen.

— — Der Calvinisten Grausambkeit, 1586. Printed by David Sartorius at Ingolstadt?

p. 178. **Campian, Edmund.** Leben vnd Leyden, 1588. Compiled from various sources; not translated from the work named: delete author statement.

p. 183. **Carion, Johann.** Chronica. Two anonymous German editions, 1533 and 1534, are entered under **Egenolff, Christian,** *Printer* (p. 262).

p. 188. **Cattaro.** This heading should be inserted before the two editions of Newe zeyttung, [1564].

p. 195. **Charles V.,** *Emperor of Germany.* Triumphierlich einreiten, 1535. The date of publication should read: 1536.

p. 196. **Charlier de Gerson, Jean.** [*Works.*] Prima (secunda) pars operum. Inuentoriū, 1494. IB.2178. Pt. 3 now acquired also.

p. 203. **Christian Songs.** Drey Schöne Christliche Lieder, [1600?]. Add imprint: [*Michael Manger: Augsburg?*].

— **Christians.** Speculum exemplorum. (4 editions.) A further edition of this text is entered under the heading **Speculum** (p. 824).

p. 206. **Chytraeus, David.** Oratio continens historiam Henrici Leonis, 1556. Date should read: 1555.

p.220. **Conrad,** *Bishop of Würzburg.* Ausschreiben, 1542. Imprint should read: [*Johann Petreius: Nuremberg*].

— **Conrad,** *Bruder.* Ein newes Lied, [1540?]. Date should read: [1560?].

p.221. **Coornhert, Dierick.** Abrahams Wtganck, 1575. Pressmark should read: 11557.de.20.

p.226. **Cranmer, Thomas.** A confutatiō, [1557?]. Date should read: [1556?].

p.227. **Crautwald, Valentinus.** Ein nuczbar Edell Buchleinn, 1524. This work is anonymous, and merely translated by Crautwald.

p.235. **D., L.A.** Both works entered under these intitials are by Lorenz Albrecht.

p.238. **Dedekind, Friedrich.** Grobianus. *Tr.* C. Scheidt. *Magdeburg,* [1600?]. Delete this entry: a seventeenth-century book.

p.246. **Discipulus.** Liber pmptuarij exemploɽ, [1474?]. Entry should now read: Sermones discipuli de tempe. (Liber pmptuarij exemploɽ. De miraculis Marie virgīs.) [By Joannes Herolt.] [*Ulrich Zel: Cologne,* 1474.] fol. IB.2963(impf.)

p.250. **Dobneck, Johann,** *Cochlaeus.* Warhafftige Historia, 1547. The date is a misprint, and should read: 1547[1537].

p.252. **Doner, Laurentius.** Ein warhafftige Historia, 1535. The supplied imprint should read: [*Heirs of Friedrich Peypus?: Nuremberg*].

p.253. **Dorpius, Heinrich.** Warhafftige Historie, 1536. 3906.cc.31. For [*G. Rottmaier*] read: [*J. Petreius*]. The edition catalogued as "*s.n.* [1550?] 4°", 3906.b.16, is part (sig. F2–L4) of a Tübingen, 1582 edition of Lucas Osiander: Ein Predig von dem Widertauff, and should be deleted from this heading.

p.255. **Du Bellay, Guillaume.** Kriegs Regiment, 1594. Imprint should read: *In verlegung P. Fischers:* [*Frankfort; J. Foillet:*] *Mümpelgart.*

p.256. **Duerer, Albrecht.** Vier bücher von menschlicher Proportion, [1550?]. Cancel this entry: a seventeenth-century book.

p.262. **Egenolff, Christian,** *Printer.* Chronic, 1533 and 1534. This is the Chronica of Johann Carion in the version edited by Melanchthon.

p.274. **Epistola.** Epistola cuiusdam puellæ Romanæ, [1510?]. Date should read: [1513 or 1514].

p.276. **Erasmus, Desiderius.** [*Letters.* — *Single Letters.* — *Ad Laurentium Campeium.*] Vrsach. *s.n.* [1530.] 3834.aa.35. Imprint should read: [*Georg Ulricher: Strasburg,* 1531].

p.277. — [*Adversus Pseudoevangelicos.*] Contra quosdam, [1529]. 847.c.10. Imprint should read: [*Christian Egenolff: Strasburg,* 1530].

p.279. — [*Colloquia.* — *Selections.*] Ain besonder schöner Dialogus, 1545. Add the imprint: [*Hans Kilian: Neuburg*].

p.282. — [*Lingua.*] Von der Zung. *s.n.* [1544?]. Imprint should read: [*Balthasar Beck: Strasburg,* 1544].

— — [*Moriae encomium.*] Μορίας ἐγκώμιον. [*M. Schürer? Strasburg?* 1520?] 820.d.37(1). Imprint should read: [*Lazarus Schürer: Schlettstadt,* 1520]. This copy wants the colophon leaf.

p.283. — [*Paraclesis.*] Paraclesis Teütscht. [*J. Pruess? Strasburg,* 1522?]. Imprint should read: [*Heirs of Matthias Schürer: Strasburg,* 1520].

— — [Another edition.] *s.n.* [1522?] 3925.c.38. Add imprint: [*Joerg Nadler: Augsburg,* 1520].

p.286. **Ess, Nicolaus van.** Margarita euangelica, 1545. In fact, translated by Eschius from the anonymous Dutch Die grote euangelische Peerle.

p.288. **Euclid.** [*Elementa.*] Elementorum libri XV. *Expensis I. B. Ciotti: Coloniæ,* 1591. Ciotti was a Venice publisher. The Cologne imprint is false; printed by Johann Feyerabend at Frankfort on the Main.

p.288f. **Eulenspiegel, Tyll.** This work is by Hermann Bote.

p.289. **Euripides.** Τραγωδίαι όκτοκαίδεκα. The order of the two "issues" dated [1558?] should be transposed. That described as "another issue of pt.1" is a separate edition, and its title-border bears the device, not of J. Secer of Hagenau, but of Johann Schott of Strasburg; its imprint should read: [*Peter Braubach: Frankfort,* ca.1553], pressmark G.8561. The edition in 2 pt. should be redated [ca.1555], pressmarks 999.a.5; G.8559, 60.

p.293. **F., A.** Ein nüw lied, [1544?]. Should be entered under the heading **Delden.** A.F. are the printer's initials, and the imprint should read: [*Augustin Friess: Zürich*].

— **Faber, Henricus.** Compendium musicæ, 1591. A later edition is entered under **Gumpelzhaimer** (p.378).

p.294. **Faber, Joannes,** *of Augsburg.* Oratio funebris, 1519. Pressmark should read: 610.e.1.

p.295. Insert the references: **Fabri, Johann,** *of Schlettstadt.* Planctus ruine ecclesie. See Planctus. — Tractatus de ruine ecclesie planctu. See Tractatus.

p.296. **Fabricius, Georgius,** *Chemnicensis.* De metallicis rebus obseruationes. Delete this reference.

p.301. **Ferrari, Antonio de',** *Galateo.* De situ Iapygiæ, 1558. The edition with the false Basle imprint (662.a.7) was in fact printed by Francesco Savio at Naples about 1645.

— **Ferrariis, Albertus de.** Author is identical with Albertus Trottus (p.871).

p.303. **Fiera, Baptista.** Coena, 1530. Delete this entry. The book is an imperfect copy of texts which should begin with Helius Eobanus: Bonae valetudinis conservandae praecepta, and is so entered in this Supplement.

p.308. **Flacius, Mathias,** *Illyricus.* Widerlegung eines Kleinen Deutschen Caluinischen Catechismi, 1563. This copy lacks the last leaf bearing the colophon. The imprint and date should therefore be enclosed in square brackets and the pressmark be followed by: (impf.).

p.310. **Foeniseca, Joannes.** The title of the only work under this heading should begin with the word Opera.

— **Folz, Hans.** Vitas patrum, [1525?]. Imprint and date should read: [*Peter Wagner: Nuremberg,* ca.1495]. Pressmark now IA.7989.

p.311. **Forster, Georg.** Selectissimarum mutetarum partim quinque, partim quatuor vocum tomus primus, 1540. Description should now read: Tenor. (Discantus. Altus. Bassus.) 4 pt. Pressmark now: K.4.b.24 & K.11.e.2(2).

p.315. **Francis,** *of Assisi, Saint.* Alcoranus Franciscanorum, 1543, *etc.* The author of the Liber conformitatum was Bartholomaeus de' Rinonichi, not B. Albizzi.

p.317. **Francus, Jacobus,** *pseud.* [i.e. **Conrad Memmius.**] Only two of the five entries under this heading are properly there: Iehoua vindex, and De rebus Gallicis commentatio, both 1590. The other three (Calendarij historici relatio, 1595, Relatio historica quinquennalis, 1595, and Warhafftige Beschreibung, 1597) should be entered under a new heading: **Francus, Jacobus**, *pseud*. [i.e. **Conrad Lautenbach**]. Of these, the two with the fictitious imprint *Walstatt* were published at Frankfort on the Main.

p. 320. **Freundburger, Johannes.** Change to **Freund, Johannes.**

p. 322. **Friese, Tilemannus.** Under this new heading insert from p. 863 the entry under the erroneous heading **Tilemannus, Friedrich.**

p. 325. **Fuchs, Jacob.** Von dē vereelichten standt, 1523. Printed at Strasburg by the Heirs of Reinhard Beck, not J. Schwan.

p. 328. **Fundling, Johann.** Anzaigung, 1526. Add: [A variant.] 3905.ee.91.

— **G., P.** Der Ewangelisch burger. The edition tentatively ascribed to Strasburg was in fact printed by Jörg Nadler at Augsburg.

p. 329. **Galen.** [*Two or more Works.*] Francisci Valesii commentaria in Galeni libros. *F. de Franciscis & I. B. Ciotti ære: Coloniæ*, 1594. Francesco de Franceschi and Giovanni Battista Ciotti were publishers at Venice. The Cologne imprint is false; printed by Johann Feyerabend at Frankfort on the Main.

p. 338. **Gengenbach, Pamphilus.** Add: Wie der Hailig Vatter. See Adrian VI., *Pope.*

p. 340. **Gerardus**, *Zutphaniensis.* De spiritualibus ascēsionib⁹, [1490?] 8°. Entry should now read: De spiritualibus ascēsionib⁹. (Gr̄arū actiões de vita mediatoris d'i.) [*Johann Prüss: Strasburg*, ca.1490.] 8°. IA. 1725 & IA. 1726.

p. 346. **Germany. — Charles V.**, *Emperor.* Zwey Keyserliche vneynige . . . gepott Luther betreffend. [*L. Cranach & C. Döring: Wittenberg*,] 1524. 4°. 1226.a.42; 697.h.4(9)(impf.). Two editions from the same press are confused here. The pressmarks should read: 1226.a.42 (Benzing 1937). [Another edition.] 3906.e.38; 697.h.4(9)(impf.) (Benzing 1938).

p. 347. — — New Zeyttung Kaiserlicher Maiestat Kriegsubūg in Franckreich, [1536]. Imprint should read: [*Wolfgang Meyerpeck: Zwickau*].

p. 348. — — Antwort auff Bapst Pauli des III. ausschreiben [25 Aug. 1542], 1543. Imprint should read: [*Johann Petrejus: Nuremberg*].

p. 349. — — [Interim, 15 May 1548.] Bekentnuss vnnd Erklerung auffs Interim, 1549, is by Joannes Aepinus.

— — — — Interim. Ein neues Lied, [1548]. The author is Cyriacus Schnauss, and the imprint should read: [*C. Schnauss: Coburg*].

p. 350. — **Ferdinand I.**, *King of the Romans.* Abdruck der Römisch. Kön. Maiest. Declaration, 1555. Add imprint: [*Valentin Bapst: Leipzig*].

p. 354. — **Reichstag.** [*Appendix.*] Eyn Christenlicher Ratschlag, [1526]. Not by M. Luther.

p. 357. **Gesen, Johann.** This heading should read: **Gese, Johann.**

— **Gesner, Conrad.** Add: *See* also Bolovesus, Conradus, *pseud.*

p. 365. **Grammatik.** Die Rotwelsch Grammatik, [1540?]. Add imprint: [*Rudolf Deck: Basle*].

p. 367. **Greek Language.** Εἰσαγωγὴ πρὸς τῶν γραμμάτων ἑλλήνων, [1505?]. Imprint should read: [*Nicolaus Marschalk: Erfurt*, 1502].

p. 370. **Gretser, Jacob.** This heading should precede Apologeticus, 1600, wrongly attached to the preceding heading **Greserus, Hieronymus.**

p. 378. **Gumpelzhaimer, Adam.** Compendium musicæ, 1600. Pressmarks now: Hirsch I.237: K.2.c.2(impf.). This is a work of Henricus Faber edited by Gumpelzhaimer. An earlier edition is entered under Faber (p.293).

p. 381. Insert reference: **Halle,** *on the Saale.* — **Collegiate Church.** See Maurice, Saint, and Mary Magdalen, Saint.

p. 384. **Hauptartikel.** Dye Grundtlichen vnd rechten hauptartickel aller Baurschafft, [1525?]. Imprint should read: [*Melchior Ramminger: Augsburg,* 1525], and the pressmark: 3906.b.72.

p. 386. **Hedio, Caspar.** Chronica, 1558. 4520.ee.2. Printed by Paul & Philipp Köpfel, not W. Köpfel.

p. 392. **Henricus,** *de Hassia.* Secreta sacerdotū, [1505?]. Imprint should read: [*Cornelis de Zieriksee: Cologne*].

p. 393. — Speculu3 anime, [1500?]. Imprint, date and pressmark should read: [*Heinrich von Neuss: Cologne,* 1509?] C.142.a.30.

p. 396. **Henry III.,** *King of France.* Ein schön new Lied, 1576. The imprint should be deleted and replaced by *s.l.*

— Insert the following references: **Henry Julius,** *Duke of Brunswick-Wolfenbüttel.* Der Caluinische Post-Reuter. See P., I.N.A.B.I.S. Comœdia von Vincentio Ladisslao. See L., H.I.D.B.E.L.E.P.I.H.A.

p. 397. **Herilacus, Pamphilus.** Aquarum natura et facultates. *Expensis I.B. Ciotti: Coloniæ,* 1591. Ciotti was a Venice publisher. The Cologne imprint is false; probably printed by Johann Feyerabend at Frankfort on the Main.

p. 409. **Hofmann, Christoph.** The reference should read: *See* Odofrancus, C., *pseud.*

p. 411. **Holthusius, Joannes.** Compendium, 1577. Date should read: 1567.

p. 417. **Horst, Jacob.** De aureo dente, 1593. Date should read: 1595.

p. 419. **Hovaeus, Antonius.** Odarum precum hymnorum liber, 1566. This is a separate issue of pt.2 of De arte amandi Christum libri.

p. 425. **Hutten, Ulrich von.** Opera poetica, 1538. Imprint should read: [*Krafft Müller: Strasburg*].

p. 427. — Nemo. *In edibus Stribilite: Erffordie,* [1512?]. Date should read: [1510].

p. 428. **Hymnals.** [*German.*] Schöne Christliche Gesenge zum begrebnus der todten, [1540?]. Add: [By Michael Weisse].

p. 445. **Jesus Christ.** Ein spruch von Christo, [1530?]. Imprint should read: [*Wolfgang Meyerpeck: Zwickau,* ca.1535?].

— — Von dem vntrenlichen vngenäten Rock Iesu christi, 1512. This is the text generally known by the name Orendel.

p. 458. **John**[Cassianus], *Saint.* [De Institutis cenobiorum], 1485. Entry should now read: De Institutis cenobiorum. (Collationes sanctorum patru3.) [*Johann Amerbach:*] *Basilee,* 1485. fol. IB.37287; IB.37287a(impf.).

p. 459. **John,** *Stobaeus.* Insert: Senarii græcanici quingenti. See Nachtigall, Otmar.

p. 467. **Karsthans.** Gesprech biechlin neüw Karsthans, [1520?]. Add: [By Martin Bucer]. The imprint and date of both editions should read: [*Heirs of Matthias Schürer: Strasburg,* 1521].

— **Kautz, Jacob.** Syben Artickel, [1527]. Imprint should read: [*Johann Schoeffer: Mainz*].

p.470. **Kinthisius, Jodocus.** The entry under the erroneous heading: **Rinthisius, Johann** (p.741) should be moved here.

p.474. **Knoefelius, Johannes.** Newe Teutsche Lieder, 1581. Imprint should read: [*Katharina Gerlach: Nuremberg*].

p.478. **Kunstbuechlein.** Delete the erroneous source of this text given within square brackets.

p.480. **L., H.I.D.B.E.L.E.P.I.H.A.** Comœdia von Vincentio Ladisslao, 1599. Add: [By Henry Julius, Duke of Brunswick-Wolfenbüttel]. Printed by Konrad Horn.

p.483. **Lange, Andreas** *of Eger* and *Pfarherr zu Clagenfurt* are identical.

p.488. **Lautenbach, Conrad.** Add the reference: See also Francus, Jacobus, *pseud*. [i.e. C. Lautenbach].

p.497. **Liddel, Duncan.** Disputationum physiologicarum quinta (sexta — nona — postrema), 1597. Pressmark should read: 1179.b.1(14–17); [another issue of no.5] T.518(6).

p.498. **Lied.** Ein new Lied von dem Jüngsten tage. H. Khol: Regenspurg, [1550?]. Kohl was in Vienna in 1550. Redate [ca.1555?].

p.500. **Lieder.** Zwey schöne Lieder. *A. Geglerin: Augspurg*, [1555?]. Date should read: [ca.1559].

— — Zway schöne Lieder, Das Erst, Wo soll ich mich hin keren, [1590?]. Date should read: [1570?].

p.509. **Liturgies.** — **Latin Rite.** — **Directories.** — **Würzburg.** [Order of Divine Service, 1517]. Pressmark should read: C.18.e.3(28).

p.511. — — **Missals.** [*Appendix.*] Missæ defunctæ epicedion, 1543. Pressmark should read: 11409.a.15.

p.515. — — **Rituals.** — **Lubeck.** [Benedictionale Lubicense, 1485?]. This text was erroneously identified and ascribed to the wrong press. The entry should read: **Liturgies.** — **Rituals.** — **Odense.** [Agenda Ottoniensis.] *Vellum.* [*Johann Snel: Lubeck, 1485?*] 4°. IA.9983.

p.519. — **Lutheran.** — **Pomerania.** Karcken Ordening, 1542. Imprint should read: [*Georg Rhau: Wittenberg*].

p.520. — **Moravians.** Ein Gesangbuch, [1544]. K.2.h.10. Date should read: [ca.1556].

p.524. **Lonicer, Johann.** Gericht büchlin, 1523. Title should read: Bericht büchlin.

p.536. **Luther, Martin.** [*Collections of Sermons.*] Zwo schöne tröstliche Predig. [*G. Rottmaier: Nuremberg,*] 1537. Printed by Johann Petrejus, not Rottmaier.

p.539. — [*Biblical Commentaries.*] Ein Kurtze vnd klare anlaitung wie das bûch der offenbarung Iohannis zuuerstehn sey, 1530. Add imprint: [*Johann Petrejus: Nuremberg*].

p.540. — [*Disputations.*] Sentencia quod doctrina legis in ecclesia sit necessaria. *s.l.* 1538. 4°. 3906.dd.8(8). Add imprint: [*Hieronymus Andreae: Nuremberg*].

— — [*Adversus armatum virum.*] Aduersus armatum virum Cokleum. *s.n.* [1523.] 4°. 3905.bb.69. Add imprint: [*Johannes Rhau-Grunenberg: Wittenberg*].

p.541. — [*An den Durchlauchtigen Albrecht.*] An den durchleüchtigen Herren. [*Nuremberg,*] 1532. 4°. 3905.bb.73. Printed by Jobst Gutknecht.

p. 542. — [*An die Ratsherrn.*] De constituendis scholis, [1525]. Date should read: [1527].
p. 544. — [*Brief an den Kardinal Erzbischof von Mainz.*] Ein Brieff. [*J. Klug?: Wittenberg?*, 1530.] 8°. Imprint should read: [*Melchior Sachse: Erfurt*].
p. 547. — [*Christlicher Ratschlag.*] Eyn Christenlicher Ratschlag. This work is not by Luther: delete the reference.
p. 548. — [*De abroganda Missa.*] De abroganda missa priuata sententia. *s.l.* Feb. 1522. 4°. 3906.dd.8(1). Add imprint: [*Johann Singriener: Vienna*].
p. 549. — [*De libertate Christiana.*] Epistola Lutherana. *s.l.* 1520. 4°. 697.h.27. Add Imprint: [*Johann Singriener: Vienna*].
p. 550. — [*De votis monasticis.*] The description of the edition in German entered as follows: [Another edition.] *s.n.* [1522.] 4°. 3905.b.39(impf.) should read: [Von den geystlichen vnd kloster gelübtē vrteyll.] [*Heirs of Matthias Schürer: Strasburg*, 1522.] 4°.
— — [*Den auserwählten Christen.*] Den uszerwöhltē lieben Freünden gottes. [*Strasburg?*]1523. 4°. 3905.bbb.19. Imprint should read: [*Heirs of Reinhard Beck: Strasburg*].
p. 551. — [*Epistel oder Unterricht.*] Von den hailgen Epistel. *s.l.* 1522. 4°. 3905.c.25. Add imprint: [*Silvan Otmar: Augsburg*].
— — — Von den hailgen Epistel. *s.l.* 1522. 4°. 3905.c.26. Add imprint: [*Melchior Ramminger: Augsburg*]. (Benzing 1218.)
— — [*Epistola ad Henricum VIII.*] Epistola ad Henricum VIII. Responsio regis. *s.n.* [1527.] 8°. 1020.e.2(2). Add imprint: [*Peter & Georg Apianus: Ingolstadt*]. This copy is imperfect, wanting the Epithalamia.
— — — Epistola ad Henricum VIII. Responsio regis. *s.n.* [1527.] 8°. 697.c.3. Add imprint: [*Johann Setzer: Hagenau*].
p. 552. — [*Etliche Artikelstücke.*] Ettlich Artickel so M. Luther erhalten wil wider dye gantzen Satans schule. [*Erfurt?*, 1530.] 4°. 3905.c.45. Imprint should read: [*Jakob Stoeckel?: Eilenburg?*,]1530.
— — — Artickel von der Christlichen kirchen gewalt. [*Nuremberg?*,] 1531. 4°. 3905.c.47. Imprint should read: [*Friedrich Peypus: Nuremberg*].
— — [*Etliche Schlüsse.*] Etliche Schlüsse, 1546. Add imprint: [*Georg Rhau: Wittenberg*].
p. 553. — [*Formula missae.*] Die weyse der Mess. *s.n.* [1524.] 4°. 3905.ee.80. Add imprint: [*Johann Schäffler: Constance*].
— — [*Freiheit des Sermons.*] Eyn Freyheyt dess Sermons. [*Augsburg*, 1518.] 4°. 3905.c.58. Imprint should read: [*Friedrich Peypus: Nuremberg*,] 1518.
p. 554. — [*Hauptstück des Neuen Testaments.*] Das Huptstuck des ewigen vnd newen testaments. *s.n.* [1522.] 4°. 3905.c.68. Add imprint: [*Johann Eckhart: Speyer*]. The date should read: [1523].
— — [*Kurze Form der zehn Gebote.*] Eyn kurtz form der zehen gebott. [*Basle?*, 1520.] 4°. 3905.c.81. Imprint should read: [*Valentin Curio: Basle*].
p. 556. — [*Missive an einen gebornen Grafen.*] Ain Missiue. [*Augsburg*, 1521.] Printed by Melchior Ramminger.
p. 558. — [*Schöne Predigt von dem Gesetz.*] Ein schöne Predigt von dem Gesetz. *s.n.* [1537.] 4°. 3905.cc.47. Add imprint: [*Hieronymus Andreae: Nuremberg*].
— — [*Sehr tröstliche Predigt.*] Ein ser tröstliche vñ schöne Predigt. [*Wittenberg?*,] 1538. 4°. Imprint should read: [*Hieronymus Andreae: Nuremberg*].

p. 559. — [*Sendbrief an Herzog Georg.*] Sendtbrief an den Durchleuchtigen Hertzog Georgen. *s.n.* [1526.] 4°. 3905.ee.74. Add imprint: [*Peter Schöffer the Younger: Worms*].

p. 560. — [*Sermon am Palmtag.*] Sermon am Palmtag. [*Augsburg,* 1522.] Printed by Heinrich Steiner.

p. 567. — [*Sermon von den sieben Broten.*] Ein Sermon von den siben broten. *s.n.* [1523.] 4°. 3908.ccc.39. Add imprint: [*Heirs of Reinhard Beck: Strasburg*].

p. 568. — [*Sermon von der Hauptsumma.*] Vō der haubtsum̄a. *s.n.* [1526]. Add imprint: [*Heinrich Steiner: Augsburg*].

— — [*Sermon von dreierlei gutem Leben.*] Eynn Sermon. [*Erfurt,* 1521.] 4°. 3905.dd.13. Printed by Matthes Maler.

p. 570. — [*Unterricht auf etliche Artikel.*] Vnderrichtung vff etlich Artickel. [*Strasburg,*] 1523. 4°. 3905.dd.66. Printed by Johann Grüninger.

p. 571. — [*Unterricht der Beichtkinder.*] Ein vndterricht der Beicht kinder. *s.n.* [1521.] 4°. 3905.ee.75. Add imprint: [*Johann Singriener: Vienna*].

— — [*Unterrichtung wie sich die Christen.*] Wie weit Mosy dienst. *s.l.* 1538. Add imprint: [*Philip Ulhart: Augsburg*]. This text is incorrectly identified, and should be entered under [*Biblical Commentaries*] (p. 536) as a sermon on the book of Genesis.

— — [*Vermahnung an alle Pfarrherrn.*] Ein Vermanung. *s.l.* 1546. Add imprint: [*Melchior Sachse: Erfurt*].

— — [*Vermahnung an die Geistlichen.*] [Another edition.] H. Lufft: Wittemberg, 1530. 3905.dd.53. For *H. Lufft* read: *J.klug*.

p. 572. — [*Vermahnung zum Sakrament.*] Vermanung zum Sacrament. [*Strasburg,*] 1541. 8°. Printed by Wendelin Rihel.

p. 573. — [*Von beider Gestalt.*] Vō beyder gestalt. [*Strasburg,* 1522.] 4°. 3905.dd.102. Printed by the Heirs of Matthias Schürer.

p. 576. — [*Warnung an seine lieben Deutschen.*] Warnunge an seine liebe Deutschen. *s.n.* [1546?] 3905.e.64. Imprint should read: [*Hans Daubmann: Nuremberg?,* ca. 1546?]. It is thought possible this may date from Daubmann's later period at Königsberg.

p. 577. — [*Welche Personen verboten sind.*] Welche person verpoten sind tzu ehlichen. *s.n.* [1522.] 4°. 3905.ee.5. First word should read: Wilche. Add imprint: [*Johannes Rhau-Grunenberg: Wittenberg*]. (Benzing 1234.)

— — [*Wider das Papsttum.*] Aduersus papatum. [*Strasburg?,*] 1545. Imprint should read: [*Georg Rhau: Wittenberg*].

— — [*Wider den Eisleben.*] Ein Schrifft, 1549. Add imprint: [*Christian Rödinger: Magdeburg*].

p. 578. — [*Wider die mörderischen Rotten.*] Wider die Reubischen vnd Mordischen rotten der Bawren. [*J. Setzer: Hagenau,* 1526]. Imprint should read: [*Peter Quentel: Cologne*].

p. 580. — [*Marginal Notes.*] Auslegung etzlicher Trostsprüche. [*Wittenberg?,* 1547.] 4°. 3905.bbb.28. Imprint should read: [*Wolfgang Stürmer: Erfurt,* 1547].

— — Ausslegung Etlicher Trostsprüch. *s.n.* [1547.] 4°. 3905.bbb.27. Add imprint: [*Johann Petrejus: Nuremberg*].

— — [*Appendix.*] Der Bock dryt frey auff disen plan. [Another edition.] *s.l.* 1525. Add imprint: [*Philip Ulhart: Augsburg*].

p. 581. — — Sepultura Lutheri, [1538.] Add: [By Justus Menius.]

p. 582. — — Ein Wellische Lügen schrifft. [Another edition.] *s.l.* 1545. Add imprint: [*Hans Guldenmund: Nuremberg*].

p. 589. **Malverda, Pedro de.** Heading should read: **Malvenda, Pedro de.**

p. 593. Insert the heading: **Maranta, Robertus** before the final two entries erroneously under **Maranta, Bartolommeo** (Praxis, 1598, and Speculum, 1586).

p. 594. The first entry under **Marcellus, Joannes** should have the heading: **Marcellus,** *pseud.*

— The heading **Marianus,** *de urbe Senarum* should read: **Socinus, Marianus,** *the Elder,* and the entry in consequence correctly be placed on p. 818.

p. 596. **Mary,** *the Blessed Virgin.* Der beschlossen gart, 1505. In the imprint, for [*Sodalitas Celtica*] read: [*Pinder's Printer*].

p. 609. **Melanchthon, Philipp.** Catechismus. Tr. C. Brusch. The pressmarks of the two editions have been transposed. That of 1544 is at 3504.aa.49, and that of [1550?] at 3504.aa.50.

p. 610. — De iustificatione, 1531. Imprint should read: [*Johannes Prael: Cologne*].

p. 612. — Historia de vita et actis M. Lutheri, 1555. Add imprint: [*David Zöpfel: Frankfort a.M.*].

— — Annotationes in Euangelium Ioannis, 1543. Date should read: 1532.

p. 613. — Loci communes, 1521 (two editions). The first, printed by Adam Petri at Basle, should have the date: 1521 [1522]. The second is erroneously ascribed to Melchior Lotter the Younger at Wittenberg, and should have the imprint and date: [*Eucharius Cervicornus: Cologne,*] 1521 [1522].

— — — Die haupt artikel, [1523?]. Imprint should read: [*Heinrich Gran: Hagenau: for*] *I. Knobloch: Strassburg.*

p. 615. — [*Selections.*] Gewise lehr, 1560. Imprint should read: *Christoph Heuss[ler]:* [*Nuremberg,*]1560.

p. 616. **Mélibée.** Diss ist der brun des Radts, 1504. Add: [An abridged translation from the "Liber consolationis et consilii" of Albertanus Judex].

p. 617. **Menius, Justus.** Insert the reference: Sepultura Lutheri. *See* Luther, Martin. [*Appendix*].

p. 619. **Mercator, Gerardus.** Atlas, 1595. Pressmark should read: Maps C.3.c.3,4(impf.).

p. 620. **Methodus.** Methodus geometrica, 1598. Add: [By Paul Pfinzing].

p. 626. **Moltherus, Menradus.** Romanorum pontificum omnium uita, [1528]. Imprint should read: [*Johann Setzer: Hagenau*].

p. 629. **Mors, Roderigo,** *pseud.* The lamentacion, [1542]. Delete the suggested imprint [*L. Mylius?: Bonn?*].

p. 634. **Muentzer, Thomas.** Ausslegung des andern vnterschyds Danielis, 1524. Imprint should read: [*Müntzer's Printer:*] *Alstedt,* 1524.

p. 635. **Munster. — Anabaptists.** Warhafftiger bericht, [1535]. Printed by Jakob Frölich.

p. 638. **Musculus, Andreas.** Vom Hosen Teuffel, 1555. Add the imprint: [*Johann Eichorn: Frankfort a.d.O.*].

p.642. **Nachtigall, Otmar.** Senarii græcanici quingenti, [1515?]. This text is by John Stobaeus.

p.644. **Nausea, Fridericus,** *Bishop.* De locustis, [1534]. Date should read: [1544].

p.645. **Nazarei, Judas,** *pseud.* Delete the tentative identification with Joachim von Watt.

— — Insert: [Vom alten und neuen Gott.] Ein Vnterschyd zů erkennen den almechtigen got. See Unterschied.

p.647. **Nepos, Cornelius.** Vita M. Catonis [and other matter], [1505]. 1308.d.9(impf.). Delete this entry. A perfect copy now acquired, entered under Wolphius, Thomas.

— **Netherlands.** [Before 1581.] — **Charles V.** Ordnung, Statuten vnd Edict, [1540]. Add imprint: [*Johann Petrejus: Nuremberg*].

p.648. — [*Appendix.*] Newe zeytung auss dem Niderlandt, auss Rom, auss Neapolis, [1523]. Imprint should read: [*Friedrich Peypus: Nuremberg*].

p.649. **Niavis, Paulus.** Three distinct works are confused in this entry. Dialogus ad latinum idioma perutilissimus is the same work as Latinum ideoma pro parvulis (iuvenibus) editum. The work entered as a Leipzig, 1494 edition of the latter is in fact Latina ideomata; the work entered as an edition printed by M.Landsberg, Leipzig 1495?, is in fact Latinum ideoma pro noviciis editum.

p.655. **Noot, Jan van der.** Theatrum das ist Schawplatz, 1572. Imprint should read: [*Gottfried Cervicornus: Cologne*].

p.658. **Ochino, Bernardino.** Ain Gesprech der flaischlichen vernunfft, [1548]. Date should read: [1546].

— **Ociorus, Tarquinius.** Experimenta, [1555?]. Date should read: [1557].

p.660. **Oecolampadius, Joannes.** Quod expediat. [*P. Schoeffer: Mainz*, 1522]. For *Mainz* read: *Worms*.

p.661. **Olmo, Giovanni Francesco.** De iis, 1576. Delete the suggested printer's name.

p.662. **Onus.** Onus Ecclesiæ, 1531. Delete the attribution to J. Ebser, and substitute: [By Berthold Pirstinger, Bishop of Chiemsee?]. Another issue, with printed attribution to Ebser, is entered on p.959.

p.663. Insert the reference: **Orendel.** See Jesus Christ. Von dem vntrenlichen vngenäten Rock Iesu christi.

p.666. **Osiander, Andreas.** Was zu Marpurgk in Hessen, 1529. Date should read: [1530].

p.668. Insert the reference: **Ostrofrancus, Christophorus,** *pseud.* [i.e. Christoph Hofmann.] See Odofrancus.

p.670. **P., I.N.A.B.I.S.** Der Caluinische Post-Reuter, 1592. Add: [By Henry Julius, Duke of Brunswick-Wolfenbüttel], and the imprint: [*Konrad Horn: Wolfenbüttel*].

p.673. **Papacy.** Von der erschrocklichen Zurstörung vnnd Niderlag dess gäntzen Bapstumbs, [1550?]. Add: [By Martin Schrot], and correct the imprint and date thus: [*Hans Gegler: Augsburg,* 1558].

p.675. **Paris. — Université.** Apologia qua patrocinatur M. Lutheri propositionibus à theologis Parrhisiensibus damnatis, 1531. Printed at Nuremberg not by Johann Petrejus, but by Friedrich Peypus.

p.676. **Pasquino,** *pseud.* Insert the following entry, incorrectly catalogued under **Scaliger, Julius Caesar**: Pasquillus. Ad neminem. [An attack on Andreas Osiander.] *s.n.* [ca.1550?] 8°. 11515.a.33.

p.678. **Paul,** *von Prag.* Mysterium nouum, 1572. Date should read: 1582.

p.691. **Philastrius,** *Saint.* De omnibus hæresibus, 1539. This entry is wrongly filed, and should follow that under **Philaretus, Gilbertus.**

p.692. **Philip II.,** *King of Spain.* Warhafftige Zeitungen, [1557]. Add the imprint: [*Ambrosius Kirchner: Magdeburg?*].

p.695. **Pickhart, Jesuwalt,** *pseud.*[i.e. **Johann Fischart.**] Die Wunderlichst, Vnerhörtest Legend, 1593. Cancel this entry: a seventeenth-century book.

p.697. **Pinder, Ulrich.** Four works have erroneous ascriptions to the press of the Sodalitas Celtica. In each case, for [*Sodalitas Celtica*] read: [*Pinder's Printer*].

p.700. **Pius II.,** *Pope.* [Cosmographia.] Asiæ Europaq͡3 descriptio, 1531. Perfect copy now acquired. Pressmark should read: Davis II, 296; 582.a.2(impf.).

p.701. **Placitus, Sextus.** De medicamentis ex animalibus libellus, 1538. Pressmarks should read: 954.c.28; [a variant] 540.d.34(2, 3).

p.702. **Planctus.** Plāctus ruinę ecclesię, [1520?]. Add: [By Johann Fabri].

p.705. **Plinius Secundus, Caius.** In Caii Plinii Secundi Naturalis historiæ I. & II. cap. libri XXX. commentarius, 1548. Author of this work is Étienne de l'Aigue.

p.708. **Pol, Sebastian.** Heading should read: **Pollio, Simphorianus,** and the entry should be moved to p.709.

p.710. **Ponet, John.** A Shorte Treatise, 1556. Printed by Paul & Philipp Köpfel, not W.Köpfel.

p.711. **Pontanus, Joannes Baptista.** Heading should read: **Pontanus, Joannes Jovianus.**

p.713. **Post-Reiter.** Der post Reutter bin ich genandt; two editions, 1590 and 1591. Insert: [By Georg Rollenhagen].

p.714. **Practica.** Eyn warhafftig Practica. *Anstat Nolt: Speir,* [1525?]. Date should read: [ca.1540?]. Pressmark now 1608/622.

p.716. **Procopius,** *of Caesarea.* De rebus Gothorum Persarum ac Vandalorum libri vii, 1531. Insert: 2 pt. Pressmark should read: 9135.f.18; [pt.2 only] 692.f.6(4).

p.718. **Prussia. — Nobility.** Ad S.R.M. legatorum nobilitatis ducatus Prussiæ literæ insinuatoriæ appellationis à se interpositæ, [1585]. Cancel this entry: printed by Aleksy Rodecki at Cracow.

p.722. **Rabus, Ludovicus.** Der Heiligen Gottes Zeügen Historia, 1552. Imprint should read: *Durch B.Becken Erben.*

p.724. **Rantzau,** *House of.* Genealogia Rantzouiana, [1585] and [1587]. Pressmarks should read: 606.c.31(1) and (2).

p.741. **Rinthisius, Jodocus.** The name is Kinthisius, and the entry should be moved to p.470.

p.742. **Rivius, Joannes.** De consolandis ægrotantibus, [1546]. Printed by Johann Oporinus?

p. 747. **Rome,** *the City.* [*Appendix.*] Declaratio Iubilei futuri Romæ anno M.D.L., [1550]. This first text by Pietro Paulo Vergerio.

p. 757. **Romming, Johannes.** Pentitētiarius. *F. Peypus: Nurmbergæ,* [1522?]. Date should read: [ca. 1515].

p. 759. **Ruell, Ebert.** Ein güthertzig bedencken. [Another edition], 1526. Add the imprint: [*Gabriel Kantz: Altenburg*].

p. 768. **Sachs, Hans.** Ein gesprech zwischen dem Todt vnd zweyen Liebhabenden, [*Nuremberg?,* 1550?]. Imprint and date should read: [*Georg Merkel: Nuremberg,* 1555].

— — Kladredt, [1550?]. Date should read: [ca. 1555?].

p. 770. — Der Todt ein Endt, [1550?]. Date should read: [ca. 1555?].

p. 775. **Sambucus, Joannes.** Obsidio Zigethiensis descripta. *R. Hofhalter: Viennæ,* [1556]. Date should read: [1558].

p. 777. **Satan.** Expostulation vnd strafschrifft Satane mit hertzog Heintzen von Braunschweig, [1541?]. Add: [By Johann Lening].

p. 782. **Scaliger, Julius Caesar.** Pasquillus. (Scaliger delapsus ex cœlis cœlorum), [1560?]. This work should be entered under the heading: **Pasquino,** *pseud.* (p. 676), as follows: Pasquillus. Ad neminem. [An attack on Andreas Osiander.] *s.n.* [ca. 1550?] 8°. 11515.a.33.

— **Scarperia.** Eyn erschrockenliche newe Zeitung. [*Strasburg?,* 1542]. Imprint should read: [*Jakob Fröhlich: Strasburg*].

p. 784. **Schatzger, Caspar.** De cultu & ueneratione sanctorum. *s.n.* [1525?]. Imprint and date should read: [*Sigmund Grimm: Augsburg?,* 1522 or 1523?].

p. 786. **Schenck, Hieronymus.** Honestissime virginis nobilitatis descriptio. [*M. Schubart?: Würzburg?,* 1504]. Imprint should read: [*Johann Weissenburger: Nuremberg*].

p. 789. **Schirmeister, Stephanus.** Add epithet: *of Eilenburg.*

p. 791. **Schnauss, Cyriacus.** Insert: Interim. Ein neues Lied. See Germany. — Charles V., *Emperor.*[Interim, 15 May 1548].

— **Schneider, Hans.** Wye der Romisch künig. [*Nuremberg?,* 1520?]. Imprint and date should read: [*Peter Wagner: Nuremberg,* 1500].

p. 792. **Schoener, Johann.** De nuper . . . repertis insulis, [1523]. Delete "(Globus geographicus)" and the second pressmark. No plates are present. Imprint should read: [*Johann Petrejus: Nuremberg*].

p. 797. **Schrot, Martin.** Add the reference: Von der erschrockenlichen Zurstörung vnnd Niderlag dess gäntzen Bapstumbs. See Papacy.

p. 798. **Schwarm,** *Doctor, pseud.* Ein schöne kurtzweylig Fassnacht Predigt, [1560?]. Add imprint: [*Matthäus Franck?: Augsburg?*].

p. 800. **Schwarzenberg, Johann von,** *Baron.* Ain Lied mit vorgehender anzaygung, [1530?]. Date should read: [1534]. This is extracted from Der Teütsch Cicero, 1534.

p. 803. **Schwenckfeld, Caspar,** *Herr von Ossing.* Von der Anbettung Christi, [1543]. Date should read: [1546?].

p. 804. **Scotus, Romoaldus.** Summarium rationum, 1588. Printed, not by D. Sartorius at Ingolstadt, but by Heinrich Bock at Trier.

p. 813. **Sibyls.** [*Appendix.*] Ein Ausstzug etlicher Practica, [1530?]. Imprint and date should read: [*Nickel Schmidt: Leipzig,* 1527]. Pressmark now 1608/734(2).

p.818. The heading **Socinus, Marianus** should read: **Socinus, Marianus,** *the Younger,* to distinguish his two entries from the work of Marianus Socinus the Elder which is erroneously entered under **Marianus,** *de urbe Senarum* on p.594.

— **Solinus, Caius Julius.** I. Camertis in Solini πολυίστωρα [*sic*] enarrationes. Index, 1520. Add to the imprint: *impensis Lucae Alantse.* The format is fol, not 4°. Pressmark should read: C.32.m.5(2).

p.823. **Spangenberg, Cyriacus.** Von der Ewigen Vorsehung, 1567. The title given should be preceded by the words: De praedestinatione.

p.824. **Speculum.** Speculum exemplorum, 1485. Further editions of this text are entered under the heading **Christians** (p.203).

p.826. **Spira, Francesco.** Ein erschröckliche Historia, 1564. Delete the suggested place of printing. Leonhard Nassinger's whereabouts at this date are not known.

p.829. **Stand.** Von dem Eelichē standt, [5120?]. Date should read: [1520?].

p.830. **Staphylus, Fridericus.** Vrsprung vnnd Anfang der Antichristlichen Lehre, 1563. Add imprint: [*Heinrich Geissler: Regensburg?*].

p.833. **Stimulus.** Stimulus beneficiatorum, 1509. Perfect copy now acquired, pressmark C.175.m.25.

p.837. **Strauss, Jacob.** Haubstuck vnnd Artickel Christlicher leer wider den wucher. [*J. Schwan: Strasburg,* 1523]. Printed by the Heirs of Reinhard Beck, not Schwan.

p.844. **Susenbrotus, Joannes.** Epitome toporum, [1540?]. Date should read: [1560?].

p.846. **Sylvius, Peter.** Luthers vnd Lutzbers eintrechtige vereinigung. [*Leipzig?,*] 1535. Imprint should read: [*Michael Blum: Leipzig*].

p.847. **Synodus.** Synodus auium, 1558. Insert: [By Jacobus Greselius].

p.848. **Tagweise.** Ein schöne Tagweyss, [1590?]. Insert imprint: [*Michael Manger: Augsburg?*].

p.849. **Tannstetter Collimitius, Georg.** Practica gemacht zü Wienn, [1523?]. Pressmark should read: C.71.h.14(18).

p.850. **Taufbuechlein.** Das Tauffbüchlin, 1524. This is not by Martin Luther. Add imprint: [*Heirs of Matthias Schürer: Strasburg*].

p.851. **Temesvár.** Sibenbürgische Victoria, [1596?]. The question-mark can be removed from the date.

p.858. **Thomas,** *Aquinas, Saint.* [*Quaestiones de veritate.*] Questiones disputate, 1475. Perfect copy now acquired. Pressmarks now: IB.3480; IB.3480a(impf.).

p.862. **Thylesius, Antonius.** De coronarum generibus commentarius, 1531. First pressmark should read: 604.a.1(1).

p.863. **Tilemannus, Friedrich.** Heading should read: **Friese, Tilemannus.**

p.864. **Toltz, Johann.** Eyn Kurtz handbüchlyn, 1526. Imprint should read: [*Gabriel Kantz: Zwickau*].

p.867. **Tractatus.** Tractatus de ruine ecclesie planctu; two editions, [1495?] and [1520?]. Add: [By Johann Fabri].

p.871. **Trottus, Albertus.** Author identical with Albertus de Ferariis (p.301).

p.872. **Troy.** Ein hübsche histori. [Another edition.] [*B. Kistler:*] *Straspurg,* 1499 [1500?]. Imprint and date should read: [*Johann Knobloch:*] *Straspurg,* 1499 [ca.1509].

p. 879. **United Brethren.** Catechismus, 1555. Add imprint: [*Hans Daubmann: Königsberg?*].

— **Unterricht.** Ain klarer vnterricht wider etliche Trück, 1531. Add: [By Pilgram Marbeck], and the place: [*Strasburg?*].

— **Unterschied.** Ein Vnterschyd zů erkennen den almechtigen got, 1521. This bears the author's name: Judas Nazarei.

p. 882. **Valeriano Bolzani, Giovanni Pierio.** De honoribus, 1513. 11409.c.55. This copy lacks the last leaf bearing the printer's device, which is however present in an otherwise fragmentary copy (sig. C only) at 11515.b.74.

p. 886. **Vehe, Michael.** Wie vnderschydlicher weiss. *M.Blum: Leipzig*, 1531. Date should read: 1532.

p. 888. **Vergerio, Pietro Paulo,** *Bishop.* Della camera et statua della madonna, 1554. Add imprint: [*Ulrich Morhart's widow: Tübingen*].

p. 889. **Veridicus, Didymus,** *Henfildanus, pseud.* [i.e. **Thomas Stapleton.**] Apologia, [1592?] Printed in Antwerp?

— **Vermigli, Pietro Martire.** Dialogus de vtraque in Christo natura. *C. Froschouerus: Tiguri*, 1561. This is the edition of November 1561 (not August).

p. 895. **Virdung, Sebastian.** Musica getutscht, [1511]. Pressmarks now: K.8.c.9; [a variant] Hirsch I.594.

p. 896. **Virgilius Maro, Publius.**[*Works.*] Opera. H. Petri: Basileæ, [1547]. Imprint and date should read: *Ex officina Henricpetrina: Basileæ,* [1575].

— — — Opera. *Ex officina Henricpetrina: Basileæ,* 1561. Imprint should read: *Per Henricum Petri: Basileæ.*

p. 902. **W., B.** Wie der Lycaon von Wolfenbüttel, 1542. Add: [By Burkard Waldis].

p. 905. **Walther, Rudolph.** Nabal, [1550?]. Date should read: [1549].

p. 907. **Watt, Joachim von.** Delete the reference to Nazarei, Judas.

p. 908. Insert the reference: **Weisse, Michael.** Schöne Christliche Gesenge zum begrebnus der todten. See Hymnals.[*German*].

p. 909. **Werböcz, Stephanus de.** Tripartitum opus. *I. Syngrenius: [Vienna,* 1550?]. Date should read: [1561].

p. 911. **Wernstreyt, Friderich,** *pseud.* Add to the heading: [i.e. **Sebastian Franck**].

p. 916. **William V.,** *Duke of Juliers, Cleve and Berg.* Ein bericht vnd zeitunge der ergangnē schlacht, [1543]. Add the imprint: [*Wolfgang Meyerpeck: Zwickau*].

p. 920. **Witekind, Hermann.** De sphæra mundi, 1590. Date should read: 1590 (1574★). This is a reissue by Harnisch of sheets printed by Mayer in 1574.

p. 926. **Wolfenbuttel.** Warhafftige beschreybung der Belegerung, [1542]. Add: [By Burkard Waldis].

p. 929. **Wurtemberg. — Christopher,** *Duke.* New landtrecht, 1554. Add imprint: [*Ulrich Morhart's widow & heirs: Tübingen*].

p. 933. **Zasius, Joannes Udalricus.** Delete the name Joannes.

p. 937. **Zwingli, Ulrich.** [Ad Carolum.] The Rekening, 1543. Imprint should read: *Zijrik* [*Widow of C.van Ruremunde: Antwerp*]. — The rekenynge, 1548. Imprint should read: *R. Wyer:* [*London;*] Ziiryk. Both Zürich imprints are false.

p.939. — Eyn kurtze klare sum̃, [1535?]. Delete "(impf.)" after the second pressmark.

p.952. **Liturgies. — Rituals. — Passau.** The second item under this heading is incorrectly entered, and should have the subheading *Salzburg* (not *Passau*).

p.959. **Ebser, Johann,** *Bishop.* Onus ecclesiæ, 1531. Thought to be by Berthold Pirstinger, not Ebser. Pressmark should read: 4050.l.6.

p.960. **Geschmuck.** Add: [By Ambrosius Blaurer]. Imprint should read: [*Christoph Froschauer: Zürich,* 1526?].

p.961. **Harryson, Johan,** *pseud.* Yet a course, 1543. The imprint is fictitious; printed by Antonius Goinus at Antwerp.

p.963. **Mercator.** Mercator iurisperitus, 1599. Add: tom.1. 2 pt. Wanting tom.2.

p.969. **Apffel, Michael.** The works indexed for 1572 & 1573 should be redated 1582 & 1583 respectively.

p.971. **Auslasser, Hans.** For *Augsburg* read: *Schwaz.*

— Insert reference: **Avena, Heinrich.** *See* Mueller, Jakob, and Avena, H.

— **Awerbach, Mathys.** For *Mainz* read: *Aschaffenburg.*

p.975. **Baumann, Georg,** *Breslau.* Should be distinguished from the Erfurt printer of the same name, whose son he was.

p.976. **Bechtermuentze, Nicolaus.** For *Eltril* read: *Eltville.*

— **Beck, Balthasar.** 1542: for Barrera read: Baviera.

— — 1552: Rabus, L. This entry belongs under **Beck, Balthasar,** *Heirs of.*

p.979. **Berg, Johann vom,** and **Neuber, U.** The 1544 entry under Liturgies.
— *Moravians* should be moved to 1556.

p.980. **Bergen, Gimel,** *the Younger.* The works of 1598, 99 erroneously indexed under this heading belong to Gimel Bergen the Elder and/or his heirs.

p.981. **Binder, Henrick.** The works of 1582–7 erroneously ascribed to this printer were printed by Hans Binder.

p.982. **Birckmann, Arnold.** The works dated 1559–62 were printed by Arnold Birckmann the Younger.

p.984. **Bock, Niclas.** Was a publisher at Leipzig, not Frankfort.

— **Boerner, Johann.** For *Erfurt* read: *Leipzig.*

p.985. **Brandis, Matthaeus.** Under 1485?, delete the index entry for Liturgies. — Rituals. — Lubeck.

p.986. **Braubach, Peter,** *Frankfort.* Delete the 1558? entry for Euripides.

p.989. **C., W.** Printer identical with W., C. (p.1201).

p.994. **Ciotti, Johann Baptist.** Was bookseller in Venice. The Cologne imprints are false.

p.1004. **Egenolff, Christian,** *Frankfort.* Delete the 1538 entry under Hutten, U. von.

p.1009. **Episcopius, Nikolaus,** *the Elder* and **Eusebius.** For *Elder* read: *Younger.*

p.1011. **Fabricius, Paul.** Identical with Julius Paulus Fabricius.

— Add the reference: **Fabritius, Walther,** and **Gymnich, J., III.** *See* also Monocerotis, Ad intersignium.

p. 1015. **Feyerabend, S. Carl.** Name is Sigmund Carl Feyerabend.
— **Fischer, Peter,** *Muempelgart*. The work indexed for 1594 was published by Fischer at Frankfort, and printed by J. Foillet at Muempelgart.
p. 1017. **Franciscis, Franciscus de.** For *Cologne* read: *Venice*.
p. 1018. **Franck, Matthaeus.** Imprints with suggested dates later than 1570 should be redated, as Franck died in 1568 and his widow was succeeded in 1570 by Michael Manger, whom she married in 1569. The Holthusius edition of 1577 appeared in fact in 1567; that of 1579 was printed by Manger and is wrongly ascribed to Franck in the index.
— **Franck, Matthaeus,** *Heirs of.* The date should read: 1570?
— **Frischmut, Hans.** The work of 1543 was printed by Frischmut in Halle.
p. 1026. **Froschauer, Christoph.** One of the two items by J. Susenbrotus indexed for 1540? (Epitome toporum) should be redated 1560? For the erroneous entry: 1550? Nabal, substitute: 1549: Walther, R. Nabal.
p. 1031. **Gastel, Jörg.** Delete the 1523 entry under Netherlands.
— **Gegler, Agathe.** The date should read: 1559?
p. 1035. **Getz, Paul.** Identical with Paul Goetz (p. 1036).
p. 1038. **Gran, Jobst.** A further item is indexed under the identical Jost Kran (p. 1082).
p. 1041. **Grueninger, Bartholomaeus.** Delete the entry for 1521.
p. 1050. **Haans, Hartmann.** Name should read: **Han, Hartmann** (son of Weigand Han).
— **Hachenberg, Paul von.** Identical with Paul, *von Hachenburg* (p. 1121).
— Add reference: **Hamer, Johann.** *See* Jamer.
p. 1051. Add reference: **Han, Hartmann.** *See* Haans, H.
p. 1056. **Hermann,** *of Emden*. For *Strasburg* read: *Hamburg*.
p. 1058. **Herwagen, Johann,** *the Younger,* and **Oporinus, J.** For *Younger* read: *Elder*.
— **Heuss, Christoph.** This is an abbreviated form of name for Christoph Heussler of *Nuremberg* (not *Wittenberg*).
p. 1060. **Hochstraten, Johan.** Should read: **Hillen (Hoochstraten), Johannes.**
p. 1063. **Hueter, Simon.** The work indexed for 1581, printed at Freiberg, was published by Hueter at *Leipzig*.
p. 1065. **Jacob, Cyriacus.** Under 1545, for Rinthisius read: Kinthisius.
— Insert the reference: **Jacobus,** *de Pforzheim*. *See* Wolff, J.
— **Jobin, Bernhard.** Delete the 1576 entry under Henry III., *King of France,* and the 1593 entry under Pickhart, J.
p. 1069. **Kestlin, Hermann.** Identical with Hermann Kaestlin (p. 1067).
p. 1070. **Kistler, Bartholomaeus.** Delete the second of the two editions indexed for 1499 under Troy.
— **Klug, Josef.** Delete the entry for 1530 under Luther, M. [*Brief an den Cardinal zu Mainz*].
p. 1071. **Knappe, Hans.** Delete the entry for 1524.
p. 1076. **Koberger, Anton.** The work indexed for 1515 was published by Anton Koberger *the Younger*.

p. 1078. **Koelhoff, Johann,** *the Younger.* Delete the entry under 1500.

p. 1079. **Koepfel, Wolfgang.** The three works indexed for 1556 & 1558 were printed by Paul & Philipp Koepfel, not Wolfgang.

— **Kohl, Hans,** *Ratisbon.* The entry indexed for 1550? under Lied should be redated 1555?

p. 1082. **Kran, Jost.** Identical with Jobst Gran (p. 1038).

p. 1092. **Lotter, Melchior,** *the Younger.* Delete the 1521 entry for Melanchthon, P., Loci communes.

p. 1098. **Maier, Johann,** *Heidelberg,* 1590. Cancel this entry.

p. 1103. **Meinberger, Friedrich.** Identical with Meynberger, Fridericus (p. 1105).

p. 1104. **Mellerstadt, Caspar de.** For *Strasburg* read: *Bremen.*

— **Menius, Matthias.** For *Görlitz* read: *Danzig.*

— **Merkel, Georg.** The two entries indexed for 1550 should be redated [ca. 1555?].

p. 1105. **Meyerpeck, Wolfgang.** Delete the entry for 1535 under Doner, L.

— **Meynberger, Fridericus.** Add the entry indexed under Meinberger, Friedrich (p. 1103).

p. 1106. **Monocerotis, Ad intersignium,** *Cologne.* This was the publishing-house directed by Walther Fabritius with the assistance of Johann Gymnich III.

p. 1108. **Muelen, Lorenz von der.** Delete the index entry for 1542.

p. 1110. **Mueller, Krafft,** and **Fabricius, Blasius.** The work of 1549 was printed by Krafft Mueller's widow and Fabricius.

p. 1111. **Nassinger, Leonhard.** The work indexed for 1564 was printed at an uncertain place other than Vienna.

p. 1112. Add the reference: **Neuss, Johann von.** *See* Johann, *von Neuss.*

— **Nolt, Anastasius.** The work indexed for 1525? should be redated: ca. 1540?

p. 1114. **Oporinus, Johann.** 1549: for Auerbachius read: Amerbachius.

p. 1118. **Oswaldt, Johann.** For *Basle* read: *Augsburg.*

p. 1120. **Otmar, Valentin.** German Theology is correctly filed under 1543, but the date is misprinted 1533.

p. 1121. **Paul,** *von Hachenburg.* Add the two entries indexed under Hachenberg, Paul von (p. 1050).

p. 1124. **Petrejus, Johann.** Delete the entry for 1531 under Paris. — *Université.*

p. 1128. **Petri, Heinrich.** The entry under 1547 for Virgilius Maro, P. [*Works.*] should be moved to 1575.

p. 1130. **Peypus, Friedrich.** The work of J. Romming indexed for 1522 should be redated: ca. 1515.

p. 1131. — Add the reference: *See* also Pinder's Printer. The works of 1535 were printed by the Heirs of Friedrich Peypus.

— **Pfeil, Johann.** The work indexed for 1495 was printed at *Ratisbon,* not *Bamberg.*

p. 1132. Insert: **Pinder's Printer (Friedrich Peypus),** *Nuremberg* 1505–10. The five works from this press are erroneously indexed under **Sodalitas Celtica** (p. 1182).

p. 1134. Insert **Printer of Francisci, Quodlibetica decisio**, *Schrattenthal* 1501. 1501 Francisci, M.

p. 1138. **Pruess, Johann,** *the Younger.* Delete the 1522? entry for Erasmus, D. [*Paraclesis*] and the 1525 entry for the work of J. Bugenhagen.

p. 1143. **Rabe, Bechtold.** For *Frankfort* read: *Wittenberg.*

p. 1146. **Ramminger, Melchior.** Delete the 1527 entry under Kautz, J.

p. 1148. **Reichardt, Hans.** Delete this entry. Reichardt was not Müntzer's printer in Allstedt.

— **Reinheckel, Andreas.** The work indexed for 1579 belongs to Reinheckel at *Augsburg* (with Philip Ulhart the Younger).

p. 1153. **Rhodius, Jonas.** Identical with Jonas Rosa (p. 1157).

p. 1154. **Richolff, Georg.** Add *the Younger*; identical with the printer subsequently at Lübeck.

p. 1156. **Rihel, Wendelin** and **Hieronymus,** 1561. This is Wendelin Rihel *the Younger.*

p. 1157. **Rollan PP,** *Heidelberg* 1597. Possibly a false imprint.

— **Rottmaier, Georg.** The work of 1529 indexed under Osiander should be redated: 1530. The two works indexed for 1536 & 1537 were printed by Johann Petrejus, not Rottmaier.

p. 1160. **Sachse, Melchior.** Delete the entry for 1542 under Liturgies.

— **Salomo, Blasius.** For *Basle* read: *Leipzig.*

p. 1162. **Sartorius, David.** Delete the 1588 entry under Scotus, R.

p. 1163. **Schenck, Wolfgang.** The entry for 1502 *Ars [Ars notariatus] should appear under Georg Schenk of Nuremberg, not W. Schenck of Erfurt.

— **Schenwetter, Johann Theobald.** For *Oberursel* read: *Frankfort.*

p. 1166. **Schmied, Peter.** Delete this entry.

p. 1170. **Schoeffer, Peter,** *the Younger.* The work indexed for 1522 was printed at *Worms,* not *Mainz.*

p. 1171. **Schoener, Johann.** Delete the work indexed under *Kirchehrenbach* for 1523. Delete the sub-heading *Nuremberg* 1524. The work of 1524 was printed at *Kirchehrenbach.*

p. 1173. **Schott, Johann.** Delete the 1528 entry under Moltherus, M.

p. 1174. **Schubart, Martin.** Delete this entry.

p. 1175f. **Schuerer, Matthias.** The works indexed for 1520 & 1521 belong to the Heirs of M. Schuerer. The 1520? entry for Erasmus, D. [*Moriae encomium*] should be deleted.

p. 1176. **Schultes, Hans.** Add the following entry: 1600 **Ehingen, G. von.

p. 1177. **Schwan, Johannes.** Delete the two entries for 1523, which were printed by the Heirs of Reinhard Beck.

p. 1181. **Setzer, Johann.** The edition indexed under Luther, M. [*An die Ratsherrn*] for 1525 should be redated: 1527. That of [*Wider die mörderischen Rotten*] under 1526 should be deleted. Three of the entries indexed for 1532 (s.v. Bible, Hesiod, Hippocrates) and the three for 1533 were printed by the Heirs of J. Setzer.

— **Setzer, Johann,** *Heirs of.* Delete the 1534 entry for J. Agricola.

— Insert the reference: **Seuberlich, Lorenz.** See Sueberlich, L.

— **Seybold, Heinrich.** Delete the entry for 1530 under Fiera, B.

— **Singriener, Johann.** The 1534 entry for Nausea, F. should be moved to 1544.

p.1182. **Singriener, Johann,** *the Younger.* The entry for 1550? under Werböcz should be moved to 1561.

— **Smesmann, Abraham.** The work of 1594 by Pithopoeus is incorrectly indexed under *Speyer*; it was printed at *Heidelberg.* Under *Speyer,* insert a 1595 edition of Heresbach's Rei rustica. It is not yet possible to determine which works were printed by Smesmann's Heirs.

— **Sodalitas Celtica.** The works indexed for 1505–10 were in fact printed on Ulrich Pinder's private press (by Friedrich Peypus).

p.1184. **Spiess, Johann.** The entry for 1578 should be dated 1580.

p.1185. — Delete *Wittenberg,* 1593. The work indexed for that year, printed in Wittenberg, was no doubt published by Spiess at Frankfort.

p.1186. **Steiner, Heinrich.** Under 1524, for Ryschner read: Rychsner.

p.1187. — The work of J. von Schwarzenberg indexed for 1530? should be redated: 1534.

p.1188. **Steinius, Nicolaus.** For *Cologne* read: *Frankfort on the Main.*

p.1190. **Stoeckel, Wolfgang.** The work of 1504 was printed in *Wittenberg,* not *Leipzig.*

p.1192. **Striblita, Sebaldus.** The work indexed under Hutten for 1512 should be redated: 1510.

p.1196. **Trebelius, Hermann.** Cancel this entry.

p.1198. **Ulhart, Philip,** *the Younger.* Delete the 1576 entry.

p.1199. Insert the reference: **Veszler, Kilian.** *See* Wetzler, K.

p.1201. **Wacker, Johann.** Should read: **Wacker, Jacob.**

p.1203. **Wattenschne, Johann.** Delete the entry for 1543.

p.1205. **Wechel, Johann.** The work by H. Porsius indexed under 1588 is in fact dated 1583.

p.1205f. **Wechel, Johann,** and **Schmidt, P.** For **Schmidt, P.** read: **Fischer, P.**

p.1206. **Weiditz, Christoph,** and **Kanehl, David.** The date should read: 1538.

— **Weidlin, Caspar.** For *Bamberg* read: *Nuremberg.*

— **Weigle, Bernhard.** For *Bamberg* read: *Würzburg.*

p.1211. **Werdemueller, Marcus.** For *Basle* read: *Zurich.*

— Insert the reference: **Werly, Josias.** *See* Woerli, J.

p.1212. **Willerus, Elias.** For *Ingolstadt* read: *Augsburg.*

p.1217. **Wolrab, Nikolaus.** The work of J. Dobneck indexed under 1547 should be redated: 1537.

— **Wyer, Richard.** For *Zurich* read: *London.*

— **Wylicx, Derek.** The index entry for the work by D. Coornhert (1575) is misdated 1593.

— **Wyriot, Nikolaus.** The work of 1584 belongs to his widow.

p.1223. **Harnisch, Anna.** She was the widow of Wilhelm Harnisch. For *Frankfort* read: *Neustadt a.d. Haardt.*

REPLACEMENT OF BOOKS
destroyed during the War of 1939-45

On pp.941-958 of the STC of 1962 is a list of those books which were destroyed but for which entries remain in the General Catalogue. The following have been replaced; frequently their pressmarks have been altered.

Augsburg. — Preachers. Gegründte Christliche Antwort der Euangelischen Predicanten in Augspurg. Auff Georgen Müllers Send vnd Trostbrieff. *Valentin Schönigk: Augspurg*, 1586. 4°.   4427.df.4(1). Now 1608/1690

Augustine, *Saint.* [*De fide et operibus.*] De fide et operibus. *Hero Alopecius: [Cologne,]* 1527. 8°.   3224.aa.38(4). Now 1506/47(2)

— [*De natura et gratia.*] De natura et gratia. *Apud Heronem Alopecium: Coloniæ,* 1527. 8°.   3224.aa.38(2). Now 1506/47(3)

Bible. — Psalms. [*Polyglott.*] Psalterium. *Lat. & Ger. Caspar Hochfeder: Metz,* 1513. 4°.   3365.ff.30. Now 1560/3338

— **Gospels. — Harmonies.** Harmoniæ Euangelicae libri IIII. *Gr. & Lat.* Annotationum liber unus [by Andreas Osiander]. 2 pt. *Per Hieronymum Frobenium & Nicolaum Episcopium: Basileæ*, 1537. fol.
    3225.f.4. Now 1502/480

— **Romans.** In sanctissimam Pauli ad Romanos epistolam Heinrychi Bullingeri commentarius. [With the text.] *Apud Christoph. Frosch.: Tiguri,* 1533. 8°.   3265.aaa.37. Now 1607/2747

— **Colossians.** Die Epistel Pauli zů den Collossenseren durch Erasmū vsgelegt. [With the text.] *Tr.* Leo Juda. *Durch Christophorū Froschouer: Zürich,* 1521. 4°.   3265.aaa.7. Now 1509/3074

— **Titus.** In epistolam Pauli ad Titum enarratio prælecta à Iacobo Schenck. [With the text.] *Nicolaus Vuolrab: Lipsiæ,* 1542. 8°.   3267.a.23(2)

Bullinger, Heinrich. In Acta Apostolorum commentariorum libri VI. *Apud Christophorum Froschouerum: Tiguri,* 1533. 8°.
    3265.aaa.5. Now 1607/2748

Charles II., *Emperor of Germany.* Liber precationum. *Ed.* Felicianus Ninguarda. *Ex typographia Dauidis Sartorii: Ingolstadii,* 1583. 8°.
    3356.a.10. Now C.127.dd.15

Christian People. Ritus baptizandi. Wie man vor etlichen hundert jaren der Christenleute kinder getaufft hat. *Tr.* Georg Witzel. *Durch Franciscum Behem: zu S. Victor ausserhalb Mentz,* 1541. 4°.
3356.b.9. Now 1608/4789

Ecard, Georg. Sechzehē predig von der waren vñ falschen Kirchen [and other sermons]. *Leonhart Reinmichel: Laugingen,* 1594. 8°.
4423.e.2. Now RB.23.a.1761

Eisengrein, Martin. Missale. *Apud Wolfgangum Ederum: Ingolstadii,* 1578. 12°.
3395.b.1. Now 1606/1331

Fabri, Joannes, *Bishop.* Sermones habiti Pragæ de eucharistiæ sacramento. *Ioannes Faber Emmeus: apud Friburgum Brisgaudiæ,* 1529. 4°.
4426.bb.3. Now 1609/1021

Fabris, Melchior de. Von der Martins Gans. Ein Predig. *Im Closter zů Thierhaupten,* 1595. 4°. 4426.aaa.16. Now 1609/4536

Franck, Caspar. Vom Catholischen namen vnd wesen zwo Predigen. *Bey Dauid Sartorio: Ingolstat,* 1581. 4°. 4424.h.17. Now 1578/1233

Gallus, Nicolaus. Von der Witwen Son zu Nain. *Durch Hañsen Khol: Regenspurg,* 1553. 4°. 4424.g.11. Now C.190.a.13

Geiler, Johann, *von Kaisersberg.* Sermōes de tēpore ℟ de sctīs accomodandi. [With other matter.] 3 pt. *Joannes Grünīger: Argētine,* 1515. fol.
4425.h.4. Now C.175.n.2(1)

Germany. — **Reichstag.** Abschiedt des Reichsstags zů Augspurg Anno M.D.xxx. gehalten. *Durch Johannem Schöffer: Meyntz,* 1531. fol.
5604.h.18. Now C.144.d.13

Jonas, Justus. Annotationes oder Anzaygungen vber das Bůch der Apostelgeschicht. *Durch Siluanum Otmar: Auspurg,* 1525. 4°.
3265.bb.41. Now 1608/4531

Kettenbach, Heinrich von. Ain sermon oder predig von der Christlichen kirchen. [*Silvan Otmar: Augsburg,*] 1522. 4°. 4426.aa.6. Now 1609/4445

Liturgies. — **Latin Rite.** — **Missals.** — **Passau.** Missale Patauieñ. Opera ℟ impensis *Johannes Winterburg: Wienne,* 1503. fol. 3395.f.20. Now L.18.a.6

— — — **Benedictines.** [*Germany.*] Missale ordinis sancti Benedicti p̄ Germaniam. p̄ *Thomā Ansshelmum: Hagenoie,* 1518. fol.
3395.f.1. Now L.17.b.10

— — **Rituals.** — **Constance.** Obsequiale simul ac Benedictionale iuxta ritum ecclesiæ Constantiensis. *Per Alexandrum & Samuelem VVeissenhornios: Ingolstadij,* 1560. 4°. 3395.c.25. Now RB.23.a.2480

— — — **Mainz.** Agenda ecclesiae Moguntinensis. *Franciscus Behem: Moguntiæ,* 1551. fol. 3366.bb.12. Now C.106.f.14

— — **Paroissiens.** Hymni et collectae, item euangelia, epistolæ.. *Apud Geruinum Calenium & hæredes Iohannis Quentel: Coloniae,* 1573. 16°.
3355.aa.9. Now RB.23.a.1762

— **Lutheran Churches.** Das Testamēt Jhesu Christi, die Mess. *Tr.* Joannes Oecolampadius. *Jörg Gastel: Zwickaw,* 1523. 4°.
3356.b.26. Now Cup.406.j.8

Luther, Martin.[*Biblical Commentaries.*] Praelectio in Psalmum CXXVII. *Per Georgium Rhauu: Vuittembergæ,* 1534. 8°. 3265.aa.37(2). Now 1607/4451

— — Das fünffte, sechste vnd siebend Capitel S.Matthei ausgelegt. *Joseph Klug: Wittemberg,* 1532. 4°. 3226.bb.6. Now C.109.n.23

— — In epistolam Pauli ad Galatas commentarius. [*Melchior Lotter: Leipzig*, 1519.] 4°. 3265.cc.14. Now C.127.dd.17

— [*Auslegung des Vater unser.*] Ausslegunge des hayligen vatter vnsers. *Durch Siluanum Ottmar: Augspurg*, 1520. 4°. 3225.b.16. Now 1609/5963

Manlius, Nicolaus. Von des Herrn Christi Leiden zwo Predigten. *Georgen Rhawen Erben: Wittemberg*, [1551.] 4°. 4426.df.29(4). Now RB.23.a.2481

Meckhart, Johann. Drey Christenliche Predigen wider das vermeint Fegfewr der Papisten. *Vlrich Morharts Wittib: Tübingen*, 1561. 8°.
4423.a.1. Now 1568/6287

Meier, Georg, *Professor.* Ein tröstliche Predigt vber das Euangelium Lucæ j. *Hans Lufft: Wittemberg*, 1549. 4°. 4423.c.8. Now 1608/5539

— Ein tröstliche Predigt von der Krafft der Aufferstehung Jhesu Christi. *Hans Lufft: Wittemberg*, 1568. 4°. 4426.df.28(7). Now 1608/2661

Melanchthon, Philipp. Scholia in Epistolam Pauli ad Colossenses. *Per Iosephum Clug: Vitebergæ*, 1534. 8°. 3265.aa.37(1). Now 1607/4629

Mylius, Georg. Ein Christliche Predigt vom alten vnd newen Babel. *Hans Kraffts Erben: Wittenberg*, 1585. 4°. 4426.aaa.50

— Zwo Christliche Predigen. *Bey Georgen Gruppenbach: Tübingen*, 1584. 4°.
4426.aaa.49. Now 1608/3726

Nase, Johann. Ein schöne tröstliche Neweiarspredig. *Beym jungen Alexander Weissenhorn; in verwaltung vnd kosten Annæ Weissenhornin: Ingolstatt*, 1572. 8°. 4428.df.5. Now 1607/6081

Ochino, Bernardino. XX. Predigē. *Tr. Joseph Höchsteter. Bey Hannsen Kilian: Neuburg*, 1545. 4°. 4423.e.37. Now 1568/6195

Peter [Canisius], *Saint.* Notæ in Euangelicas lectiones. *Ex officina Abrahami Gemperlini: Friburgi Heluetiorum*, 1591. 4°. 3227.e.8. Now 1570/1416

Philosophia. Dialogus philosophie de ritu omni verborum venustate editus. *Ed.* Georg Ebner. *In officina Joannis Weyssenburger:* [*Nuremberg,*] 1509. 4°.
4424.d.1(6). Now 1609/3935

Pitonius, Peter. Ein Leychpredig. *Bey dem Petreio: Nürnberg*, 1542. 4°.
4427.aaa.34. Now 1578/6402

Reuschlin, Caspar. Hippopronia. *B. Jobins Erben: Strassburg*, 1599. fol.
7906.i.10. Now 1605/591

Russ, Wolfgang. Ein guete nützliche predig von dem rechten güten glauben. [*Hans Schobser: Munich,*] 1523. 4°. 4426.df.28(3). Now 1608/4664

Schwenckfeld, Caspar. Ausslegung des Euangelij Luce ij. *s.l.* 1596. 4°.
4423.bb.13(2). Now 1609/4447

— Ausslegung des Euangelij Luce 5. *s.l.* 1596. 4°.
4423.bb.13(8). Now 1609/4446

— Ausslegung des Euangelij Luce 6. *s.l.* 1596. 4°.
4423.bb.13(7). Now 1609/3680

— Ausslegung des Euangelij Luce 15. *s.l.* 1596. 4°.
4423.bb.13(6). Now 1609/2113

Sermon. Ein Sermon vō zweyerley wercken. *Wolff. Stöckel:* [*Leipzig*, 1522.] 8°. 4428.a.25. Now 1607/4635

Zegerus, Nicolaus. Scholion in omnes Noui Testamenti libros. 3 pt. *Hæredes Arnoldi Birckmanni: Coloniæ Agrippinæ*, 1553. 8°. 3225.de.34(1)

The following nine books, which were destroyed in the War, were not recorded as such in 1962:

Annaberg. Fewer Ordenung. *M. Lotther: Leiptzigk,* [1530.] 4°. 5549.a.6

Berne. [*Appendix.*] Die predigen so vonn den frömbden Predicanten, die zu Bernn vff dem Gespräch gewesen, beschehen sind. *C. froschouer: Zürich,* 1528. 8°. 4426.de.25

Hoffmann, Simon. Ain sermonn geschen am Ostertag zu der frwe messe zu Stolbergk. *Michael Büchfürer: Erffurdt,* 1523. 4°. 4423.aa.1

Medler, Nicolaus. Eine Predigt uber das Evangelion Luce XIIII. von dem Wassersüchtigen. [*Leipzig?*] 1548. 4°. 4423.aa.35

Reuschlin, Caspar. Hippiatria. [*B. Jobin:*] *Strassburg,* 1593. fol. 7905.k.15(2)

Sack, Bartholomaeus a. Theses de acquirenda hereditate. *Tubingae,* 1588. 4°. 5510.c.32

Sarcerius, Erasmus. In Matthaeum Evangelistam justa scholia. *Francoforti,* 1538. 8°. 3225.a.34(1)

Wimpfen. Reformation vñ Ordnung der Statt Wympffen. *s.l.* 1544. fol. 5604.h.27(4)

Zuinglius, Huldericus, *the Younger.* Sermones XXX. in undecimum caput Epistolæ ad Hebræos. Petri Pictaviensis Genealogia sanctorum Patrum. 2 pt. *Per Leonhardum Ostenium: Basileae,* 1592. fol. 4425.i.2

Index I

INDEX OF PRINTERS AND PUBLISHERS
in this Supplement

Entries marked † are among the amendments to the 1962 catalogue (pp.71–87); those marked †† among the additions to the list of destroyed books (p.96).

Adam, Danyel
Prague
1586 Codicillus, P.

Adelmann, Bernard
Augsburg
1522 John VI., *Patriarch*

Adler, Aegidius
Vienna
1552 Coturnossius, G.
1552? Lazius, W. Tituli

See also **Kohl, H.**, and **Adler, A.**

Alantse, Leonardus and **Lucas**
Vienna
1517 Nannus Mirabellius, D.

Alantse, Lucas
Vienna
1520 Solinus, C. J.
1520 †Solinus, C. J.

Albinus, Bernard
Speyer
1596 Hatzger, A.

Albrecht, Lorenz
Lübeck
1595 Estienne, H.
1600 Sturtzius, C.

Alectorius, Ludwig, and **Soter, Jacobus,** Heirs of
Cologne
1576 Graminaeus, D.
1578 Cologne. — *Universität*

Amerbach, Johann
Basle
1484? Turrecremata, J. de

Amerbach, Johann, Petri, J., and **Froben, J.**
Basle
1507? Ficino, M.

Andreae, Hieronymus, *Formschneider*
Nuremberg
1537 †Luther, M. [*Schöne Predigt*]
1538 † — [*Disputations*]
1538 † — [*Sehr tröstliche Predigt*]

Andreae, Lambert
Cologne
1590 Chimarrhaeus, J.

Angermayer, Andreas
Ingolstadt
1599 Fornerus, F.

Anonymus, Adam, *pseud.*
Augsburg
1545 Erasmus, D. [*Enchiridion*]

Anshelm, Thomas
Pforzheim
1509 Bebelius, H.

Hagenau
1520 Melanchthon, P. Integræ

Antonius, Wilhelm
Hanau
1595 Collibus, H. à
1599 Affelmann, J.

Apianus, Peter and **Georg**
Ingolstadt
1527 †Luther, M. [*Epistola ad Henricum*]

Apiarius, Matthias
Berne
1543 Lampadius, A.

Apiarius, Samuel
Basle
1569 Bible. [*Spanish*]
1581 French Border

Arnt, *von Aych*
Cologne
1525? Wacker, S.

Aurik, Jacob, *pseud.*
Emden
1534 Joye, G.

Baer, Hans
Coburg
1530 Luther, M.[*Auf das Schreien*]

Baerwald, Jacob
Leipzig
1553 Sarcerius, E.
1556 Pollicarius, J.

Eisleben
1554 Eisleben.—*Synod*

Baerwald, Jacob, *Heirs of*
Leipzig
1575 Luther, M. [*Catechismus*]

Baerwald, Zacharias
Leipzig
1589 Vhessel, H.

Balhorn, Johann
Lübeck
1535? German Vigil

Bapst, Valentin
Leipzig
1544 Leipsic.—*Rat*
1546 Anhalt
1548 Stigel, J.
1550 Leipsic.—*Rat*
1550? Tabulae
1551 Leipsic.—*Rat*
1552 Luther, M. [*Catechismus*]
1555 George, *Prince.* Conciones
1555 Germany.—Ferdinand I., *King of the Romans.* Abdruck
1555 Linacre, T.

Bapst, Valentin, *Heirs of*
Leipzig
1558 Bible. [*Selections.—German*]

Barsages, Jean
Frankenthal
1578 Pacificus, H.

Bassée, Nikolaus
Frankfort on the Main
1567 Strawe, C.
1571 Grimaldi Robio, P.
1573 Nomenclatura
1574 Chasseneux, B. de. Consuetudines
1590? Sultzerus, J.
1596 Decimator, H.
1600 Malleus

Bassée, Nikolaus, and **Beller, Johann**
Frankfort on the Main
1573 Paleotti, G.

Baum, Theodor
Cologne
1574 Mandagotus, G.

Baumann, Georg
Erfurt
1557 Hiltstein, J.
1558 Bible.—*Psalms.* [*Selections.—German.—Single Psalms. 90*]
1559 Greff, W.
1561 Musculus, A. Vom Missbrauch
1583 Erbenius, N.

Breslau
1595 Bornmann, Z. Astrolabium
1596 — Astra
1600 Sarcephalus, C.

Baur, Hans
Innsbruck
1591 Bible.—*Liturgical Epistles.* [*Polyglott*]

Beck, Balthasar
Strasburg
1539 Strasburg. — Rat
1540 — —
1544 †Erasmus, D. [*Lingua*] Ger.

Beck, Balthasar, and **Meyer, Michael**
Strasburg
1531 Josephus, F.

Beck, Johann
Erfurt
1580 Dinckel, J.

Beck, Reinhard, *Heirs of*
Strasburg
1523 †Fuchs, J.
1523 †Luther, M. [*Den auserwählten Christen*]
1523 † — [*Sermon von den sieben Broten*]
1523 †Strauss, J. Haubstuck

Beckenth, Balthasar, *pseud.*
Strasburg
1531 BIBLE.—*Isaiah*

Becker, Matthaeus
Frankfort on the Main
1598 Uffenbach, P.

Behem, Franz
Mainz
1544 Kuchenmeister, A.
1548 Sedelius, W.
1550 Wild, J.
1558 —
1559 Seneca, L. A. [*Letters*]
1581 Loosaeus, C.

Behem, Kaspar
Mainz
1583 Leucht, V. (2)
1586 Rândenburgh, R.

Beller, Johann
See **Bassée, Nikolaus,** and **Beller, J.**

Berg, Adam
Munich
1565 Bavaria
1565 Quichelbergus, S.
1567 Gameren, H. de
1567 Klostermair, M.
1567 Raspergerus, C.
1575 Stoeckelius, A.
1580 Khirchmarius, B.
1584 Kreitman, M.
1585 Wispeckius, W.
1596 Dilbaum, S.
1599 Anisius, M. Siben

Berg, Johann vom, and **Neuber, Ulrich**
Nuremberg
1544 Bugenhagen, J.
1550 Heyden, S. Pædonomia
1550 Liturgies.—*Antiphoners*
1556 Ulmer, J. C.
1562 Schoener, A.

Berg, Johann vom, *Heirs of,* and **Neuber, Ulrich**
Nuremberg
1564 Schmidlap, J.
1565 Liturgies.—*Antiphoners*

Bergen, Gimel
Dresden
1590 Albinus, P.

Bertram, Anton
Strasburg
1586 Linck, J.

Beyer, Johann
Leipzig
1590 Artomedes, S.
1592 Raphelt, M.
1595 Leipsic.—*Rat*

Birckmann, *House of*
Cologne
1589 Faunteus, L. A.
1594 Stapleton, T. (2)

Birckmann, Arnold, *Heirs of*
Cologne
1554 Curtius, J.
1562 Plutarch. [*Vitae parallelae*]
1564 V., S. G.

Birckmann, Johann
Cologne
1559 Zichenius, F.
1572 Llwyd, H.

Blum, Michael
Leipzig
1526 Toltz, J.
1535 †Sylvius, P.
1539 Spangenberg, J.
1539 Willich, J.

Bock, Heinrich
Trier
1588 †Scotus, R.

Bock, Niclas
Leipzig
1579 Thomingius, J.

Boeckler, Martin
Freiburg i. Br.
1593 Possevino, A.
1595 Peter [Canisius], *Saint*

Boerner, Johann
Leipzig
1592 Raphelt, M.

Boettiger, Gregorius
Leipzig
1495? Jacobus, *de Clusa*

Bohmberg, Nikolaus
Cologne
1574? N., H. Comoedia
1580? N., H. Terra pacis

Brachfeld, Paul
Frankfort on the Main
1598 Uffenbach, P.

Brandis, Marcus
Merseburg
1479? Tractatus

Brandis, Moritz
Leipzig
1489 Valentinus, *Licentiatus*

Magdeburg
1497 Gemma

Braubach, Peter
Hagenau
1534 †Agricola, J. Sybenhundert

Hall (Suabia)
1539 Melanchthon, P. Loci communes

Frankfort on the Main
1544 Luther, M. [*Von den Juden*]

1545 Hoffmann, C.
1553 Christian Faith
1553? †Euripides. [*Works*]
1555? † — —
1564 Micyllus, J. Syluarum

Brehm, Heinrich
Mainz
1596 Venatorius, D.

Brenner, Anton and **Walter**
Neubrandenburg
1556 Alberus, E. Wider die verfluchte lere

Brittelmann, Zacharias
Trier
1576 Liturgies. — *Rituals.* — *Treves*

Brylinger, Nikolaus
Basle
1546 Ovidius Naso, P. Mctamorphoseon

Buchfuehrer, Michael
Erfurt
1523 Cronberg, H. von
1523 Culsamerus, J. Aduersus
1523 ††Hoffmann, S.

Bumgart, Hermann
Cologne
1502 Poeta
1510? Haich, H.

Burger, Andreas
Ratisbon
1593 Wigand, J. (2)

Burger, Johann
Straubing
1562? Jaeger
1562? Lied. Ain new
1562? — Ein schön geistlich
1564 Tagweise

Ratisbon
1568 Diemmairus, J. De criminibus
1570 — Declaratio
1575 Herbst, G.
1575? Vergleichung
1588 Calendarium
1588 V., I.D.D.I.

Buys, Albert, and **Oridryus, Johann**
Duesseldorf
1563 Ovelius, J.

Caesar, Anton
Cologne
1550? Margaret, *Saint*

Calenius, Gerwin, and **Quentel, J.,** *Heirs of*
Cologne
1562 Gruenfelt, F.
1588 Luis, *de Granada*

1590 Pistorius, J. Badische
1591 — De vita

Cervicornus, Eucharius
Cologne
1517 Montanus, J.
1522 Dati, A.
1522 †Melanchthon, P. Loci communes
1528 Erasmus, D. [*Colloquia*]
1532 Bible. [*Epistles*]
1535 Clichtoveus, J.
1536 Agrippa, H. C.

Marburg
1537 John, *Chrysostom*

Cervicornus, Gottfried
Cologne
1572 †Noot, J. van der

Cholinus, Maternus
Cologne
1556 Gerardus, A.
1561 Treflerus, F.
1562 Schopper, J. (2)
1566 Fabricius, A.
1566 Hovaeus, A.
1570 Rabe, J. J.
1577 Kromer, M.
1585 Briegerus, J.

Ciotti, Johann Baptist
Venice
1587 Picciolus, A.
1588 Molina, L.
1589 Hippocrates

Closterdruckerei
Tegernsee
1573 Jacobus, *Bishop*
1576 Liturgies.—*Occasional Prayers*
1580 Anisius, M. Carmen

Closterdruckerei
Thierhaupten
1591 Wagner, B.
1592 Muntz, G.

Collegium Novum, *Wittenberg*
See **Rhau-Grunenberg, J.**

Commelinus, Hieronymus
Heidelberg
1593 Basil. *Saint*

Coninx, Arnout
Antwerp
1592 England. — Elizabeth I.

Coppenius, Aegidius
Antwerp
1557 Goltz, H.

Coppenius, Aeigidius, *the Younger*
Antwerp
1572 Ortelius, A.
1573 —

Cornelis, *de Zierikzee*
Cologne
1505? †Henricus, *de Hassia.* Secreta
1510? Quadrivium
1511 Arithmetica

Corvinus, Christoph
Frankfort on the Main
1583 Feyerabend, S.
Herborn
1600 Whitaker, W.

Cranach, Lucas, and **Doering, Christian**
Wittenberg
1524 Bible. — Psalms. [*German*]

Cratander, Andreas
Basle
1519 Luther, M. [*Disputations*]
1530 Muenster, S.
1537 Aristotle

Creussner, Friedrich
Nuremberg
1474 Sixtus IV., *Pope*
1493 Donatus, A.
1493? Regula
1493 Regulae

Curio, Hieronymus
Basle
1543 Mueller, J.

Curio, Valentin
Basle
1520 †Luther, M. [*Kurze Form*]
1521 Evangelical Penitence

Dačický, Jiří Jakubův
Prague
1570 Farkas, M.

Dalbin, Bernard
See **Albinus, B.**

Daschitsky, Georg
See **Dačický, J. J.**

Daubmann, Hans
Nuremberg
1546? †Luther, M. [*Warnung*]
Koenigsberg
1555 †United Brethren. Catechismus
1564 Steinbach, J.

Day, John
London
1554 Confession

Deck, Rudolf
Basle
1540? †Grammatik

Deffner, Georg
Leipzig
1581 Heidenreich, E. Sechs vnd zwantzig
1581 — Vierzehen

Diest, G. van
See **Coppenius, Aegidius**

Dietrich, Alexander Philip
Nuremberg
1596 Haendl, J.
1596 Most, W.

Dietz, Ludwig, *Heirs of*
Rostock
1559, 60 Chytraeus, D. De lectione

Dolgen, Merten von
Erfurt
1571 Regebrand, G.

Donat, Paul
Magdeburg
1587 Papa, A.
1596 Crato, A.

Dorcastor, Nicholas, *pseud.*
Wittenberg
1554 Confession

Dorn, Hans
Brunswick
1520 Mueller, J.

Drach, Peter, *the Younger*
Speyer
1505? Liturgies. — Missals. — Lübeck

Dreher, Konrad
Erfurt
1572 Eberbach, A.

Dumaeus, Govert
Antwerp
1534 Joye, G.

Eckhart, Johann
Speyer
1523 †Luther, M. [*Hauptstück*]
1525 Bible. — Appendix. — New Testament

Eder, Wolfgang
Ingolstadt
1579 Rotmarus, V.
1583 Lucius, C. De variis
1583 Mary, *the Blessed Virgin.* — Congregatio
1586 Brunnenfelser, S.
1586 Eyssvogel, J.
1588 Nase, J. Angelus
1588 — Præludium
1589 — Leuita
1593 Wagner, B.
1594 Melemius, A.
1595 Andreae, C.

Egenolff, Christian
Strasburg
1530 †Erasmus, D. [*Adversus Pseudoevangelicos*]

Frankfort on the Main
1531 Gebrauch
1531 Koebel, J.
1533 Frankfort-on-the-Main. — Ministers
1534 Geldenhaurius, G.
1535 Kunstbuechlein
1538 Lucian, *of Samosata*. [*Works*]
1538 Sturm, C.
1539 Micyllus, J. Ratio
1544 Melanchthon, P. Catechesis
1549 Schelling, V.
1550 Melanchthon, P. Erotemata
1550 — Initia

Marburg
1541 Livius, T. [*Selections*]

Egenolff, Christian, Heirs of
Frankfort on the Main
1557 Loss, L. Annotationes
1563 Cicero, M. T. [*Supposititious Works*]
1567 Paganus, P.
1577 Kling, M.
1577 Spaniards
1595 Heupoldus, B.
1597 Goldwurm, C.

Egenolff, Paul
Marburg
1593 Valerius, C.
1595 Vulteius, H.

Eichorn, Andreas
Frankfort on the Oder
1580 Papenburgerus, H.
1589 Crugerius, P.
1590 Caminaeus, B.
1592 Radtmann, B.
1600? Loss, L. Arithmetices

Eichorn, Johann
Frankfort on the Oder
1549 Dedekind, F.
1553 Schuirphius, H.
1555 †Musculus, A. Vom Hosen Teuffel
1562 Schosserus, J.
1568 Lasius, C.
1571 Musculus, A. (2)

Emmel, Samuel
Strasburg
1558 Spangenberg, C. Der weyse

Emlos, Theophyll, *pseud.*
Basle
1540? Solme, T.

Emser's Printer
Dresden
1524 Emser, H.

Episcopius, Eusebius
Basle
1572 Isocrates

Episcopius, Eusebius, and **Nikolaus,** Heirs of
Basle
1571 Irenaeus, *Saint*

Erben, Nikolaus
Lich
1597 Rennecherus, H.

Erlinger, Georg
Bamberg
1523 Spandugino, T.
1524 Bodenstein, A.

Ewald, Daniel
Cologne
1576 Arnhem

Faber, Abraham
Metz
1597 †Boissard, J. J.

Faber, Joannes, *pseud.*
Augsburg
1592 England. — Elizabeth I.

Faber, Johann
Freiburg i. Br.
1538 Zasius, J. U.

Fabricius, Blasius
Strasburg
1554 Goniaeus, J.

Falckenburg, Heinrich
Cologne
1590 Chimarrhaeus, J.

Ferber, Augustin
Güstrow
1582 Celichius, A.

Greifswald
1585 Marcus, J.
1585 Suflon, A.

Rostock
1596 Schyrlentz, H.

Feyerabend, Johann
Frankfort on the Main
1574 Chasseneux, B. de Consuetudines
1579 — Catalogus
1588 Molina, L.
1589 Hippocrates
1590 Matthioli, P. A.
1591 Bible. — *New Testament*. [*German*]
1591 †Euclid. [*Elementa*]
1591 †Herilacus, P.

1594 †Galen. [*Two or more Works*]
1597 †Boissard, J. J.

Feyerabend, Johann and **Sigmund**
Frankfort on the Main
1578 Livius, T.

Feyerabend, Sigmund
Frankfort on the Main
1571 Grimaldi Robio, P.
1572 Milis, J. de
1572 Vázquez de Menchaca, F.
1582 Amman, J.
1583 Feyerabend, S.
1583 Stammbuch

Fischer, Peter
Frankfort on the Main
1591 Bible. — New Testament. [German]

Fischer, Peter, and **Tack, Heinrich,**
Heirs of
Frankfort on the Main
1590 Matthioli, P. A.

Flach, Martin
Strasburg
1493 Sermones
1494 —

Flach, Martin, *the Younger*
Strasburg
1519 Felman, T.

Fleischmann, Georg
Würzburg
1595 Steeghius, G.
1596 Upilio, C.

Fluvius, Rupertus, *pseud.*
[*No place named*]
1595 Poyssel, E.

Foillet, Jakob
Muempelgart
1588 Riolan, J.
1591 Macchiavelli, N. Discorsi
1593 Bauhinus, J. (2)
1593 Porta, G. B. della
1594 †Du Bellay, G.
1597 Flamand, C.
1598 Bauhinus, J.
1599 Colonne, G.delle
1599 Macchiavelli, N. Il principe

Formica, Leonhard
Vienna
1595 Ruef, T.
1599 Dalnerus, A.

Foxe, Francis, *pseud.*
Strasburg
1530 Hortulus

Franck, Matthaeus
Augsburg
1560? Berckenmeyer, J.

1560? Berckringer, M.
1560? Christian. Ein new
1560? Gletting, B. (2)
1560? Hebenstreit, C. Ein news
1560? Jacob, *the Patriarch*
1560? Lazarus, *Saint*
1560? Lied. Ein geystliches
1560? — Ein schöns
1560? Lieder. Zwey schöne
1560? Lobgesang
1560? †Schwarm, *Doctor*
1560? Vogel, N.
1560? W., B.
1565? Gigas, J.
1565? Joseph, *the Patriarch*
1565 Lochner, Z. Probier Büchlein
1568 Roth, S.

Francke, Johann
Magdeburg
1582 Pomarius, J.
1597 Agrippa, H.C. De nobilitate
1599? A., H.I.B.A.L.D.E.H.

Fratres Ordinis Eremitarum
Nuremberg
1483? Vincent [Ferrer], *Saint*

Friess, Augustin
Zurich
1544? †F., A.
1547 Hooper, J.

Frisius, Ewardus
See **Oostfreese, E.**

Fritsch, Ambrosius
Görlitz
1586 Jacob, N.
1587 Papa, F.
1592 Crusius, M.

Froben, Ambrosius and **Aurelius**
See **Oporinus, Johann,** and **Froben, A.** and **A.**

Froben, Hieronymus
Basle
1534 Lucian, *of Samosata.* [*Dialogues*]

Froben, Hieronymus, and **Episcopius, N.**
Basle
1532 Erasmus, D. [*Apophthegmata*]
1544 Maffeus, R.
1549 Dionysius, *of Halicarnassus*
1560 Pachymeres, G.

Froben, Hieronymus, Herwagen, J., and **Episcopius, N.**
Basle
1529 Erasmus, D. [*Two or more Works*]
1529 Muenster, S.

Froben, Johann
Basle
1521 Tertullianus, Q. S. F.
1522 Bible. — *Epistles*. [*Latin*]
1525 Elijah ben Asher

Froelich, Jakob
Strasburg
1535 †Munster. — *Anabaptists*
1542 †Scarperia
1557 Luther, M. [*Disputations*]

Froschauer, House of
Zurich
1588 Walther, R.

Froschauer, Christoph
Zurich
1526? †Geschmuck
1528 ††Berne. [*Appendix*]
1531 Haller, B.
1539 H., C.
1549 Casa, G. della [*Appendix*]
1550 Blum, H.
1551 Bullinger, H.
1560 Cicero, M. T. [*Two or more Works*]

Froschauer, Christoph, *the Younger*
Zurich
1565 Murer, J.
1568 Ephemerides
1577 Stuck, J. W.
1584 Bible. — *Ecclesiastes*
1584 Montenay, G. de

Froschauer, Hans
Augsburg
1501 Liturgies. — *Missals*. [*Appendix*]
1502 Locher, J. Threnodia
1506? — De cometa

Fuchs, Hero
Cologne
1527 Augustine, *Saint*. [*De spiritu*]
1539 Evax, *King*

Fuhrmann, Valentin
Nuremberg
1580? Rausch, *Bruder*
1592 Caesius, G.

Furter, Michael
Basle
1496? Cube, J. von
1506? Carthusia

Gastel, Jörg
Zwickau
1523 Pastoris, H.
1524 Amandus, G.

Gaubisch, Urban
Eisleben
1558 Caelius, M. Von der Kinder
1561, 64 Bible. — *Corinthians*

1561 Spangenberg, C. Chronicon
1562 Flacius, M. Ein Sendbrieff
1563 Helmreich, A.
1563 Luther, M. [*Auslegung*]
1563 Magdeburg, J.
1563 Spangenberg, C. Von der geistlichen
1566 Hoppenrod, A.
1580 Porta, C.
1581 Neander, M.

Gegler, Hans
Augsburg
1558 †Papacy

Geissler, Heinrich
Ratisbon
1561 Glait, O.
1562 Flacius, M. Kurtze anwort
1563 †Staphylus, F.

Gemperlin, Abraham
Freiburg (Switzerland)
1594 Lucerne. — *Rat*
1595 Peter [Canisius], *Saint*

Gennep, Jaspar von
Cologne
1549 Gropper, J.
1549 Insulanus Menapius, G.
1549 Treves, *Council of* (2)

Gerlach, Dietrich
See **Neuber, Ulrich,** and **Gerlach, D.**

Gerlach, Katharina
Nuremberg
1581 †Knoefelius, J. Newe
1587 Matthesius, J. Diluvium

Gerlach, Katharina, and **Berg, J. vom,** *Heirs of*
Nuremberg
1576 Solis, V.

Gerlach, Katharina, *Heirs of*
Nuremberg
1592 Taurellus, N. Carmina
1593 Crusius, J.

Gessner, Andreas
Zurich
1553 England. — *Church of England*. [*Articles*]
1558 Werdmueller, O.

Gessner, Andreas, and **Wyssenbach, Rudolf**
Zurich
1552 Euonymus, *Philiatrus*

Gessner, Jacob
Zurich
1560? Gesner, C.
1563 Crolachius, H.
1563 Vives, J. L.
1564 Christian. Erinnerung

1564 Christian Life. Das Christenlich Läben
1564 Werdmueller, O.
1566 Fabricius, G.

Ghotan, Bartholomaeus
Magdeburg
1483? Polichius, M.

Goetz, Paul
Strasburg
1530 Bible. — Appendix. [*Concordances*]

Goinus, Antonius
Antwerp
1543 †Harryson, J.

Golsenus, Sebastianus, *pseud.*
Lüneburg
1533 Philalethes, *Hyperboraeus*

Goltz, Hubert
Bruges
1557 Goltz, H.

Gottfried, *von Kempen*
Cologne
1585 †Calvinistic Cruelty
1588, 89 Eytzinger, M. von
1594 Stapleton, T. (2)

Gotz, Nicolaus
Cologne
1475? Henricus, *de Wrimaria*
1475? Modus

Graeber, Paul
Halle
1597 Agrippa, H. C. De nobilitate

Graf, Stephan Melechus
Freiburg i. Br.
1579 Lorich, J.

Gran, Heinrich
Hagenau
1518 Cicero, M. T. [*Supposititious Works*]
1519, 20 Hollen, G.
1523? †Melanchthon, P. Die haupt artikel
1527 Agapetus

Grevenbruch, Gerhard
Cologne
1588 Kuehn, J.
1594 Denss, A.
1600 Jansonius, P. A.

Greyff, Michael
Reutlingen
1480 Rhodes

Grimm, Hans
Strasburg
1546 Culman, L.

Grimm, Sigmund
Augsburg
1522? †Schatzger, C.
1523 Melanchthon, P. Annotationes

Grimm, Sigmund, and **Wirsung, M.**
Augsburg
1522 John VI., *Patriarch*

Gronenberg, Simon
Wittenberg
1579 Grunius, J.
1581 Jagenteufel, A.

Grosse, Henning
Leipzig
1585 Weller, H.
1594 Franck von Franckenstein, V.
1596 Leipsic. — Rat
1597 Reusner, N.
1599 Schultes, J.

Gruener, Hans
Ulm
1527 Saum, C.
1529 Pollio, S.

Grueninger, Johann
Strasburg
1494 Liturgies. — *Hymnals*
1509? Modus
1521 Geiler, J. Das buoch
1523 †Luther, M. [*Unterricht auf etliche Artikel*]
1529 Jābir ibn Ḥaiyān

Gruner, Salomon
Jena
1595 Mylius, G. Zehen

Gruppenbach, Georg
Tübingen
1577 Heerbrand, J.
1579 Frischlin, N. Hildegardis
1581 Pappus, J.
1588 Heilandus, S.
1597, 98 Guntherus, *Cisterciensis*

Guarin, Thomas
Basle
1563 Gerardus, A.
1569 Bible. [*Spanish*]

Guelfferich, Hermann
Frankfort on the Main
1551 Boltz, V.
1553 Luther, M. [*Catechismus*]

Guenther, Johann
Prossnitz
1550 Terentius, P.

Guenther, Wolfgang
Leipzig
1550 Salfeld, B.

1551 George, *Prince*. Von dem hochwirdigen
1551 Liturgies. — *Church of England*
1552 George, *Prince*. Zwo predigten
1554 Wagener, B.

Guldenmund, Hans
Nuremberg
1545 †Luther, M. [*Appendix*.] Ein Wellische

Gutknecht, Christoph
Nuremberg
1545? Hildebrand, *Hero*

Gutknecht, Friedrich
Nuremberg
1550? Bible. — *Psalms*. [*Selections*. — *German*. — *Single Psalms*. 91]
1555? Friedrich, *Count*
1555? Jesus Christ. Ein schön
1555? Lieder. Zwey

Gutknecht, Jobst
Nuremberg
1520 Camillus, E.
1532 †Luther, M. [*An den Durchlauchtigen Albrecht*]
1539 Christian Devotion
1541 Heilbronn

Gymnich, Johann, I.
Cologne
1531 Bible. — *Epistles*
1532 Vives, J. L. De disciplinis
1533 Ornithoparchus, A.
1537 Mancinellus, A. Speculum
1538 Bible. — *Epistles*. [*Latin*]
1539 Alardus
1544 Welpius, H.

Gymnich, Johann, I., *Heirs of*
Cologne
1544 Erasmus, D. [*De conscribendis epistolis*]

Gymnich, Johann, the *Younger*
Cologne
1570 Termineus, P.
1576 Mizauld, A.
1577 Menochius, J.
1588 Cujacius, J.
1591 Patrizi, F.
1592 Duranti, J.E.
1593 Boudinius, J.
1593 Verhaer, F.

Gymnich, Martin
Cologne
1545 Erasmus, D. [*De copia verborum*]
1546 Schopper, J.
1549 Erasmus, D. [*Adagia*]

Hamsing, Hermann
Nuremberg
1553 Heyden, S. Die Einsetzung

Han, Weigand
Frankfort on the Main
1558? Widmann, A. J.

Hans, *von Erfurt*
Worms
1521 Schnaitpeckh, J.

Hantzsch, Andreas
Muehlhausen
1587 Sachs, M.
1595 Calerus, A.

Hantzsch, Georg
Leipzig
1550, 51 Alesius, A.
1553 Pollicarius, J.
1556 Faber, H.
1556 Matthesius, J. Zwo

Harnisch, Matthaeus
Heidelberg
1575 Candidus, J.

Neustadt a.d. Haardt
1580 Pezel, C. Der 107. Psalm
1581 Sturmius, J.
1587 Pezel, C. Examen
1595 Scultetus, A.

Harscher, Matthias
Basle
1554 Erasmus, D. [*Colloquia*]

Hartmann, Friedrich
Frankfort on the Oder
1597 Pelargus, C. Hypomnemata
1598 Buentingus, G.

See also **Hartmann, Johann** and **F.**

Hartmann, Johann and **Friedrich**
Frankfort on the Oder
1595 Pelargus, C. Lusus

Heinrich, *von Aich*
Würzburg
1588 Dietmannus, G.
1588 Driel, G.
1589 Dithmarus, R.
1590 Clencherus, P.

Heinrich, *von Neuss*
Cologne
1509? †Henricus, *de Hassia*. Speculum

Henricpetri, Sebastian
Basle
1573 Taurellus, N.
1574 Polybius
1575 †Virgilius Maro, P. [*Works*]
1582 Ryff, W. H.
1584 Calepinus, A.

Henricus, Nikolaus, *the Younger*
  Munich
  1599 Guevara, A. de
  1600 Molitor, J.
Hergot, Hans
  Nuremberg
  1527 Wagner, G.
Hergotin, Kunigunde
  Nuremberg
  1530 Althamer, A. Catechismus
Herwagen, Johann
  Basle
  1526 Ferrandus, F.
  1554 Achilles Tatius
Heumann, Friedrich
  Mainz
  1509 Conradus, *de Zabernia*
Heussler, Christoph
  Nuremberg
  1560 †Melanchthon, P. [*Selections*]
Heussler, Leonhard
  Nuremberg
  1587 Otthe, J.
Hieber, Georg
  Vienna
  1597 Schielborg, H.
Hillen (Hoochstraten), Johannes
  Antwerp
  1528 Tyndale, W. (2)
  1529 Brightwell, R.
  1530 Bible. — *Appendix.* [*English*]
  1530 Dialogue
  1530 T., W.
Hillen, Michiel
  Antwerp
  1533 Philalethes, *Hyperboraeus*
Hist, Conrad
  Speyer
  1497? Wimpheling, J.
Hittorp, Gottfried
  Cologne
  1522 †Melanchthon, P. Loci communes
  1532 Bible. — *Epistles*
Hock, Alexander
  Tübingen
  1575 Frischlin, N. Epistolæ
  1582 Osiander, L.
Hoeltzel, Hieronymus
  Nuremberg
  1523 Luther, M. [*Brief*]
  1524 Bodenstein, A.
Hofer, Hans
  Augsburg
  1540? Schiff

Hofer, Hans, *Heirs of*
  Augsburg
  1584 Ephemerides
Hoffhalter, Raphael
  Vienna
  1558 Ransanus, P.
Hoffmann, Georg
  Freiberg (Saxony)
  1583 Juncker, M.
  1588 Tilisch, E.
Hofmann, Gregor
  Worms
  1551 Scheidt, C.
Horn, Konrad
  Wolfenbüttel
  1571 Gogrevius, M.
  1571 Selneccer, N.
  1587 Satler, B.
  1589 Julius, *Duke*
  1589 Rigeman, P.
  1592 †P., I.N.A.B.I.S.
  1597 Kempe, Z.
  1599 †L., H.I.D.B.E.L.E.P.I.H.A.
Huber, Gregor
  See **Hieber, Georg**
Hueter, Simon
  Frankfort on the Main
  1568 Gottingen
Huettich, Guenther
  Jena
  1571 Heshusius, T. Oratio de synodis
Hupfuff, Matthias
  Strasburg
  1508 Tollat, J.
Husner, Georg
  Strasburg
  1475? Abusiva
  1479 Jacobus, *de Voragine*
  1503 Vincent [Ferrer], *Saint*
Isengrin, Michael
  Basle
  1542 Plutarch. [*Moralia*]
  1546 Vergilius, P.
Jacob, Cyriacus
  Frankfort on the Main
  1545 Beccadelli, A.
  1546 Rodler, H.
  1549 Tritheim, J.
Jamer, Johann
  Frankfort on the Oder
  1533 Petrus, *Anspach*
Jason, Gabriel, *pseud.*
  Aygenstein
  1576 France. — *Henry III.*

Jobin, Bernhard
Strasburg
1574 Cilicius, C.
1574 Neusidler, M.
1576 Droet, P.
1579 French News
1585 Henry IV., *King*
1588 Henry I., *Duke*
1588 Nachenmoser, A.
1593 ††Reuschlein, C.

Jobin, Bernhard, Heirs of
Strasburg
1595 Nachenmoser, A.

Jobsson, Wernher, *pseud.*
Leyden
1588 Nachenmoser, A.

Johann, *von Neuss*
Cologne
1552 Innocent III., *Pope*

Kachelofen, Conrad
Leipzig
1490 Mary, *the Blessed Virgin*
1494 Versor, J.

Freiberg (Saxony)
1495 Liturgies. — Missals. — Meissen

Kalt, Nikolaus
Constance
1598 Hyeble, C.

Kantor, Jan Had
Prague
1555 Collinus, M. Nomenclatura
1557 Heyden, S. Puerilium

Kantz, Gabriel
Altenburg
1525 Bible. — Appendix. [*Concordances.* — *German*]
1525 Philip, *Landgrave*. Ein Christlich
1525 Zymmermann, A.
1526 †Ruell, E.

Zwickau
1526 †Toltz, J.
1527 Luther, M. [*Auf des Königs*]
1529 Guethel, C.

Kauffmann, Paul
Nuremberg
1595 Taurellus, N. Emblemata
1600 Altdorf. — *Schola*

Keschedt, Peter
Cologne
1595 Laurus, G.

Keyser, Anton
See **Caesar, A.**

Keyser, Martin de
Antwerp
1530 Hortulus
1531 Bible. — *Isaiah*
1532 Abell, T.
1532 Pope

Kilian, Hans
Neuburg
1545 †Erasmus, D. [*Colloquia.* — *Selections*]

Kirchner, Ambrosius
Magdeburg
1557? Faber, G.
1557 †Philip II., *King*
1558 Kollekten
1560 Wigand, J.

Kirchner, Ambrosius, the Younger
Magdeburg
1587 Papa, A.
1596 Crato, A.

Kirchner, Wolfgang
Magdeburg
1560 Heshusius, T. Das Jesu
1574 Bible. — *Proverbs*

Klosterdruckerei
See **Closterdruckerei**

Klug, Josef
Wittenberg
1525 Luther, M. [*Brief*]
1530 †— [*Vermahnung an die Geistlichen*]
1530 Schrick, M.
1536 Barnes, R.
1540 Collinus, M. Elegia
1540 Melanchthon, P. De officio
1540 Schenck, J.
1545 Melanchthon, P. Enarratio
1546 Creutziger, C., *the Elder*

Knappe, Hans
Erfurt
1512? Vegetius Renatus, F.

Knobloch, Johann
Strasburg
1509? †Troy
1520? Spruch. Ein neüwer
1525 Bible. — *Proverbs*. [*Latin*]
1527 Ignatius, *Saint*

Knobloch, Johann, the Younger
Strasburg
1551 Eppendorff, H. von. Kriegsübung
1555 Vegius, M.

Knoblochtzer, Heinrich
Heidelberg
1491? Rome, *Church of*. — Curia

Knorr, Nikolaus
Nuremberg
1562 Osterreicher, A.
1565? Adam. Ein new geistlich Lied
1565? Model, G.
1566 Waldner, W.

Koberger, Anton
Nuremberg
1496? Dorsprunner, A.
1510 Petrus, *Lombardus*

Kobian, Valentin
Durlach
1530 Annotatio

Koelhoff, Johann
Cologne
1475 Thomas, Aquinas. [*Quaestiones de veritate*]
1479 Jacobus, *de Voragine*
1482 Antonius, *de Parma*
1488 Boethius, A.M.T.S.

Koepfel, Paul and **Philipp**
Strasburg
1556 †Adamo, A, di
1556 †Ponet, J.
1558 †Hedio, C.

Kohl, Hans
Ratisbon
1545 Nuber, V.
1555 Bericht

Adlersberg (Kloster)
1556 †Brandenburg-Anspach and Baireuth

Heidelberg
1558 George John, *Count*

Kohl, Hans, and **Adler, Aegidius**
Vienna
1548 Bible. — *Psalms.* [*Selections.* — *Latin*]

Kohl, Paul
Ratisbon
1525 Bible. — *Liturgical Epistles.* [*German*]

Kolbe, Andreas
Marburg
1545 Asclepius Barbatus, N. Sortium

Kolbe, Augustin
Marburg
1578 Frese, R. Carmen

Koler, Johann
Nuremberg
1565? Bible. — *Psalms.* [*Selections.* — *German*]
1565? — — — — [*Single Psalms.* 23]
1565? Jonas, J. [*Appendix*]
1565? Lied. Ein schön new

Kote, Georg
Halberstadt
1595 Dolearius, J.

Krafft, Johann
Wittenberg
1553 Heshusius, T. Oratio in qua
1558 Orth, Z.
1561 Creutziger, C., *the Younger.* Propositiones
1563 Bible. — *Liturgical Epistles.* [*German.* — *Low German*]
1564 Theodoricus, S.
1565 Melanchthon, P. [*Letters*]

Krafft, Johann, Heirs of
Wittenberg
1580 Bible. — *Galatians*
1580 Siberus, A.
1585 †Mylius, G.
1591 Thomas [More], *Saint*
1597 Habermann, J.

Kreutzer, Veit
Wittenberg
1545 Sacrobosco, J. de
1546 Nabod, A.
1546 Scharschmied, F.
1549 Melanchthon, P. Disputatio
1552 Rebhun, P.

Kreutziger, Hans
Neisse
1561 Rigelius, S.
1563 Liubichts, J.
1574 —

Kreydlein, Margaretha
Nuremberg
1565? Nuremberg. [*Appendix*]

Kriegstein, Melchior
Augsburg
1546 B., J.
1550 Mahediah

Kruffter, Servatius
Cologne
1525 Luther, M. [*Wider die mörderischen*]

Kuendig, Jakob
Basle
1556 Frantz, W. (3)
1561 Acronius, J.

Kunne, Albrecht
Memmingen
1485 Perottus, N.

Lamberg, Abraham
Leipzig
1594 Fischer, B.
1596 Bible. — *Liturgical Epistles.* [*German*]
1597 Ingolstetterus, J.

Lamprecht, Josse
Wesel
1554 Sampson, T.

Landsberg, Martin
Leipzig
1490? Saxony, *the Duchy*
1494? Helias, P.
1494? Vallibus, H. de
1495? Huguccio, *Bishop*

Lange, Werner
See **Omichius, Franz,** and **Lange, W.**

Lantzenberger, Michael
Leipzig
1594 Franck von Franckenstein, V.
1595 Cicero, M. T. [*Selections*]

Lechler, Martin
Frankfort on the Main
1568 Gottingen
1582 Amman, J.

Lehmann, Zacharias
Wittenberg
1589 Liturgies. — *Lutheran*
1590 Posselius, J.
1593 Nymann, H.

Leonardus, *de Aich*
Nuremberg
1529 Gechauf, T. De uirtute

Liechtenstein, Petrus
Venice
1502 Liturgies. — *Breviaries.* — *Salzburg*

Lieskau, Achatius
Halle
1591 Heshusius, T. [*Letters*]
1592 Kittelman, C.

Lipp, Balthasar
Mainz
1600 Suarez, F.

Lochner, Christoph, and **Hofmann, J.**
Nuremberg
1590 Schopper, J.
1592 Crusius, J.

Lonicer, Adam, Cnipius, J., and **Steinmeyer, P.**
Frankfort on the Main
1577 Kling, M.

Lotter, Melchior
Leipzig
1507 Persius Flaccus, A.
1511 Plautus, T.M.
1514 Burchardi, U.
1514 Tuberinus, J.
1519 Erasmus, D. [*Letters*]
1519 Virgilius Maro, P. [*Bucolica*]
1520 Malaciola, T. C.
1530 ††Annaberg

Lotter, Melchoir, *the Younger*
Wittenberg
1524 Pflug, J.

Lotter, Michael
Magdeburg
1550 Civilius, M.
1550 Magdeburg
1552 Flacius, M. Wider den Euangelisten
1553 Westphal, J.

Lucius, Jakob
Rostock
1575 Chytraeus, D. Oratio
Helmstedt
1589 Boekel, J.
1589 Hofmann, D.
1589 Smidenstet, H.
1591 Creissius, J.
1593 Caselius, J. Ἐπιτάφιος
1593 Pfafrad, C.
1593 Satler, B.
1595 Caselius, J. Ad Mathiam
1595 Frenzelius, S. Monomachia
1595 Plutarch. [*De curiositate*]

Lucius, Jakob, *Heirs of*
Helmstedt
1598 Hefftrich, M.

Lucius, Jakob, *the Younger*
Helmstedt
1600 Trusted, J.

Lucius, Ludwig
Heidelberg
1562 Bologna. — *Università*

Ludwig, *von Renchen*
Cologne
1502? Schiphower, J.

Luetzenkirchen, Wilhelm
Cologne
1593 France. [*Appendix*] Kurtzer
1596 Albert, *Cardinal*

Lufft, Hans
Wittenberg
1525 Gespraechbuechlein
1525 Rhegius, U.
1539 Homer
1550 Meier, G. Eine Predig
1555 Bible. — *Liturgical Epistles.* [*Latin*]
1560 — *Galatians*
1563, 64 — *Timothy*
1564 Wittenberg. — *Academia*
1567 Meier, G. Commonefactio
1570 Leipsic. — *Academia*

> *Koenigsberg*
1550 Osiander, A.
1551 —

Lufft, Hans, *pseud.*
> *Marburg*
1528 Tyndale, W. (3)
1529 Brightwell, R.
1530 Bible. —*Appendix*. [*English*]
1530 Dialogue
1535 Tyndale, W.

Lynne, Walter
> *London*
1550 Jesus Christ. The true

Maler, Matthes
> *Erfurt*
1516? Zutrinker
1521 †Luther, M. [*Sermon von dreierlei*]
1521 W., J. E. M.
1522 Culsamerus, J. Eyn wiederlegung
1522 Guethel, C.
1523 Eobanus, H.
1524 Bartholomaeus [Arnoldi]

Manger, Michael
> *Augsburg*
1569 Sulz, M. C. von
1570? Reuss, M.
1572 Hungarian Disease
1572 Metri, N. de
1572 Nostredame, M. de
1575? Lobgesang
1582 Holthusius, J.
1584 Winckler, N.
1587 Ovidius Naso, P. Tristia
1588 Kuenste
1590? Lied. Ein Lied
1590? — Ein schön news
1590? Octavian, *Emperor*
1590? Osterreicher, A.
1590? †Tagweise
1598 Schwarzenberg, A. von
1600? †Christian Songs

Marne, Claude, and **Aubry, Jean**
> *Frankfort on the Main*
1588 Foesius, A.
1592 La Ramée, P. de
1599 Talaeus, A.
1600 Calvinius, J.

Marschalk, Nicolaus
> *Erfurt*
1502 †Greek Language

Martin, *von Werden*
> *Cologne*
1508 Losow, C.
1510 Poeta

Martin, Jost
> *Strasburg*
1599 Vogel, H.

Mayer, Johann
> *Heidelberg*
1570 Brantius, J.
1574 †Witekind, H.
1575 Candidus, J.

Mayer, Johann
> *Neustadt a.d. Haardt*
1579 Strigelius, V.

Mayer, Johann, Heirs of
> *Neustadt a.d. Haardt*
1579 Pezel, C. Der LXVII. Psalm

Mayer, Sebald
> *Dillingen*
1558 Amerbachius, G.
1559 Pole, R.
1559 Rutland, J. C.
1560 Noguera, J.
1562? Porcia, B. di
1566 Mary, *Queen*
1572 Perpinianus, P. J.

Mechler, Esaias
> *Erfurt*
1590 Mirus, M.
1590 Mylius, G. Eilff

Meissner, Johann
> *Magdeburg*
1600 Bible. —*Psalms*. [*Selections.* — *Latin*]

Melantrich, Georg
> *Prague*
1579 Makowinus a Makowa, V.

Melchior, *von Neuss*
> *Cologne*
1534 Bede, *the Venerable*
1545 Carvaialus, L.
1545 Gardiner, S.

Merkel, Georg
> *Nuremberg*
1550? Sachs, H. Der gantz
1555 †— Ein gesprech

Messerschmidt, Georg
> *Strasburg*
1551 Eppendorff, H. von. Kriegsübung

Meyer, Michael
> See **Beck, Balthasar**, and **Meyer, M.**

Meyerpeck, Wolfgang
> *Zwickau*
1532 Kuenste
1535? †Jesus Christ. Ein spruch
1536 †Germany. — Charles V.
1543 †William V., *Duke*
1544 Klein Leupsch

Mierdman, Steven
> *Antwerp*
1545 Catechism

1545 Christian. The lamētacyon
1545 Erasmus, D. [*Enchiridion*]
1546 R., L.
1550 Jesus Christ. The true

Milchthaler, Leonhard
Nuremberg
1540 Kolbenschlag, S.

Miller, Johann
Augsburg
1514 Turks

Moellemann, Stephan
Rostock
1560, 61 Chytraeus, D.
1581 Aeschylus
1581 Distelmeier, C.
1583 Caselius, J. Henrico
1584 — Laudatio
1584 Demetrius, *Phalereus*
1588 Caselius, J. Ill.mo
1592 Chytraeus, D.
1595 Estienne, H.
1595 Euripides
1596 Caselius, J. Ἰουλέιον
1596 Gunarius, H.
1597 Mancinus, G. Honori
1600 — In honorem
1600 Sturtzius, C.

Morhart, Ulrich
Tübingen
1546 Schradin, J.

Morhart, Ulrich, Widow of
Tübingen
1554 †Vergerio, P. P.
1554 †Wurtemberg. — Christopher, *Duke*
1556 Meichsner, J. H. Handtbüchlin
1561 Wicknerus, A.
1567 Terentius, P.

Mueller, Christian, *the Elder*
Strasburg
1561 Scalichius, P.
1566 Naegelin, M.

Mueller, Christian, *the Elder, Heirs of*
Strasburg
1568 Luther, M. [*Catechismus*]

Mueller, Georg
Wittenberg
1593 Frenzelius, S. Epigrammatum
1594 — Ad Germaniam

Mueller, Krafft
Strasburg
1538 †Hutten, U. von. Opera
1544 Melanchthon, P. Philosophiæ

Mueller, Krafft, Widow of
Strasburg
1548 Melanchthon, P. Commentarius

Müntzer's Printer
Allstedt
1524 †Muentzer, T.

Mylius, Arnold
Cologne
1589 Faunteus, L. A.
1594 Baldesano, G.
1594 Stapleton, T. (2)
1600 Suarez, F.

Mylius, Christian
See **Mueller, C,**

Nadler, Joerg
Augsburg
1520 †Erasmus, D. [*Paraclesis*] Ger.
1524? †G., P.

Nassinger, Leonhard
Vienna
1584 Scherer, G.

Nerlich, Nikolaus
Leipzig
1595? Sachs, M.

Neuber, Ulrich, and **Gerlach, Dietrich**
Nuremberg
1566 Roggius, N.

Neuber, Valentin
Nuremberg
1550? Cana
1555? Apostles' Creed
1555? Abraham, *the Patriarch*
1555? Adam. Ein klag Liedt
1555? B., L.
1555? Bible. — Psalms. [Selections. — German. — Single Psalms. 22]
1555? — — [— — — *63*]
1555? — — [— — — *91*]
1555? — — [— — — *103*]
1555? — *Appendix.* [*Miscellaneous*]
1555? Christians
1555? Hymnals. [*German*]
1555? Kettner, L.
1555? Lazarus, *Saint.* Zwey
1555? Lied. Ein geistlich
1555? Lieder. Zwey schöne
1555? Lord's Prayer
1555? Reihen Lieder
1555? Sachs, H. Ein schön
1555? Spruch. Ein hübscher
1560? Bible. —*Appendix.* [*Psalms*]
1560? Lieder. Drey geistliche
1560? — Drey geystliche
1560? — Drey schöne
1560? — Zwey schöne
1560? Plonick
1560 Sachs, H. Die Zerstörung
1560? Schnauss, C.
1566 Bel
1583 Lochner, Z. Tractätlein

Nolt, Anastasius
Speyer
1542 Reuschius, J.

Novesianus, Joannes
See **Johann,** *von Neuss*

Nycolson, Henry, *pseud.*
Wesel
1546 R., L.

Oeglin, Erhard
Augsburg
1520 Oecolampadius, J.

Omichius, Franz, and **Lange, Werner**
Güstrow
1582 Celichius, A.

Oostfreese, Eewardus
Emden
1584 Frese, R. Tragica (2)

Oporinus, Johann
Basle
1545 Camerarius, J. Elementa
1546 †Rivius, J. De consolandis
1546 — De erroribus
1547 Mexia, P.
1547 Plutarch. [*Vitae parallelae*]
1547 Rivius, J. De stultitia
1550 Marlianus, J. B.
1550 Rivius, J. De perpetuo
1551 Bible. —*Ecclesiasticus*. [*Greek*]
1551 Lazius, W. Commentariorum
1555 Micyllus, J. Arithmeticæ
1556 Neander, M.
1557 Fox, J.
1566 Schardius, S.

Oporinus, Johann, and **Froben, Ambrosius** and **Aurelius**
Basle
1565 Lycosthenes, C.

Oporinus, Johann, Heirs of
Basle
1580? Isocrates
1591 Schutz, H.

Oridryus, Johann
See **Buys, Albert,** and **Oridryus, J.**

Ostein, Leonhard
Basle
1592 Henricpetri, J.
1592 ††Zuinglius, H.

Osterberger, Georg
Koenigsberg
1579 Oderbornius, P.
1591 Bible. —*Liturgical Epistles*.
[*Lithuanian*]
1597 Eccard, J.
1600 Francisci, A.

Otmar, Johann
Reutlingen
1488 Liturgies. —*Missals*. [*Extracts*]

Otmar, Silvan
Augsburg
1517 Augsburg, *Diocese of*. — Synod
1522 Germany. — Charles V.
1522 †Luther, M. [*Epistel*]
1534 Schueler, G.

Otmar, Valentin
Augsburg
1555 Euclid

Palthenius, Zacharias
Frankfort on the Main
1596 Decimator, H.
1596 Magirus, J.
1598 Metius, A.

Peetersen, Henrick
Antwerp
1533 Frith, J.
1535 Tyndale, W.

Perna, Peter
Basle
1559 Themistius, *Euphrada*
1560 Bairo, P.
1560? Betti, F.
1562? Ochino, B.
1573 Wecker, H. J.
1577 Giovio, P.
1578 Châteillon, S.
1578 Theorian

Perna, Peter, Heirs of
Basle
1587 Wecker, H. J.

Pessus, Gerardus, *pseud.*
Danzig
1595 Nauntelius, R.

Peter, *von Friedberg*
Mainz
1494? Tritheim, J.

Peterle, Michael
Prague
1577 Elogii, C.
1585 Martini, L.

Petrejus, Johann
Nuremberg
1523 †Schoener, J. De nuper
1527 Pirckheimer, B.
1529 Rome. — Justinian I. [*Institutiones*]
1530 †Luther, M. [*Biblical Commentaries*.
— *Revelation*]
1536 †Dorpius, H.
1537 †Luther, M. [*Collections of Sermons*]
1539 Magnesius, E.
1540 †Netherlands. — Charles V.
1541 Stigel, J.
1542 †Conrad IV., *Bishop*

1542 Peckham, J.
1543 †Germany. — Charles V.
1547 †Luther, M. [*Marginal Notes*]

Petri, Adam
Basle
1520 Luther, M. [*Smaller Collections*]
1521 Pfruendenmarkt
1522 Valla, G.

Petri, Andreas
Eisleben
1567 Greitz. — *Preachers*
1568 Brunswick. — *Ministers*
1568 Spangenberg, C.
1584 Vischer, C.

Mansfeld
1574 Irenaeus, C.

Petri, Heinrich
Basle
1528 Rome. — *Emperors*. — Theodosius II.
1533 Coccius, M. A.
1535 John, *of Damascus*
1540 Bock, G.
1541 Statius, P. P.
1550 Mikropresbutikon
1577 Giovio, P.

Petri, Heinrich, and **Perna, Peter**
Basle
1561 Santbech, D.

Petri, Johann
Passau
1486 Herbarius

Petrus, de Olpe
Cologne
1477? Bible. —*Appendix*. [*Miscellaneous*]

Peypus, Friedrich
Nuremberg
1518 †Luther, M. [*Freiheit des Sermons*]
1520? Erasmus, D. [*Concio*]
1521 Rothenburg
1523 †Netherlands. [*Appendix*] Newe zeytung
1525 Luther, M. [*Eine schreckliche Geschichte*]
1529 Gechauf, T. De uirtute
1530 Tiber
1531 †Paris. — *Université*
1533 Luther, M. [*Biblical Commentaries*]

Peypus, Friedrich, Heirs of
Nuremberg
1535 †Doner, L.

Pfeil, Johann
Bamberg
1504 Kratwol, H.
1512 Ratisbon, *Diocese*

Philadelphus, Theophilus, *pseud.*
Aresdorf
1578 Châteillon, S.

Pinus, ad insigne
Augsburg
1600 Muret, M. A.

Pistor, Johann
See **Beck, J.**

Plantin, Christoph
Antwerp
1580–4 Ortelius, A.

Platter, Thomas
Basle
1538 Pomponius Laetus, J.

Portenbach, Jeremias
Erfurt
1564 Hebenstreit, J.

Prael, Johannes
Cologne
1531 †Melanchthon, P. De iustificatione
1531 Sententiae
1532 Bible. — *Pentateuch*

Printer of Aristeas
Erfurt
1483? Solomon, *King*

Printer of Barbatia
Strasburg?
1495? Barbatia, A.

Printer of Capotius
Leipzig
1488? Praecepta

Printer of Dares
Cologne
1470? Rome. — *Paul II., Pope*

Printer of Dictys
Cologne
1470? Bernard, *Saint*

Printer of Historia S. Albani
Cologne
1472? Nider, J.

Printer of Hundorn
Erfurt
1494 Negligentiae

Printer of Jordanus
Strasburg
1500? Bertrandus, *de Turre Cura*

Printer of Sermones Thesauri novi
Strasburg
1486 Sermones

Pruess, Johann, the Elder
Strasburg
1490? Fasciculus

1498? Bible. — *Psalms*. [*Latin*]
1500? — — —
1502 Formulare
1505 Wolphius, T.
1507 Dionysius, N.

Quentel, Arnold
Cologne
1595 Luis, *de Granada*

Quentel, Heinrich
Cologne
1494 Aristotle. [*Ethica*]
1494? Speculum
1500 Cordiale

Quentel, Heinrich, Sons of
Cologne
1514 Murmelius, J.

Quentel, Johann
Cologne
1546 Gersonites, *Landavus*

Quentel, Johann, Heirs of
Cologne
1552 Ruysbroeck, J. van

See also **Calenius, Gerwin,** and **Quentel, J.,** Heirs of

Quentel, Peter
Cologne
1526 Damasus, *Pope*
1526 †Luther, M. [*Wider die mörderischen Rotten*]
1532 Alardus

Rabe, Georg
Frankfort on the Main
1572 Vázquez de Menchaca, F.
1574 Laetus, E.
1578 Livius, T.
1579 Chasseneux, B. de. Catalogus

Rabe, Georg, Feyerabend, S., and **Han, W.,** Heirs of
Frankfort on the Main
1569 Posthius, J.

Rabe, Georg, and **Han, W.,** Heirs of
Frankfort on the Main
1563 Meichsner, J. H. Hoch oder
1563 Schmidenstedt, H.

Raesfeldt, Lambert
Muenster
1591 Michaelis, P.
1592 Liturgies. — *Rituals*. — *Munster*

Ramminger, Melchior
Augsburg
1521 †Luther, M. [*Missive an einen Grafen*]
1522 †— [*Epistel*]
1525 †Hauptartikel

1530? †Blindenspiegel
1540? Susanna

Ratdolt, Erhard
Augsburg
1509? Froeschel, V.

Reinhardt, Hieronymus
Muehlhausen
1587 Sachs, M.

Reinheckel, Andreas
Neisse
1587 Taeucher, D.
1594 Edmund [Campian], *Saint*

Reinmichel, Leonhard
Lauingen
1591, 95 Heilbrunner, J.

Retro Minores
Cologne
1497 Annius, J.
1499 Evagatorium

Retsch, Thomas, and **Haberklee, W.**
Culmbach
1552? Vermahnung

Reusner, Christoph
Rostock
1600 Sturtzius, C.

Rhambau, Hans
Leipzig
1560 Trubius, L.
1570 Gordonio, B. de

Rhau, Georg
Wittenberg
1532 Antichrist
1534 Listenius, N.
1542 †Liturgies. — *Lutheran*. — *Pomerania*
1545 †Luther, M. [*Wider das Papsttum*]
1546 †— [*Etliche Schlüsse*]
1548 Alberus, E. Von den Zeichen

Rhau, Georg, Heirs of
Wittenberg
1549 Sarcerius, E.
1550 Krage, T.
1551 Goldwurm, C. Die schöne
1556 Eber, P.
1556 Finck, H.
1559–62 Wittenberg. — *Academia*

Rhau-Grunenberg, Johannes
Wittenberg
1520 Lonicer, J.
1522 †Luther, M. [*Welche Pesonen*]
1523 †— [*Adversus armatum virum*]
1523 Savonarola, G.
1525 Raut, G.

Rhode, Franz
Marburg
1534 Asclepius Barbatus, N. Oratio
Danzig
1558 Galen

Richel, Bernard
Basle
1481 Tudeschis, N. de

Richel, Josias
Strasburg
1561 Xenophon
1565, 66 S., I.
1590 Golius, T.

Richolff, Georg, *the Younger*
Hamburg
1530 Aepinus, J.

Richter, Wolfgang
Frankfort on the Main
1600 Malleus

Richzenhan, Donat
Jena
1561 Curtius, V.
1579 Utzinger, A. (2)
1592 Strigenitz, G.

Rihel, Josias
Strasburg
1575 Bible. — Psalms. [*Latin*]

Rihel, Theodosius
Strasburg
1568 Specker, M.

Rihel, Wendelin
Strasburg
1541 †Luther, M. [*Vermahnung zum Sakrament*]
1541 Thomas, H.
1555 Treatise

Riswick, Otto à
Erfurt
1596 Sartorius, J.

Roedinger, Christian
Magdeburg
1548 Germany. — Charles V. (2)
1549 †Luther, M. [*Wider den Eisleben*]
1549 Rabshakeh
1550 Germany. — Charles V.
1552 Melanchthon, P. De oppido

Roedinger, Christian, *the Younger*
Jena
1569 Jena. — *Academia*

Ross, Wilhelm
Magdeburg
1582 Pomarius, J.

Ruedem, Henning
Hanover
1548 Sylvanus, J.

Ruelius, Cunradus
Wittenberg
1559, 62 Wittenberg. — *Academia*

Ruremunde, Christoffel van, Widow of
Antwerp
1540 Solme, T.
1543 Joye, G.
1543 †Zwingli, U. Ad Carolum

Rusch, Adolf
Strasburg
1477? Vincentius, *Bellovacensis*

Rynmann, Johann
Augsburg
1502 Liturgies. — Breviaries. — Salzburg
1518 Cicero, M. T. [*Supposititious Works*]
1519, 20 Hollen, G.

Sachse, Melchior
Erfurt
1527 Rome, *the City*
1530 †Luther, M. [*Brief an den Kardinal*]
1546 †— [*Vermahnung an alle Pfarrherren*]

Sacon, Jacques
Lyons
1510 Petrus, *Lombardus*
1515, 16 †Alexander, *de Ales*

Sadeler, Johann
Munich
1590? Lasso, O. di

Sartorius, Adam
Ingolstadt
1598 Hund, W. Bayrisch
1600 Fachineus, A.
1600 †Gretser, J. Apologeticus
1600 Rosignoli, B.

Sartorius, David
Ingolstadt
1580 Laymannus, M.
1582 Hund, W. Metropolis
1582 Lucius, C. Brevis
1584 Turner, R.
1586 †Calvinistic Cruelty
1588 Nicephorus
1589 Hendschele, T.
1589 Pistorius, J. Thesium
1589 Valentia, G. de
1590, 91 Raedt, H. A. de
1590 Tramenus, L.
1593 England. — Elizabeth I.
1593 Milius, E.

Sauer, Johann
    Frankfort on the Main
  1597 †Boissard, J. J.
  1600 Plinius Secundus, C.

Schaeffler, Johann
    Constance
  1524 †Luther, M. [*Formula missae*]

Scharffenberg, Crispin
    Goerlitz
  1548 S., F. K.
    Breslau
  1570? Heidenreich, E. Hauss liedlein
  1575? Lieder. Zwey

Schirlentz, Nickel
    Wittenberg
  1521 Maurice, *Saint,* and Mary Magdalen, *Saint*
  1523 Beyer, D.
  1524 Caelius, M. Wie
  1526 Beyr, L.
  1532 Athanasius, *Saint*

Scleich, Clemens, and **Schoene, A.**
    Wittenberg
  1570 Creutziger, C., *the Younger.* Propositiones theologicæ
  1572 Wittenberg. — *Academia*
  1574 Wennemeyerus, Z.
  1577 Goedeman, C.
  1578 Pulmannus, J.

Schlot, Bartholomaeus
    Lemgo
  1578 Kerssenbrock, H.

Schmidt, Jakob
    Speyer
  1524 Sachs, H. Disputatio
  1527 Sigismund, *Emperor*

Schmidt, Johann
    Porrentruy
  1595 Liturgies. — *Rituals.* — *Basle*
  1599 Binsfeldius, P.
  1600 Porrentruy

Schmidt, Nickel
    Leipzig
  1527 †Sibyls. [*Appendix*]
  1529 Sylvius, P.

Schmidt, Peter
    Arnstadt
  1548 Holtzhausen

Schmidt, Peter
    Frankfort on the Main
  1578 †Amman, J. Kunst
  1580 †— —
  1583 Stammbuch

Schmuck, Michael
    Schmalkalden
  1575 Bischoff, M. Ausslegung
  1577 — Eine Christliche
  1577 — Eine tröstliche

Schnauss, Cyriacus
    Coburg
  1548 †Germany. — *Charles V.* Interim

Schneider, Andreas
    Leipzig
  1571 Camerarius, J. Ἀριθμολογία

Schneider, Nikolaus
    Zittau
  1586 Quinos, B.
    Sorau
  1589 Streuber, P.
    Liegnitz
  1593 Goetling, C.
  1595 Blum, N.

Schobser, Andreas
    Munich
  1535? †Bavaria. [*Constitutional Documents*] (2)
  1545? Vincent [Ferrer], *Saint*
  1550? Mai

Schoeffer, Ivo
    Mainz
  1538 Tibertus, A.
  1541 Germany. — *Reichstag*
  1548 Evangelical War

Schoeffer, Johann
    Mainz
  1513 Liturgies. — *Rituals.* — *Mainz*
  1521 Guentherus, P.
  1523 Livius, T.
  1524 Melanchthon, P. In obscuriora
  1527 Nausea, F.
  1527 †Kautz, J.
  1529 Enchiridion
  1529 Gaius, *the Jurist*
  1529 Rome. — *Justinian I.* [*Institutiones*]

Schoeffer, Peter
    Mainz
  1478 Chaimis, B. de

Schoeffer, Peter, *the Younger*
    Worms
  1524 Gustavus, I., *King*
  1526 †Luther, M. [*Sendbrief an Herzog Georg*]

Schoene, Anton
    Wittenberg
  1583 Luther, M. [*Works*]

Schoenig, Valentin
    Augsburg
  1586 Augsburg. [*Appendix*]

Schoensperger, Johann, *the Younger*
Augsburg
1515? Sheba, *Queen of*

Schott, Johann
Strasburg
1514 Virgilius Maro, P. [*Appendix*]
1523 Brunfels, O.
1523 Stifel, M.
1527 Jesus Christ. The true
1529 Pollio, S.
1540 Eppendorff, H. von. Türckischer
1540 Leuwis, D. de
1544? Plutarch. [*Moralia*]

Schuerer, Lazarus
Schlettstadt
1520 †Erasmus, D. [*Moriae encomium*]

Schuerer, Matthias
Strasburg
1508 Athanasius, *Saint.* In Psalmos
1510 Mancinellus, A. Sermonum
1515 Ovidius Naso, P. De Ponto
1517 Nannus Mirabellius, D.

Schuerer, Matthias, *Heirs of*
Strasburg
1520 †Erasmus, D. [*Paraclesis*] Ger.
1521 Rhomanus, J.
1521 Rothenburg
1522 †Luther, M. [*De votis monasticis*]
1522 †— [*Von beider Gestalt*]
1525 †Bugenhagen, J. Etlich

Schuetz, Hieronymus
Dresden
1595 Lentz, J.

Schuhman, Hans
Prague
1591 Bacháček, M.

Schumann, Valentin
Leipzig
1529 Sylvius, P.
1530? Dungersheym, H.
1530 Proles, A.

Schwan, Johannes
Strasburg
1524 Bryssgawer, M.

Schwenck, Lorenz
Wittenberg
1560 Schorkelius, S.
1561 Theognis
1565 Gese, J.

Schwertel, Johann
Wittenberg
1567 Ferinarius, J.
1567 Wernerus, A.
1570 —

1573 Matthaeus, B.
1575 Bible. [*German*]

Seitz, Peter
Wittenberg
1538 Bible. — *Ecclesiasticus.* [*Latin*]

Seitz, Peter, *Heirs of*
Wittenberg
1555 Mensch

Seitz, Peter, *the Younger*
Wittenberg
1568 Garcaeus, J. Sterbbüchlein
1570 Bredekauu, F.

Selfisch, Samuel
Wittenberg
1563 Bible. — *Liturgical Epistles.* [*Low German*]
1589 Liturgies. — *Lutheran*

Setzer, Johann
Hagenau
1525 Bible. — *Proverbs.* [*Latin*]
1526 Suabia
1527 †Luther, M. [*Epistola ad Henricum*]
1527 Moltherus, M.
1528 †—
1530 Dickius, L.
1532 Potho, *Benedictine*

Seuberlich, Lorenz
See **Sueberlich, L.**

Seybold, Heinrich
Strasburg
1530 Eobanus, H. Bonae

Silvius, Willem
Antwerp
1578 Netherlands. — *Staten Generaal*

Singriener, Johann
Vienna
1517 Ursinus Velius, C.
1520 †Luther, M. [*De libertate Christiana*]
1520 Solinus, C.J.
1521 †Luther, M. [*Unterricht der Beichtkinder*]
1522 †— [*De abroganda Missa*]
1536 Germany. — *Ferdinand I.*

Singriener, Matthaeus
Vienna
1545 Musler, G.

Smesmann, Abraham
Heidelberg
1592 Kimedoncius, J.
1592 Stenius, S.

Smesmann, Abraham, *Heirs of*
Heidelberg
1595 Scultetus, A.

Snel, Johann
    Lübeck
1485? †Liturgies. — *Rituals.* — *Odense*

Soter, Jacobus, Heirs of
    Cologne
1579 Graminaeus, D.

Soter, Johannes
    Cologne
1521 Budé, G.
1530 Hegesippus

Soter, Melchior
    Dortmund
1550 Schopper, J.

Spiess, Johann
    Frankfort on the Main
1585 Codomannus, L.
1591 Hunnius, E. Christliche
1592 — Articulus
1592 — Catechismus
1596 — [Collections]
1596 Magirus, J.
1596 Virgilius Maro, P. [*Bucolica and Georgica*]

    Heidelberg
1583 Bible. — *Psalms.* [*Selections.* — *German.* — *Single Psalms. 91*]
1583 Schechsius, J.

Stainhofer, Kaspar
    Vienna
1574 Bible. — *New Testament.* [*Hungarian*]

Steenberch, Simon
    Deventer
1559 Overyssel

Steiner, Heinrich
    Augsburg
1522 †Luther, M. [*Sermon am Palmtag*]
1523 †Briessmann, J. Vnterricht
1523 Reychart, P.
1523 Spelt, H.
1526 †Luther, M. [*Sermon von der Hauptsumma*]
1530 Lobera de Avila, L.
1535 Kunstbuechlein
1540 Decembrius, A.
1541 Prague
1542 Bucoldianus, G.
1545 Erasmus, D. [*Colloquia*]

Steinmann, Hans
    Leipzig
1572 Hesiod
1582 Ovidius Naso, P. Metamorphoseon

Steinmann, Tobias
    Jena
1592 Leyser, P.

1595 Mylius, G. Zehen
1597 Reusner, N.

Steinmetz, Georg
    Annaberg
1560? S.; C. Die zehen

Stoeckel, Jakob
    Eilenburg
1530 †Luther, M. [*Etliche Artikelstücke*]

Stoeckel, Jakob, and **Widemar, Nikolaus**
    Eilenburg
1524 Haferitz, S.

Stoeckel, Matthes
    Dresden
1550 Saxony, the Electorate. — *Laws*

Stoeckel, Wolfgang
    Leipzig
1505 Cesar, H.
1508 Plinius Secundus, C.
1520 Chuntz, *von Oberndorff*
1520 Copp, J.
1522 Nuremberg. — *Rat*
1523 Henry VIII., *King*

    Wittenberg
1504 Spagnuoli, B.

    Dresden
1530 Dobneck, J. Erclerung

Straten, Derick van der
    Wesel
1546 Jonas, J. The true

Strauss, Nikolaus
    Prague
1596 Hàjek, V.

Stuchs, Hans
    Nuremberg
1529? Arznei
1530 Gechauf, T. Ein kurtze

Stuempfeld, Georg
    Freiberg (Saxony)
1583 Juncker, M.

Stuermer, Wolfgang
    Erfurt
1521 Roman Preacher
1523 †Briessmann, J.
1523 Plunderus, H.
1524 †Bodenstein, A. Eyn frage
1547 †Luther, M. [*Marginal Notes*]

Stuermer, Wolfgang, the *Younger*
    Leipzig
1575 Verzeichnis
1579 —

Sueberlich, Lorenz
  Wittenberg
  1597 Althamer, A. Conciliationes
  1600 Koythar, J.

Tack, Heinrich, Heirs of
  See **Fischer, Peter,** and **Tack, H.,** Heirs of

Thanner, Jakob
  Leipzig
  1499 Spagnuoli, B.
  1500? Virgilius Maro, P. [*Appendix. — Centos*]
  1507 Comedia
  1507 Juvenalis, D. J.
  1511 Picolomineus, D.

Ther Hoernen, Arnold
  Cologne
  1471? Augustine, Saint [*Supposititious Works. — Soliloquia*]
  1475? Formula

Tretter, Martin
  Frankfort on the Oder
  1502 Geiler, J. Arbor

Ulhart, Philip
  Augsburg
  1524 Langenwalde, H. von, and Schwenckfeld, C.
  1525 †Luther, M. [*Appendix*] Der Bock
  1530 Rome, *the City*
  1538 †Luther, M. [*Unterrichtung*]
  1538 Saltzman, G.
  1548 †Agricola, J. Fünfhundert
  1548 Amerbachius, V.
  1550? Linguae
  1550 Treflerus, F.
  1551 Brusch, C. Sacelli
  1563 Liturgies. — Missals

Ulhart, Philip, *the Younger*
  Lauingen
  1575 Meckhart, G.

Ulricher, Georg
  Strasburg
  1531 †Erasmus, D. [*Letters. — Single*]

Ungnad, Ivan
  Urach
  1562 Bible. — New Testament. [*Serbocroatian*]

Varnier, Hans
  Ulm
  1534 Franck, S.

Vietor, Hieronymus
  Vienna
  1515 Harmonius, J.
  Cracow
  1544 German Language

Voegelin, Ernst
  Leipzig
  1563 Strigelius, V. Arithmeticus
  1564 — Oratio
  1567 Walther, G.
  1570 Gordonio, B. de
  1572 Hesiod

Voltz, Nikolaus
  Frankfort on the Oder
  1592 Christian I., Elector
  1600 Gebhardt, J.

Wachter, Georg
  Nuremberg
  1529 Musler, J.

Wagner, Peter
  Nuremberg
  1495? †Folz, H.
  1499? Savonarola, G.
  1500 †Schneider, H. Wye

Wagner, Sebastian
  Worms
  1541 Liturgies. — Greek Rite. — Leitourgikon

Walde, Joachim
  Magdeburg
  1564 Amsdorff, N. von
  1564 Heshusius, T. [*Appendix*]
  1565 Wernerus, S.
  1570? Ilferus, L.

Waldkirch, Konrad von
  Basle
  1586 Ulmer, J. C.
  1588 Heidenstein, R.
  1593 Ars
  1597 Peerus, H.

Walther, Hans
  Magdeburg
  1530 Luther, M. [*Bekenntnis*]

Warneri, Peter
  Emmerich
  1575 D., I. L.

Warnfast, Hiob, *pseud.*
  Leyden
  1595 Nachenmoser, A.

Wechel, Andreas
  Frankfort on the Main
  1577 Wittekindus, Monachus
  1579 Du Tillet, J.
  1580 Casa, G. della
  1580 Walbeck, D. von
  1581 La Ramée, P. de

Wechel, Andreas, Heirs of
  Frankfort on the Main
  1584 Falloppio, G.
  1591 Porta, G. B. della

1592 La Ramée, P. de
1594 Estienne, H.
1599 Talaeus, A.

Wechel, Johann
Frankfort on the Main
1587 Picciolus, A.

Wechel, Johann, and **Fischer, P.**
Frankfort on the Main
1591 Variolus, C.

Weidlich, Andreas
Most
1596 Hájek, V.

Weinreich, Hans
Koenigsberg
1526 Heydeck, F. von
1548 Funck, J.
1548 Holtorpius, B.

Weiss, Hans
Berlin
1540 Agricola, J.
1541 Knaust, H.

Weissenburger, Johann
Nuremberg
1503 Stabius, J.
1504 †Schenck, H.
1507? Tockler, C.

Landshut
1515 Seneca, L. A. [*Supposititious Works*]
1516 Quercu, S. de
1520 Luther, M. [*Tractatus*]
1527 Seitz, A.

Weissenhorn, Alexander
Augsburg
1528 Huth, J.
1538 Johann, *von Eck.* Explanatio

Ingolstadt
1540 Johann, *von Eck.* Schutz red
1546 Hoffmeister, J.
1546 Montboissier, P. de
1548 Helding, M.

Weissenhorn, Alexander, II.
Ingolstadt
1550 Roth von Schreckenstein, H.
1568 Eisengrein, M. Beschaydne

Weissenhorn, Alexander, II. and Samuel
Ingolstadt
1551 Brusch, C. Monasteriorum
1551 Sedelius, W.
1567 Eisengrein, M. Ein frey

Weissenhorn, Alexander, III.
Ingolstadt
1571 Franck, C. Von dem ordentlichen
1576 Flaschius, S.

1577 Nase, J. Widereinwarnung
1577 Raspergerus, C.

Weissenhorn, Anna
Ingolstadt
1571 Franck, C. Von dem ordentlichen

Welack, Matthaeus
Wittenberg
1580 Thucydides
1584 Neander, V.

Welack, Matthaeus, *Widow of*
Wittenberg
1593 Hunnius, E. Calvinus

Wenssler, Michael
Basle
1481 Gratianus

Widemar, Nikolaus
See **Stoeckel, Jakob,** and **Widemar, N.**

Widmanstetter, Georg
Graz
1588 Ellander, B.

Willems, Conrad, *pseud.*
Münster
1533 Frith, J.

Willer, Elias
Frankfort on the Main
1600 Plinius Secundus, C.

Willer, Georg
Augsburg
1572 Metri, N. de
1572 Nostredame, M. de

Winkler, Andreas
Breslau
1542 Auctus, M.
1546 Valla, L.

Winter, Jakob
Magdeburg
1509 Wilsnack

Winterburg, Johann
Vienna
1509 Holandrinus, J.
1510? Rome. — Church. — Nicholas V.
1513 Fabri, W.

Winters, Conrad
Cologne
1478 Guido, *de Monte Rocherii*

Wipprecht, Leonhard
Jena
1590 Mylius, G. Eilff

Witte, Hans
Barth
1590 Muret, M. A.
1596 Caselius, J. Ad Casparem

Wittel, Martin
    Erfurt
    1595 Sternhals, J.
    1596 Sartorius, J.
    1600 Hess, E. F.

Woerli, Josias
    Augsburg
    1586 Venice

Wolf, Johannes
    Zurich
    1593, 94 Theodoret, *Bishop*

Wolff, Johann
    Frankfort on the Main
    1565 Solis, V.

Wolrab, Johann
    Bautzen
    1571 Leisentrit, J.

Wolrab, Michael
    Bautzen
    1581 Franck, C. Ein Trostbüchlein

Wolrab, Nikolaus
    Leipzig
    1538 Dobneck, J. De immensa

Wyriot, Nikolaus
    Strasburg
    1578 Strasburg. — *Academia*
    1579 Isaac, *Monachus*
    1581 Sturmius, J.

Zainer, Guenther
    Augsburg
    1473? Jerome, *Saint*

Zanach, Jacob
    Zerbst
    1597 Sturmius, H.

Zangarus, Joannes Baptista, *pseud.*
    Naples
    1585 Briegerus, J.

Zel, Ulrich
    Cologne
    1470? Mary, *the Blessed Virgin*

Zetzner, Lazarus
    Strasburg
    1593 Porta, G. B. della
    1596 Manuzio, P.

Zimmermann, Hans
    Augsburg
    1550? Kuenste
    1552 S., C. Ein Gebet

Zimmermann, Michael
    Vienna
    1555, 56 Reysacher, B.
    1562? Gienger, G.
    1564 Charopus, A.

Zoepfel, David
    Frankfort on the Main
    1555 †Melanchthon, P. *Historia*

Index II

CONSOLIDATED INDEX OF TOWNS
in the catalogue of 1962 and this Supplement
with dates of printers' and publishers' activity as represented in both volumes

Adlersberg
  Kohl, Hans — 1556
Alençon
  Du Bois, Simon — 1523
Allstedt
  Müntzer's Printer — 1524
Altenburg
  Kantz, Gabriel — 1524–6
Amberg
  Guldenmund, Wolf — 1558–60?
  Muelmarckart, Michael — 1578–88
  Forster, Michael — 1592–1600
Annaberg
  Guenther, Nikolaus — 1550
  Steinmetz, Georg — 1560?
Antwerp
  Hillen (Hoochstraten), Johannes — 1526–30
  Keyser, Martin de — 1528–32
  Hillen, Michiel — 1533
  Peetersen, Henrick — 1533–5
  Dumaeus, Govert — 1534
  Ruremunde, Christoffel van, *Widow of* — 1540–3
  Goinus, Antonius — 1543
  Mierdman, Steven — 1545–50
  Coppenius, Aegidius — 1557
  Plantin, Christoph — 1561–84
  Coppenius, Aegidius, *the Younger* — 1572–3
  Gallaeus, Philippus — 1572–5
  Silvius, Willem — 1576–8
  Rade, Gilles van den — 1578
  Coninx, Arnout — 1592

Arnhem
  Janson, Jan — 1597
Arnstadt
  Schmidt, Peter — 1548
Aschaffenburg
  Awerbach, Mathys — 1529
Augsburg
  Zainer, Guenther — 1468–80?
  Schuessler, Johann — 1470–3
  Ulrich & Afra, Monastery — 1470–6?
  Baemler, Johann — 1472–93
  Pflanzmann, Jodocus — 1475?
  Sorg, Anton — 1475–92
  Wiener, Johann — 1475?–80?
  Hohenwang, Ludwig — 1476?–7
  Keller, Johann — 1478–82
  Kaestlin, Hermann — 1479?–85
  Keller, Ambrosius — 1479
  Blaubirer, Johann — 1480–1
  Heyny, Christmann — 1481
  Schoensperger, Johann — 1482–1519
  Schoensperger, Johann, and Rueger, T. — 1482
  Ruegerin, Anna — 1484
  Ratdolt, Erhard — 1487–1516
  Berger, Peter — 1488–9
  Feger, Theobald — 1488
  Schobser, Hans — 1488–1500?
  Schnaitter, Christoph — 1493
  Schaur, Johann — 1494–6
  Zeissenmayr, Lucas — 1494–1502
  Froschauer, Hans — 1495–1523
  Rynmann, Johann — 1497–1522
  Otmar, Johann — 1502–15
  Schoensperger, Johann, *the Younger* — 1502–22

Otmar, Johann, and Oeglin, E.	1505
Oeglin, Erhard	1506–20
Widmann, Johann	1507–15
Oeglin, Erhard, and Nadler, J.	1508
Diemar, Georg	1510–14
Oswaldt, Johann	1510–1
Schregel, Sextus	1511
Sittich, Johann	1511–2
Otmar, Silvan	1513–38
Miller, Johann	1514–20
Ratdolt, Georg	1515–20
Grimm, Sigmund, and Wirsung, M.	1518–22
Hans, *von Erfurt*	1518–20
Nadler, Joerg	1519?–24
Ramminger, Melchior	1520–40
Grimm, Sigmund	1521–5
Adelmann, Bernard	1522
Steiner, Heinrich	1522–48
Ulhart, Philipp	1522–66
Denecker, Jobst	1523–44?
Ruff, Simprecht	1523–6
Weissenhorn, Alexander	1528–39
Schwarz, Hayyim	1533–44
Schwartzenberger, Johann	1534
Sand, Niclas vom	1535
Elchinger, Matthaeus	1540?
Hofer, Hans	1540?
Kriegstein, Melchior	1540–55?
Otmar, Valentin	1541–55
Deygerus, Joan. Valentinus	1548
Zimmermann, Hans	1549–70
Gegler, Hans	1554–8
Gegler, Agathe	1559?
Franck, Matthaeus	1560?–70?
Meyerpeck, Wolfgang, and Sorg, J.	1566
Manger, Michael	1567–1600
Ulhart, Philipp, *the Younger*	1568–79
Franck, Matthaeus, *Heirs of*	1570?
Gastel, Christoph	1570?
Rogel, Hans	1571–80
Schoenig, Valentin	1572–1600
Willer, Georg	1572–83
Reinheckel, Andreas	1579
Schultes, Hans	1580?–1600
Woerli, Josias	1580?–9
Hofer, Hans, *Heirs of*	1584
Kaeppeler, Bartholomaeus	1592–6
Pinus, Ad insigne	1594–1600
Dilbaum, Samuel	1595
Custos, Dominicus	1599–1600
Willerus, Elias	1600

Baden

Beck, Reinhard	1511

Bamberg

Printer of the 36-line Bible	1460?
Sensenschmidt, Johann	1481–7
Sensenschmidt, Johann, and Petzensteiner, Heinrich	1482–91
Sensenschmidt, Laurentius, Pfeil, J., and Petzensteiner, H.	1491
Sporer, Hans	1491–3
Bernecker, Hans, and Ayrer, M.	1493
Pfeil, Johann	1498–1518
Schoener, Johann	1521
Erlinger, Georg	1522–7
Wagner, Johann	1577–80
Horitz, Anton	1591–9

Barth

Seitner, Andreas	1584
Witte, Hans	1588–96

Basle

Ruppel, Berthold	1468?–89
Biel, Friedrich	1472?
Flach, Martin	1472?–86?
Wenssler, Michael	1472–91
Richel, Bernard	1474?–82
Amerbach, Johann	1476?–1510
Ruppel, Berthold, and Wenssler, M.	1479?
Besicken, Johann	1482–3?
Kollicker, Peter	1483–5
Printer of Modus legendi abbreviaturas	1484–5?
Kesler, Nikolaus	1486–1509
Hohenwang, Ludwig	1487
Wenssler, Michael, and Jacobus, *de Kilchen*	1488
Furter, Michael	1489?–1517
Adam, *von Speyer*	1490
Helmut, Andreas	1490
Ysenhut, Lienhart	1490
Froben, Johann	1491–1527
Wolff, Jakob, *de Pforzheim*	1492–1519
Bergmann, Johann	1494–9
Lachner, Wolfgang	1495
Petri, Johann, and Froben, J.	1496–9
Amerbach, Johann, and Froben, J.	1500
Amerbach, Johann, Petri, J., and Froben, J.	1502–12
Lamparter, Nikolaus	1505–19
Petri, Johann	1506
Petri, Adam	1509–28
Gengenbach, Pamphilus	1513?–25?
Berlaer, Theo.	1515
Froben, Johann Erasmus	1517
Cratander, Andreas	1518–37
Cratander, Andreas, and Kruffter, S.	1518
Wolff, Thomas	1519–34
Curio, Valentin	1520–30

Froben, Hieronymus	1520–59
Bebel, Johann	1523–38
Wattenschnee, Johann	1524–40
Herwagen, Johann	1526–55
Cratander, Andreas, and Bebel, J.	1527–33
Faber, Johann	1527–9
Froben, Hieronymus, and Herwagen, J.	1528–38
Froben, Hieronymus, Herwagen, J., and Episcopius, N.	1528–31
Herwagen, Johann, and Froben, J. E.	1528–38
Petri, Heinrich	1528–78
Froben, Hieronymus, and Episcopius, N.	1530–64
Bebel, Johann, and Isengrin, M.	1531–50
Isengrin, Michael	1532–57
Walder, Johann	1533–41
Resch, Conrad	1535
Westheimer, Bartholomaeus	1535?–47
Lasius, Balthasar, and Platter, T.	1536–9
Schauber, Lux	1536
Westheimer, Bartholomaeus, and Brylinger, N.	1536–7
Winter, Robert	1537–46
Brylinger, Nikolaus	1538–64
Cratander, Andreas, Heirs of	1538–52
Isengrin, Michael, and Petri, H.	1538–46
Lasius, Balthasar	1538–41
Platter, Thomas	1538–44
Oporinus, Johann	1539–68
Deck, Rudolf	1540?–4
Westheimer, Bartholomaeus, and Winter, R.	1540
Hospinianus, Leonardus	1541
Winter, Robert, and Platter, T.	1541
Brylinger, Nikolaus, and Franck, S.	1542
Curio, Hieronymus	1542–63
Beck, Reinhard.the Younger	1543–4
Oporinus, Johann, and Winter, R.	1545
Kuendig, Jakob	1546–63
Brylinger, Nikolaus, and Oporinus, J.	1549–61
Brylinger, Nikolaus, and Staehelin, B.	1551
Lucius, Ludwig	1552–7
Episcopius, Nikolaus, the Younger	1553–63
Herwagen, Johann, and Oporinus, J.	1553
Harscher, Matthias	1554
Staehelin, Bartholomaeus	1554–7
Herwagen, Johann, the Younger	1555–63
Derbilley, Jacob	1556–8
Herwagen, Johann, the Elder and the Younger	1556
Stella, Michael Martin	1556
Herwagen, Johann, the Younger, and Brand, B.	1557–8
Isengrin, Michael, Widow of	1558–60
Perna, Peter	1558–82
Ringysen, Gabriel	1559
Oporinus, Johann, and Herwagen, J., the Younger	1560–4
Guarin, Thomas	1561–91
Gymnicus, Arnoldus	1561–2
Petri, Heinrich, and Perna, P.	1561–3
Brylinger, Nikolaus, and Russinger, M.	1563–7
Oporinus, Johann, and Episcopius, N.	1564
Brylinger, Nikolaus, Heirs of	1565–82
Episcopius, Eusebius and Nikolaus, the Younger	1565
Oporinus, Johann, and Froben, Ambrosius and Aurelius	1565
Oporinus, Johann, and Herwagen, J., the Younger, Heirs of	1565
Queck, Paul	1565–70
Froben, Ambrosius and Aurelius	1566–87
Oporinus, Johann, and Episcopius, Eusebius	1566
Oporinus, Johann, and Perna, P.	1566
Episcopius, Eusebius	1567–94
Franck, Bartholomaeus	1567–8
Apiarius, Samuel	1568–90
Episcopius, Eusebius and Nikolaus, the Younger, Heirs of	1568–95
Franck, Bartholomaeus, and Queck, P.	1568
Oporinus, Johann, Heirs of	1568–91
Henricpetri, Sebastian	1569–1600
Gemusaeus, Polycarp and Hieronymus, and Han, B.	1570–1
Henricpetri, Sixtus	1570–1
Koenig, Samuel	1570
Perna, Peter, and Dietrich, Theobaldus	1570

Davantes, Pierre	1572
Christoffel, *von Sichem*	1573–7
Ostein, Daniel and Leonhard	1575
Froben, Ambrosius	1578–85?
Ostein, Leonhard	1578–92
Ziphroni, Israel	1580–3
Perna, Peter, *Heirs of*	1583–7
Waldkirch, Konrad von	1583–1600
Han, Balthasar, and Gemusaeus, H.	1584
Froben, Hieronymus, *the Younger*	1585
Foillet, Jakob	1593
Apiarius, Samuel, *Heirs of*	1595?
Gemusaeus, Hieronymus	1595
Schroeter, Johann	1597–1600
Jacob ben Abraham, *of Miedrzyrzee*	1600

Bautzen
Wolrab, Nikolaus	1555–60
Wolrab, Johann	1561–71
Wolrab, Michael	1573–98

Berlin
Weiss, Hans	1540–2
Thurneysser, Leonhard	1574–6
Hentzke, Michael	1578–80
Hentzke, Michael, *Widow of*	1580
Hentzke, Michael, *Heirs of*	1581
Voltz, Nikolaus	1582–9

Berne
Apiarius, Matthias	1537–54
Apiarius, Samuel	1554–8
Im Hof, Vinzenz	1583
Le Preux, Jean	1600

Beromuenster
Heliae, Helias	1470–3

Blaubeuren
Mancz, Conrad	1477

Bonn
Muelen, Lorenz von der	1543–5

Bremen
Mellerstadt, Caspar de	1511
Gloichstein, Dietrich	1579–85
Peters, Bernhard	1589–94

Breslau
Elyan, Caspar	1475
Baumgarten, Conrad	1503–4
Klosse, Franz	1512
Dyon, Adam	1519–30
Libisch, Kaspar	1523–4
Winkler, Andreas	1542–50?
Scharffenberg, Crispin	1554–75?
Scharffenberg, Johann	1577–88
Baumann, Georg	1590–1600

Wolcke, Andreas	1593–5
Albertus, David	1600

Bruenn
Stahel, Conrad, and Preunlein, Mathias	1495

Bruex See Most

Bruges
Goltz, Hubert	1557

Brunntrut See Porrentruy

Brunswick
Dorn, Hans	1506–20
Goltbeck, Andreas	1539

Buda
Kaym, Urban	1515–8

Burgdorf
Printer of Jacobus de Clusa	1475

Coburg
Baer, Hans	1530
Schnauss, Cyriacus	1546–52
Kroener, Valentin	1589–97

Colmar
Farckall, Amandus	1523

Cologne
Zel, Ulrich	1465?–1500?
Printer of Dares	1470?–2
Printer of Dictys	1470?–1
Ther Hoernen, Arnold	1470–82
Koelhoff, Johann	1472–93
Printer of Augustinus, De fide	1472–3
Printer of Flores S. Augustini	1472?–3
Printer of Historia S. Albani	1472?–4?
Solidi, Johann	1472?–4?
Gotz, Nicolaus	1474–80?
Bartholomaeus, *de Unkel*	1475–85?
Gops, Goiswin	1475
Printer of the Sarum Breviary	1475?
Winters, Conrad	1475?–82
Guldenschaff, Johann	1477–90
Petrus, *de Olpe*	1477–8
Quentel, Heinrich	1479–1501
Printer of Dialogus Salomonis	1480?–1
Ten Raem, Gerardus	1480?
Bell, Johannes de	1482
Ludwig, *von Renchen*	1483–1505
Theodoricus	1485
Conradus, *de Bopardia*	1486
Ther Hoernen, Peter	1486
Koelhoff, Johann, *the Younger*	1494–1500?
Bumgart, Hermann	1496–1518

Landen, Johann	1496–1515
Cornelis, *de Zierikzee*	1498?–1515?
Retro Minores	1497–1504
Quentel, Heinrich, *Sons of*	1501–19
Spot, Roloff	1501
Martin, *von Werden*	1504–16
Heinrich, *von Neuss*	1507?–22
Gutschaiff, Hermann	1512–3?
Hornken, Ludwig	1514–19
Arnt, *von Aich*	1515?–25?
Cervicornus, Eucharius	1517–41
Gymnich, Johann, I.	1517–44
Caesar, Konrad	1518–24
Caesar, Nikolaus	1518
Elisabeth, *von Werden*	1518
Hornken, Ludwig, and Hittorp, G.	1518–20
Soter, Johannes	1518–35
Cervicornus, Eucharius, and Fuchs, H.	1520–1
Krufter, Servatius	1520?–30
Quentel, Peter	1520–46
Fuchs, Hero	1522–39
Hittorp, Gottfried	1522–42
Birckmann, Arnold	1525–32
Melchior, *von Neuss*	1525–50
Birckmann, Franz	1526–9
Arnt, *von Aich, Heirs of*	1529–33
Prael, Johannes	1530–7
Johann, *von Kempen*	1531–7
Dorsten, Johann von	1532
Gennep, Jaspar von	1532–63
Johann, *von Aich*	1532?–43
Johann, *von Remunde*	1540
Schoenstenius, Johannes	1540
Gymnich, Johann I., *Heirs of*	1544
Gymnich, Martin	1545–50?
Quentel, Johann	1546–51
Birckmann, Arnold, *Widow of*	1547–50
Caesar, Anton	1550?
Hensbergius, Gerhardus	1550
Mameranus, Heinrich	1550–2
Fabritius, Walther	1552–64
Johann, *von Neuss*	1552–5
Quentel, Johann, *Heirs of*	1552–6
Sylvius, Lambertus	1552
Birckmann, Arnold, *Heirs of*	1553–81
Horst, Peter	1554–84
Cholinus, Maternus	1555–87
Soter, Jacobus	1555–61
Bathen, Johannes	1556–7
Birckmann, Arnold, *the Younger*	1559–62
Birckmann, Johann	1559–73
Calenius, Gerwin, and Quentel, *Heirs of*	1560–97
Cervicornus, Gottfried	1561–77
Birckmann, Johann, and Richwin, W.	1562–3
Richwin, Werner	1562–4
Cervicornus, Gottfried, and Baum, T.	1563
Caesar, Anton and Arnold	1564
Baum, Theodor	1565–85
Gymnich, Johann, *the Younger*	1565–96
Monocerotis, Ad intersignium	1565–70
Fabritius, Walther, and Gymnich, J., III.	1567
Heinrich, *von Aich*	1567–77
Renerus, *Tremonensis*	1567
Schreiber, Nikolaus	1567–98
Virendunck, Gerard	1567–8
Birckmann, Johann, and Baum, T.	1569
Graminaeus, Theodor	1569–72
Weiss, Jakob	1569
Caesar, Arnold	1570?
Bohmberg, Nikolaus	1573–80
Wildt, Hans	1573
Alectorius, Ludwig	1575
Alectorius, Ludwig, and Soter, Jacobus, *Heirs of*	1576–80
Birckmann, Johann, *Widow of*	1576
Ewald, Daniel	1576
Ordenbach, Martin	1576
Gottfried, *von Kempen*	1577–97
Rutus, Jaspar	1577
Soter, Jacobus, *Heirs of*	1579–82
Wierdt, Thomas von	1580
Birckmann, *House of*	1582–1600
Hohenberg, Franz	1582
Cholinus, Goswin	1585–1600
Gerhard, *von Kempen*	1585
Mylius, Arnold	1585–1600
Nettesheim, Heinrich	1585–95
Gottfried, *von Kempen*, and Nettesheim, H.	1588
Grevenbruch, Gerhard	1588–1600
Andreae, Lambert	1590–7
Falckenburg, Heinrich	1590–7
Luetzenkirchen, Wilhelm	1593–9
Bussemacher, Johann	1594–1600
Keschedt, Peter	1594–7
Buchholtz, Bertram	1595–8
Quentel, Arnold	1595–1600
Gymnich, Johann, *the Younger, Heirs of*	1596
Haack, Petrus	1596
Gymnich, Johann, III.	1597–1600
Christoffel, Johann	1598–9
Gottfried, *von Kempen, Widow of*	1598
Gymnich, Johann, *the Younger, Widow of*	1598–9

Falckenburg, Heinrich,
  Widow of — 1599
Hemmerden, Stephan — 1599
Hoberg, Hermann — 1599
Walter, Bernard — 1599–1600
Hierat, Anton — 1600

Constance
Schaeffler, Johann — 1507–24
Spitzenberg, Joerg — 1529?–31
Fagius, Paul — 1543–4
Romaetsch, Balthasar — 1545
Straub, Leonhard — 1589–98
Kalt, Nikolaus — 1597–1600

Cracow
Scharffenberg, M. — 1532
Vietor, Hieronymus — 1544

Culmbach
Retsch, Thomas, and
  Haberklee, Willibald — 1551–2?

Danzig
Rhode, Franz — 1541–58
Weinreich, Hans — 1555
Menius, Matthias — 1572
Rhode, Jacob — 1576–1600

Deventer
Steenberch, Simon — 1559

Dillingen
Mayer, Sebald — 1550?–76
Schick, Christophorus — 1560
Mayer, Johann — 1580–95

Dortmund
Soter, Melchior — 1549–50
Sartor, Albert — 1574

Dresden
Emser's Printer — 1524–5
Silvius, M. P. — 1526
Stoeckel, Wolfgang — 1526–39
Stoeckel, Mathes — 1550–97
Wolrab, Nikolaus — 1553
Bergen, Gimel — 1575–99
Morgenrodt, Andreas — 1583
Spindelmeyer, Hans — 1583
Urban, Mathes — 1583
Saxony, Hofdruckerei — 1589
Schuetz, Hieronymus — 1595

Düsseldorf
Bathen, Jakob — 1555–7
Buys, Albert, and
  Oridryus, Johann — 1563
Buys, Albert — 1583–95

Durlach
Keibs, Nikolaus — 1512?
Kobian, Valentin — 1530

Echzell *See* **Eychen Zell**

Eichstedt
Reyser, Michel — 1484–8

Eilenburg
Widemar, Nikolaus — 1522–4
Stoeckel, Jakob — 1524–30
Stoeckel, Jakob, and
  Widemar, N. — 1524

Eisleben
Baerwald, Jakob — 1554
Gaubisch, Urban — 1554–93
Petri, Andreas — 1565–92
Hoernig, Bartholomaeus — 1595–1600

Eltville
Bechtermuentze, Nicolaus — 1469

Emden
Erven, Gilles van der — 1554–66
Mijerdmann, Steven, and
  Gailliaert, Johann — 1556–8
Kinderen, Lenaart der — 1558–65
Biestkens, Nikolaus — 1559–78
Gailliaert, Willem — 1559–68
Urban, *van Collen* — 1560–4
Goebens, Goosen — 1578–9
Oostfreese, Eewardus — 1584

Emmerich
Warneri, Peter — 1575

Erfurt
Wider, Paulus — 1482
Printer of Aristeas — 1483
Printer of Bollanus — 1486?–90?
Printer of Hundorn — 1494–5?
Sporer, Hans — 1497–1500
Paul, *von Hachenburg* — 1499–1501
Schenck, Wolfgang — 1500–7
Sertorius, Enricus — 1501–2
Marschalk, Nicolaus — 1502
Stuermer, Wolfgang — 1506–51
Striblita, Sebaldus — 1510
Knappe, Hans — 1511–23
Maler, Matthes — 1512–35
Buchfuehrer, Michael — 1521–3
Loersfeld, Johann — 1523–6
Sachse, Melchior — 1525–47
Rauscher, Andreas — 1531
Golthammer, Christoffel — 1539
Dolgen, Merten von — 1543–71
Stuermer, Gervasius — 1547–56
Stuermer, Gervasius and
  Wolfgang — 1549–50
Sachsin, Barbara — 1551
Baumann, Georg — 1557–95
Portenbach, Jeremias — 1564
Dreher, Konrad — 1572
Sachse, Melchior, *the
  Younger* — 1573–88
Beck, Johann — 1580–99

Mechler, Esaias	1580–90
Riswick, Otto à	1585–96
Stockheim, Caspar	1585
Wittel, Martin	1585–1600
Preusser, Konrad Heinrich	1587
Singe, Jacob	1592–4
Zimmer, Zacharias	1592

Esslingen
Fyner, Conrad	1472–8

Ettlingen
Kobian, Valentin	1530–2

Eychen Zell
Schlot, Bartholomaeus	1582

Frankenthal
Barsages, Jean	1578

Frankfort on the Main
Murner, Beatus	1511–2
Egenolff, Christian	1531–55
Braubach, Peter	1540–67
Jacob, Cyriacus	1541–51
Guelfferich, Hermann	1543–54
Egenolff, Christian, Heirs of	1555–99
Gran, Jobst	1555
Guelfferich, Hermann, Heirs of	1555
Zoepfel, David	1555–62
Han, Weigand	1556–61
Feyerabend, Sigmund	1559–90
Han, Weigand, and Feyerabend, S.	1560
Zoepfel, David, Rasch, J., and Feyerabend, S.	1560–2
Han, Weigand, and Rabe, G.	1561–6
Bassée, Nikolaus	1562–1600
Han, Weigand, Rabe, G., and Feyerabend, S.	1562
Lucius, Ludwig	1562–73
Rabe, Georg, and Feyerabend, S.	1562–79
Zoepfel, David, and Rasch, Johann	1562–3
Feyerabend, Sigmund, and Hueter, S.	1563–82
Hueter, Simon	1563–8
Lechler, Johann	1563–4
Rabe, Georg, Feyerabend, S., and Han, W., Heirs of	1563–71
Rabe, Georg, and Han, W., Heirs of	1563–72
Lechler, Martin	1564–93
Rabe, Georg	1564–80
Schmidt, Peter	1565–95
Wolff, Johann	1565–72
Berck, Wilhelm	1566–68
Schmidt, Peter, and Feyerabend, S.	1566
Feyerabend, Hieronymus	1568–79
Han, Weigand, Heirs of	1568–74
Braubach, Peter, Heirs of	1570
Reffeler, Paul	1570?–9
Schmidt, Johann	1570?–80
Corthois, Anthony	1571
Schmidt, Peter, and Feyerabend, H.	1571
Bassée, Nikolaus, and Beller, Johann	1573
Bassée, Nikolaus, and Feyerabend, S.	1573–82
Lonicer, Adam, Cnipius, J., and Steinmeyer, P.	1573–84
Schmidt, Johann, and Lechler, M.	1573
Feyerabend, Johann	1574–99
Feyerabend, Sigmund Carl	1574–87
Han, Kilian	1574
Wechel, Andreas	1574–82
Bassée, Franz	1577–8
Feyerabend, Johann and Sigmund	1578–80
Fischer, Peter	1578–96
Feyerabend, Sigmund, and Fischer, G.	1579
Haans, Hartmann	1579–80
Spiess, Johann	1580–1600
Cambier, Robert	1581–6
Corvinus, Christoph	1582–5
Wechel, Andreas, Heirs of	1582–1600
Wechel, Johann	1582–93
Humm, Wendel	1583–8
Tack, Heinrich	1585–90
Feyerabend, S., Tack, H., and Fischer, P.	1586
Marne, Claude, and Aubry, Jean	1587–1600
Cnipius, Barbara, and Steinmeyer, M.	1589
Bassée, Johann	1590
Brachfeld, Paul	1590–1600
Bry, Theodor de	1590–8
Castelvitreus, Jacobus	1590
Fischer, Peter, and Tack, Heinrich, Heirs of	1590
Feyerabend, Sigmund, Heirs of	1591–7
Wechel, Johann, and Fischer, P.	1591–2
Wechel, Johann, Widow of	1593–4
Humm, Wendel, Heirs of	1594
Kopff, Peter	1594–1600
Osthausius, Henricus	1594
Palthenius, Zacharias	1594–1600
Sauer, Johann	1594–1600
Kollitz, Johann	1595–8
Bry, Johann Theodor de and Johann Israel de	1596–1600
Fischer, Peter, Widow of	1596
Fischer, Peter, Heirs of	1596–1600

Becker, Matthaeus	1598–1600
Cambier, Robert, *Heirs of*	1598–1600
Richter, Wolfgang	1598–1600
Steinius, Nicolaus	1598
Beatus, Romanus	1599–1600
Bry, Theodor de, *Widow of and Son*	1599–1600
Draudius, Georgius, and Angelus, P.	1599
Kollitz, Johann, *Widow of*	1599
Lechler, Johann, *the Younger*	1599
Rosa, Jonas	1599–1600
Hartmann, Melchior	1600
Willer, Elias	1600

Frankfort on the Oder

Tretter, Martin	1502
Lacher, Ambros	1506
Lamparter, Nikolaus, and Murrer, Balthasar	1507–8
Baumgarten, Conrad	1509
Schreck, Laurentius	1509
Jamer, Johann	1510–33
Wolrab, Nikolaus	1548–9
Eichorn, Johann	1549–80
Rauchart, Ulrich	1571
Eichorn, Andreas	1580–1600
Voltz, Nikolaus	1592–1600
Hartmann, Johann and Friedrich	1595–6
Hartmann, Friedrich	1597–8
Hartmann, Johann	1598

Freiberg (Saxony)

Kachelofen, Conrad	1495
Meyerpeck, Wolfgang	1553
Hoffmann, Georg	1581–94
Stuempfeld, Georg	1583

Freiburg im Breisgau

Fischer, Kilianus	1491–6?
Riedrer, Friedrich	1493–9
Schott, Johann	1503
Woerlin, Johann	1522–3?
Faber, Johann	1529–40
Graf, Stephan Melechus	1543–79
Boeckler, Martin	1593–8

Freiburg (Switzerland)

Gemperlin, Abraham	1585–96
Maess, Wilhelm	1598–9

Geneva

Stoer, Jacques	1574
Vignon, Eustathius	1588–92
Tournes, Jean de	1590–7

Goerlitz

Scharffenberg, Crispin	1548
Fritsch, Ambrosius	1568–93
Rhambau, Hans, *the Younger*	1595–9

Graz

Bartsch, Zacharias	1572
Widmanstetter, Georg	1587–1600
Schmidt, Hans	1592

Greifswald

Ferber, Augustin	1582–98

Grimma

Stoeckel, Wolfgang	1522

Güstrow

Ferber, Augustin	1582

Hagenau

Gran, Heinrich	1489–1527
Anshelm, Thomas	1516–23
Setzer, Johann	1523–32
Farckall, Amandus	1525
Seltz, Wilhelm	1528–9
Kobian, Valentin	1532–7
Setzer, Johann, *Heirs of*	1533–4
Braubach, Peter	1534–6

Halberstadt

Stuchs, Lorenz	1520–3
Trutebul, Ludwig	1522
Kote, Georg	1595

Halle

Stoeckel, Wolfgang	1520
Frischmut, Hans	1543
Lieskau, Achatius	1591–2
Graeber, Paul	1597–8

Hamburg

Borchard, Johann and Thomas	1491
Hermann, *of Emden*	1509
Richolff, Georg, *the Younger*	1529–30
Rhode, Franz	1536–7
Loew, Joachim	1548–58
Wickradt, Johann	1557–65
Wegener, Nikolaus	1570–5
Binder, Hans	1582–7
Sachse, Johann	1587
Wolff, Jacob	1588–91
Binder, Henrick	1589–97
Wolff, Jacob, *Heirs of*	1591–2
Steinbach, Heinrich	1592–3
Jandeck, Ernst	1593–4
Kretzer, Paul	1593
Dortt, François van	1596
Lucius, Jacob, *the Younger*	1596–7
Kretzer, Abraham	1597
Ohr, Philipp von	1597–9
Wolder, Theodosius	1597–8
Binder, Henrick, *Heirs of*	1598
Moeller, Hermann	1599

Hanau

Antonius, Wilhelm	1593–1600

Hanover
Ruedem, Henning   1544–8
Heddernheim
Schwarz, Hayyim   1546
Heidelberg
Printers of Lindelbach   1485–6
Knoblochtzer, Heinrich   1488–1501
Misch, Friedrich   1488
Stadelberger, Jakob   1510–15
Aperbacchus, Johann   1548
Kohl, Hans   1558–9
Kohl, Hans, *Widow of*   1560
Lucius, Ludwig   1560–2
Mayer, Johann   1563–76
Schirat, Michael, and
  Mayer, Johann   1563
Schirat, Michael   1567–75
Harnisch, Matthaeus   1573–7
Mareschal, Jean   1576–88
Mueller, Jacob   1576–85
Spiess, Johann   1582–4
Mueller, Jacob, and Avena,
  Heinrich   1585
Commelinus, Hieronymus   1587–1600
Sanctandriana Officina   1588–94
Smesmann, Abraham   1589–96
Harnisch, Josua   1593
Smesmann, Abraham,
  Heirs of   1595
Justus, Georg   1596
Mareschal, Peter   1596
Loew, Christoph   1597–1600
Rollan PP   1597
Loew, Christoph, and
  Lancelot, Johann   1598
Cambierius, Andreas   1599–1600
Voegelin, Gotthard   1600

Heilbronn
Stir, Sigismund   1507

Heinrichstadt *See* **Wolfenbuettel**

Helmstedt
Lucius, Jakob   1579–97
Brandes, Luedeke   1591
Brandes, Luedeke, *Heirs of*   1594–1600
Lucius, Jakob, *Heirs of*   1598
Lucius, Jakob, *the Younger*   1598–1600

Henricopolis *See* **Wolfenbuettel**

Herborn
Corvinus, Christoph   1586–1600

Hof
Pfeilschmidt, Matthaeus   1581–98

Ingolstadt
Printer of Lescher,
  Rhetorica   1485?–7
Printer of Celtes, Epitoma   1492

Wirffel, Georg, and Ayrer,
  Marx   1497
Lutz, Andreas   1519–23?
Apianus, Peter and Georg   1526–32
Apianus, Georg   1527
Focker, Jacobus   1530–5
Krapff, Georg   1530–7
Apianus, Peter   1534–40
Weissenhorn, Alexander   1540–9
Weissenhorn, Alexander II.   1550–69
Weissenhorn, Alexander II.
  and Samuel   1550–70
Weissenhorn, Alexander
  III.   1570–7
Weissenhorn, Anna   1571–4
Sartorius, David   1575–96
Weissenhorn, *Heirs of*   1577
Eder, Wolfgang   1578–95
Sartorius, Adam   1596–1600
Eder, Elisabeth   1597–8
Angermayer, Andreas   1599–1600

Innsbruck
Hoeller, Ruprecht   1554–8
Baur, Hans   1583–96

Isny
Fagius, Paul   1541–2

Jena
Roedinger, Christian   1554–7
Rebart, Thomas   1558–67
Roedinger, Christian, *Heirs
  of*   1558
Richzenhan, Donat   1561–1600
Roedinger, Christian, *the
  Younger*   1569
Huettich, Guenther   1571
Rebart, Thomas, *Widow of*   1572
Rebart, Thomas, *Heirs of*   1575
Steinmann, Tobias   1585–1600
Wipprecht, Leonhard   1590
Trosterus, Jacobus, and
  Knoperus, Nicolaus   1591
Gruner, Salomon   1595
Richzenhan, Salomon   1600

Juliusfriedenstedt *See* **Wolfenbuettel**

Jungbunzlau
Sturm, Jindřich   1531

Kassel
Wessel, Wilhelm   1598

Kirchehrenbach
Schoener, Johann   1524

Kirchheim
Reinhard, Marcus   1490?–1
Printer of Sankt Brandons
  Leben   1499

Koenigsberg
Weinreich, Hans   1524–53

Lufft, Hans 1550–3
Augezdecky, Alexander 1553
Daubmann, Hans 1555–69
Daubmann, Hans, Heirs of 1574–5
Osterberger, Georg 1575–1600

Lahr
Schaffner, Wilhelm 1514–5

Laibach
Mannel, Hans 1578–9

Landshut
Wurm, Hans 1501
Weissenburger, Johann 1513–31
Apianus, Martin 1574

Lauingen
Saltzer, Emanuel 1564–9
Ulhart, Philip, the Younger 1575
Reinmichel, Leonhard 1580–1600

Leipzig
Brandis, Marcus 1481–4
Kachelofen, Conrad 1485?–1516
Printer of Capotius (M. Landsberg?) 1486–90?
Brandis, Moritz 1488–90?
Schmiedhoefer, Johann 1489?–90?
Landsberg, Martin 1490?–1522
Arnoldus, de Colonia 1492–5
Boettiger, Gregorius 1492–6?
Lotter, Melchior 1495–1537
Stoeckel, Wolfgang 1496–1525
Thanner, Jakob 1498–1529
Kelner, Georg 1511
Kuna, Heinricus 1512
Schumann, Valentin 1514–40
Salomo, Blasius 1519
Schmidt, Nickel 1522–39
Blum, Michael 1525–49
Wolrab, Nikolaus 1537–51
Baerwald, Jakob 1542–70
Bapst, Valentin 1543–57
Guenther, Wolfgang 1549–54
Hantzsch, Georg 1550–60
Bapst, Valentin, Heirs of 1557–60
Rhambau, Hans 1557–80
Schmidt, Lorenz 1558
Voegelin, Ernst 1560–76
Apel, Jacob, the Elder 1570
Baerwald, Jakob, Heirs of 1570–84
Schneider, Andreas 1570–5
Steinmann, Hans 1571–88
Martorff, Johann 1572
Beyer, Johann 1575–96
Stuermer, Wolfgang, the Younger 1575–89
Bock, Niclas 1579–80
Grosse, Henning 1580–1600
Boerner, Johann 1581–92
Deffner, Georg 1581–6
Hueter, Simon 1581

Nerlich, Nikolaus 1582–1600
Baerwald, Zacharias 1585–96
Lamberg, Abraham 1587–1600
Steinmann, Hans, Heirs of 1588–90
Apel, Jacob, the Younger 1590–8
Voegelin, Ernst, Heirs of 1590–1600?
Lantzenberger, Michael 1591–1600
Voegelin, Valentin 1592–6
Schnellboltz, Franz 1597–9
Schuerer, Thomas 1597
Voigt, Bartholomaeus 1597–1600
Strach, Vinzenz 1598

Lemgo
Grothe, Franz 1563
Schlot, Bartholomaeus 1578
Grothe, Konrad 1582–8

Lich
Erben, Nikolaus 1597–8
Ketzel, Wolfgang, and Nebenius, C. 1600?

Liegnitz
Schneider, Nikolaus 1594–9

Lindau
Brem, Johann Ludwig 1595

London
Wyer, Richard 1548
Lynne, Walter 1550
Day, John 1554

Lucerne
Murner, Thomas 1527–8

Luebeck
Brandis, Lucas 1475–80?
Snel, Johann 1480?–5?
Brandis, Matthaeus 1485?–6?
Arndes, Stephan 1487–1507
Poppy Printer 1488–1500
Arndes, Stephan, Heirs of 1520
Ballhorn, Johann 1531–46
Richolff, Georg, the Younger 1547–68
Kroeger, Aswer 1564–7
Ballhorn, Johann, the Younger 1575–84
Albrecht, Lorenz 1586–1600

Lueneburg
Luce, Johann 1493
Stern, Hans 1590

Lyons
Sacon, Jacques 1509–20
Lescuyer, Bernard 1514
Myt, Jacques 1517
Pesnot, Charles 1582

Magdeburg
Ghotan, Bartholomaeus 1480–3
Ravenstein, Albrecht, and Westphal, Joachim 1483

Grashove, Johann	1486
Koch, Simon	1486–93
Brandis, Moritz	1490?–1500
Winter, Jakob	1507–9
Winter, Jakob, *Heirs of*	1513
Knappe, Hans, *the Younger*	1524
Oettinger, Heinrich	1525?–31
Barth, Hans	1528
Lotter, Michael	1529–56
Walther, Hans	1530–53
Roedinger, Christian	1540?–53
Lor, Hans	1551
Kirchner, Ambrosius	1557–60
Kirchner, Wolfgang	1560–82
Walde, Joachim	1563–70?
Ghene, Andreas	1567–95
Ghene, Andreas, and Ross, W.	1569
Ross, Wilhelm	1577–97
Francke, Johann	1579–1600
Gisecke, Mathias	1579
Meissner, Johann, and Walde, Joachim, *Heirs of*	1580
Donat, Paul	1584–99
Kirchner, Ambrosius, *the Younger*	1584–1600
Duncker, Andreas	1597–1600
Ghene, Andreas, *Heirs of*	1597
Boetcher, Johann	1599
Meissner, Johann	1600
Seitner, Andreas	1600

Mainz

Printer of the 42-line Bible	1455
Fust, Johann, and Schoeffer, P.	1457–66
Gutenberg, Johann	1460
Schoeffer, Peter	1467–1502
Neumeister, Johann	1479
Printer of the Prognostication	1480?
Reuwich, Erhard	1486–8
Gise, Johann	1489
Meydenbach, Jacob	1491–5
Peter, *von Friedberg*	1493?–1500?
Schoeffer, Johann	1503–31
Heumann, Friedrich	1509–10?
Schoeffer, Ivo	1531–51
Jordan, Peter	1532–5
Behem, Franz	1540–81
Schoeffer, Ivo, *Heirs of*	1557
Spengel, Theobald	1559
Behem, Kaspar	1568–90
Ysrael, Yakob	1584
Brehm, Heinrich	1594–8
Albin, Johann	1598–1600
Lipp, Balthasar	1599–1600

Mansfeld

Petri, Andreas	1574

Marburg

Loersfeld, Johann	1527
Rhode, Franz	1528–34
Cervicornus, Eucharius	1535–8
Egenolff, Christian	1537–43
Kolbe, Andreas	1545–60
Kolbe, Andreas, *Heirs of*	1567
Kolbe, Augustin	1571–85
Egenolff, Paul	1587–1600

Marienthal

Fratres Clerici Vitae Communis	1474–6?

Meissen

Lotter, Melchior	1520

Memmingen

Kunne, Albrecht	1482–1519

Merseburg

Brandis, Lucas	1473
Brandis, Marcus	1479?

Metz

Colini, Johannes, and Gerhardus, *de Nova Civitate*	1481–2
Hochfeder, Caspar	1499–1517
Pallier, Jehan	1547
Faber, Abraham	1587–97
Aubry, Jean	1588

Most

Weidlich, Andreas	1596

Muehlhausen

Hantzsch, Georg	1568–80
Hantzsch, Georg, *Heirs of*	1585
Hantzsch, Andreas	1587–99
Reinhardt, Hieronymus	1587

Muempelgart

Foillet, Jakob	1588–99

Muenster

Limburg, Johann	1486
Tzwyvel, Dietrich	1514
Tzwyvel, Gottfried	1545
Tzwyvel, Dietrich, *the Younger*	1564–73
Ossenbrug, Johann	1569–70
Raesfeldt, Lambert	1591–7

Mulhouse

Schirenbrand, Johann, and Schmidt, P.	1559?
Schmidt, Peter	1559–62

Munich

Schobser, Hans	1500?–28
Ostendorffer, Hans, and Zayssinger, Matheus	1505
Schobser. Andreas	1531–57
Berg, Adam	1565–1600
Sadeler, Johann	1590?

William, *Duke of Bavaria,*
   Press of   1597
Henricus, Nikolaus, *the*
   Younger   1598–1600

Neisse
Kreutziger, Hans   1558–74
Reinheckel, Andreas   1587–94

Neubrandenburg
Brenner, Anton and Walter 1556

Neuburg
Kilian, Hans   1544–57

Neudamm
Runge, Christoph   1572

Neustadt an der Haardt
Mayer, Johann   1578–9
Mayer, Johann, *Heirs of*   1579
Harnisch, Matthaeus   1580–96
Harnisch, Matthaeus, *Heirs*
   of   1597
Harnisch, Josua   1598
Harnisch, Wilhelm, *Widow*
   of   1598
Harnisch, Wilhelm, *Heirs*
   of   1600

Noerdlingen
Walther, Friedrich, and
   Hurning, Hans   1470
Scharpf, Erasmus   1542

Nuremberg
Sensenschmidt, Johann   1470–8
Koberger, Anton   1471?–1513
Sporer, Hans   1471
Creussner, Friedrich   1472?–97
Sensenschmidt, Johann,
   and Kefer, Heinrich   1473
Frisner, Andreas, and
   Sensenschmidt, J.   1474–8
Mueller, Johann,
   Regiomontanus   1474–5?
Briefftruck, Hans   1476?
Folz, Hans   1479
Fratres Ordinis
   Eremitarum   1479–91
Zeninger, Conrad   1480–2
Printer of the
   Rochuslegende   1483?–4?
Wagner, Peter   1483–1500
Stuchs, Georg   1484–1515
Hochfeder, Caspar   1491–8
Hoeltzel, Hieronymus   1500–25?
Huber, Ambrosius   1500?–1
Meurl, Johann   1501–2
Schleifer, Balthasar   1501
Sodalitas Celtica   1501–2
Schenk, Georg   1502
Fleischmann, Nicolas   1503
Weissenburger, Johann   1503–13
Pinder's Printer   1505–10
Huber, Wolfgang   1509–10
Stuchs, Hans   1509–33
Dyon, Adam   1510?
Peypus, Friedrich   1512–34
Koberger, Johann   1514–25
Gutknecht, Jobst   1515–41
Koberger, Anton, *the*
   Younger   1515–6
Schoensperger, Johann   1517
Glockendon, Georg   1519
Petrejus, Johann   1523–50
Hergot, Hans   1524–7
Andreae, Hieronymus   1525–50
Weidlin, Caspar   1525
Guldenmund, Hans   1527–45
Duerer, Albrecht, *Widow of* 1528–34
Wachter, Georg   1528–46
Leonardus, *de Aich*   1529
Hergotin, Kunigunde   1530–8?
Meldemann, Nikolaus   1530–3
Quercu, Leonhardus à   1530
Rottmaier, Georg   1530–2
Zell, Christoph   1530–5?
Resch, Wolfgang   1531–5?
Schoeffler, Hektor   1533–4
Hamer, Stephan   1534–51
Peypus, Friedrich, *Heirs of* 1535
Wandereisen, Hans   1537–40
Milchthaler, Leonhard   1538–40
Berg, Johann vom, and
   Neuber, U.   1541–63
Gutknecht, Christoph   1541?–8?
Oettel, Joannes   1541
Guenther, Johann   1542
Daubmann, Hans   1546?–50
Fabricius, Julius Paulus 1549–53
Gutknecht, Friedrich   1550–84
Neuber, Valentin   1550–84
Geissler, Valentin   1552–70
Merkel, Georg   1550?–60
Petrejus, Johann, *House of* 1552
Fischer, Bernhart   1553–63?
Hain, Gabriel   1553–6
Hamsing, Hermann   1553–4
Heller, Joachim   1553–7
Glaser, Hans   1555–8
Kramer, Johann   1555?
Kreydlein, Georg   1555?–60
Heussler, Christoph   1556–72
Weigel, Hans   1558–77
Gall, Hermann   1559
Knorr, Nikolaus   1562–92
Berg, Johann vom, *Heirs*
   of, and Neuber, U.   1564–5
Koler, Johann   1564–75?
Kreydlein, Margaretha 1565?
Neuber, Ulrich, and
   Gerlach, D.   1565–6
Glaser, Hans Wolf   1566

Neuber, Valentin, and
  Gerlach, D. 1566
Gerlach, Dietrich 1567–75
Neuber, Ulrich 1568–9
Fuhrmann, Valentin 1570–98
Heussler, Leonard 1570–97
Kempf, Pancraz 1570?
Lochner, Joachim 1570–81
Berg, Johann vom, *Heirs
  of*, and Gerlach, D. 1573
Gerlach, Katharina, and
  Berg, J. vom, *Heirs of* 1575–85
Gerlach, Katharina 1576–91
Mack, Georg 1579
Berg, Johann vom, *Heirs of* 1580–3
Bluemel, Leonard 1581
Lang, Georg 1586?
Lochner, Christoph, and
  Hofmann, J. 1589–92
Dietrich, Alexander Philip 1590?–1600
Drechsel, Wolf 1590
Hofmann, Johann, and
  Camocius, Hubertus 1590
Gerlach, Katharina, *Heirs of* 1592–4
Hofmann, Johann 1593
Kauffmann, Paul 1594–1600
Lochner, Christoph 1595–9
Knor, Hans 1596
Hulsius, Levinus 1597–9
Endter, Georg 1599
Scherff, Balthasar 1600

Oberursel
Henricus, Nikolaus 1558–98
Sutor, Cornelius 1597–1600

Oldenburg
Berendts, Werner, *Heirs of* 1599

Olmuetz
Haendl, Georg 1598

Oppenheim
Koebel, Jacob 1503–28

Ottobeuren
Benedictine Abbey 1511–13

Paris
Prévost, Nicolas 1525
Dupuys, Jacobus 1581

Passau
Alakraw, Johann, and
  Mayr, B. 1482
Mayr, Benedictus 1482
Stahel, Conrad, and Mayr,
  B. 1482
Petri, Johann 1485–93
Nenninger, Matthaeus 1587

Pforzheim
Anshelm, Thomas 1500–11
Rabe, Georg 1557–60

Porrentruy
Schmidt, Johann 1595–1600

Prague
Kantor, Jan Had 1555–7
Melantrich, Georg 1563–79
Dačický, Jiří Jakubův 1570
Schwartz, Georg 1574
Peterle, Michael 1576–95?
Adam, Danyel 1586–95
Schuhman, Hans 1591–4
Strauss, Nikolaus 1596
Schuhman, Hans, *Heirs of* 1599

Prossnitz
Guenther, Johann 1550

Pruntrut *See* **Porrentruy**

Rees
Wylicx, Derek 1575–81

Regensburg
Lienhart 1470?
Pfeil, Johann 1495
Kohl, Paul 1522–30
Kohl, Hans 1532–56
Geissler, Heinrich 1558–68
Burger, Johann 1565?–88
Burger, Andreas 1593–4
Graef, Bartholomaeus 1599–1600
Strauss, Ambrosius 1599

Reichenau
Hasselberg, Hans 1515–37

Reutlingen
Greyff, Michael 1477?–1503?
Otmar, Johann 1482–95
Hans, *von Erfurt* 1525–32

Rome
Plannck, Stephan 1491–1500
Besicken, Johann, and
  Martin, *of Amsterdam* 1500
Silber, Marcello 1518

Rorschach
Straub, Leonhard 1590–8

Rostock
Fratres Communis Vitae 1476–81
Barkhusen, Hermann 1505?
Dietz, Ludwig 1510?–58
Marschalk, Nicolaus 1515–20
Dietz, Ludwig, *Heirs of* 1559–60
Moellemann, Stephan 1560–1600
Lucius, Jakob 1564–80
Stoeckelmann, Johann, and
  Gutterwitz, Andreas 1570–2
Ferber, Augustin 1577–96
Reusner, Christoph 1597–1600?

Rothenburg
- Gros, Albrecht — 1560?
- Gros, Zacharias — 1569

Salzburg
- Wacker, Jacob — 1503
- Baumann, Hans — 1557
- Kuerner, Konrad — 1594

Sankt Gallen
- Straub, Leonhard — 1581
- Straub, Georg — 1600

Schleswig
- Wegener, Nikolaus — 1588–95
- Rantzau, Heinrich — 1591

Schlettstadt
- Schuerer, Lazarus — 1519–21
- Kueffer, Nikolaus — 1521

Schleusingen
- Hamsing, Hermann — 1555–7

Schmalkalden
- Schmuck, Michael — 1564–95
- Graf, Antonius — 1570

Schrattenthal
- Printer of Francisci, Quodlibetica decisio — 1501

Schwaebisch Hall
- Braubach, Peter — 1536–40
- Queck, Pankratius — 1543
- Frentz, Peter — 1546

Schwaz (Sigmundslust)
- Rosentaler, Caspar — 1512
- Ausslasser, Hans — 1513
- Piernsieder, Joseph — 1524–7
- Stoekhl, Jörg — 1524

Schweinfurt
- Kroener, Valentin — 1581

Simmern
- Rodler, Hieronymus — 1530–5

Solingen
- Soter, Johannes — 1538–40

Sorau
- Schneider, Nikolaus — 1589

Speyer
- Printer of Postilla scholastica — 1470?
- Printer of Gesta Christi — 1472–5?
- Drach, Peter — 1476?–1502
- Hist, Johann and Conrad — 1483–90?
- Hist, Conrad — 1492–1514
- Biber, Hartmann — 1502
- Drach, Peter, *the Younger* — 1505?–27
- Schmidt, Jakob — 1514–28?
- Eckhart, Johann — 1521?–5
- Beringer, Jacob — 1532
- Nolt, Anastasius — 1540?–2
- Albinus, Bernhard — 1579–1600
- Smesmann, Abraham — 1594–5

Staffort (Schloss)
- Albinus, Bernhard — 1599

Stendal
- Westphal, Joachim — 1488

Stettin
- Kellner, Andreas — 1589–91
- Kellner, Andreas, *Heirs of* — 1593–8
- Rhetius, Joachim — 1594
- Mueller, Martin — 1599

Strasburg
- Mentelin, Johann — 1460?–77
- Eggestein, Heinrich — 1466?–82
- Rusch, Adolf — 1467?–80?
- Printer of Henricus Ariminensis (Georg Reyser) — 1468?–80?
- Husner, Georg, and Bekenhaub, Johann — 1473
- W., C. — 1473–5?
- Husner, Georg — 1474?–1505
- Knoblochtzer, Heinrich — 1476–85?
- Georgius, *de Spira* — 1478–80?
- Eber, Jacob — 1480–3
- Printer of Jordanus — 1480?–1500?
- Printer of Legenda aurea — 1481–5?
- Grueninger, Johann — 1483–1532
- Ingweiler, Heinrich — 1483
- Printer of Vitas Patrum — 1483–5?
- Schott, Martin — 1483–98
- Printer of Sermones thesauri novi — 1484–6
- Pruess, Johann, *the Elder* — 1484–1511
- Flach, Martin — 1487–1500
- Anshelm, Thomas — 1488
- Pruess, Johann, *the Elder*, and Printer of Jordanus — 1489
- Attendorn, Peter — 1490?
- Printer of Casus breves — 1493–5
- Printer of Barbatia — 1495?
- Kistler, Bartholomaeus — 1497–1502
- Hupfuff, Matthias — 1499–1516
- Brant, Matthias — 1500?
- Ruch, Friedrich — 1500?
- Schaffner, Wilhelm — 1500–10?
- Schott, Johann — 1500–46
- Flach, Martin, *the Younger* — 1501–23?
- Waehinger, Johann — 1503
- Knobloch, Johann — 1504–28
- Schuerer, Matthias — 1508–19
- Maxillus, Georgius — 1510
- Beck, Reinhard — 1511–22
- Pruess, Johann, *the Younger* — 1513–44
- Goetz, Paul — 1514–30
- Kerner, Konrad — 1517

Knobloch, Johann, and Goetz, P.	1518
Schuerer, Matthias and Lazarus	1519
Morhart, Ulrich	1520-2
Schuerer, Matthias, *Heirs of*	1520-25
Koepfel, Wolfgang	1521-51
Beck, Reinhard, *Heirs of*	1523
Herwagen, Johann	1523-8
Schwan, Johannes	1524-6
Beck, Balthasar	1528-46
Seybold, Heinrich	1528-30
Egenolff, Christian	1529-30
Knobloch, Johann, *the Younger*	1529-57
Ulricher, Georg	1529-36
Farckall, Amandus	1530
Schoeffer, Peter, *the Younger*	1530?-2
Schoeffer, Peter, *the Younger*, and Schweintzer, J.	1530-1
Schweintzer, Johann	1530-1
Beck, Balthasar, and Meyer, Michael	1531
Albrecht, Johann	1532-7
Grueninger, Bartholomaeus	1532-8
Apiarius, Matthias	1533-6
Cammerlander, Jakob	1533-48
Froelich, Jakob	1534-57
Schoeffer, Peter, *the Younger*, and Apiarius, M.	1534-6
Rihel, Wendelin	1536-55
Mueller, Krafft	1537-45
Vogtherr, Heinrich	1538-9
Weiditz, Christoph, and Kannel, David	1538
Bund, Sigmund	1539-40
Cephalus, Stephanus	1542
Messerschmidt, Georg	1542-55
Schott, Florian	1543
Rihel, Wendelin, and Messerschmidt, G.	1544-50
Grimm, Hans	1546
Mueller, Krafft, *Widow of*	1548
Fabricius, Blasius	1549-58
Guedon, Remigius	1549
Mueller, Krafft, *Widow of*, and Fabricius, B.	1549
Beck, Balthasar, *Heirs of*	1552
Friess, Augustin	1552
Koepfel, Paul and Philipp	1554-8
Berger, Thiebold	1555-81
Emmel, Samuel	1555-67
Rihel, Wendelin, *Heirs of*	1555-9
Knobloch, *House of*	1556-8
Rihel, Josias and Theodosius	1556-7
Mueller, Christian, *the Elder*	1557-67
Rihel, Josias	1557-96
Rihel, Josias, and Messerschmidt, G.	1560
Messerschmidt, Paul	1561-3
Rihel, Theodosius	1561-1600?
Rihel, Wendelin, *the Younger* and Hieronymus	1561
Hug, Peter	1567?-71
Jobin, Bernhard	1570?-93
Mueller, Christian, *the Elder, Heirs of*	1568-70
Mueller, Christian, *the Younger*	1571-9
Wyriot, Nikolaus	1572-83
Mueller, Christian, *the Younger, Heirs of*	1580-2
Faber, Nikolaus	1582
Wyriot, Nikolaus, *Widow of*	1584
Bertram, Anton	1585-1600
Zetzner, Lazarus	1585-1600
Jobin, Bernhard, *Heirs of*	1593-1600
Martin, Jost	1593-1600
Rietsch, Andreas	1600
Rihel, Josias, *Heirs of*	1600

Straubing

Burger, Johann	1560?-4
Sommer, Andreas	1596-1600?

Stuttgart

Printer of Erwählung Maximilians	1486?
Fuerster, Marx	1598

Susch

Chiampel, Durich	1562

Tegernsee

Closterdruckerei	1573-81
Quirinus, *Abbot*	1576

Thierhaupten

Closterdruckerei	1591-9

Thiengen

Eliezer ben Naphtali Herz Treves, and Joseph ben Naphtali	1560

Torgau

Frederick William, *Duke of Saxony*	1597

Trento

Schindeleyp, Hermann	1475-6
Longo, Giovanni Leonardo	1481-2
Fracassinis, Mafeus de	1528
Gelmini, Giovanni Battista and Giacomo	1585-8
Gelmini, Giacomo	1592

Trier
Colini, Johannes, and Gerhardus, *de Nova Civitate*	1481?
Haene, Matthias	1514–17
Rotaeus, Johann	1574
Brittelmann, Zacharias	1576
Hatot, Emund	1583–5
Hatot, Emund, *Widow of*	1586
Bock, Heinrich	1588–96

Tübingen
Otmar, Johann	1498–1501
Meynberger, Fridericus	1499–1501
Anshelm, Thomas	1511–16
Breuning, Conrad	1516
Wetzler, Kilian	1516
Zuyfel, Johann	1516
Morhart, Ulrich	1523–54
Morhart, Ulrich, *Heirs of*	1554
Morhart, Ulrich, *Widow of*	1554–70
Hock, Alexander	1569–90
Gruppenbach, Georg	1573–1600
Cellius, Erhard	1599

Uelzen
Kroener, Michael	1576–1600

Ulm
Zainer, Johann	1473–1500
Dinckmut, Conrad	1480?–96
Holle, Lienhart	1482–4
Reger, Johann	1486–99
Schaeffler, Johann	1492?–9
Hauser, Hans	1495?
Gruener, Hans	1521–32
Varnier, Hans	1531–8
Franck, Sebastian	1537
Varnier, Hans, *the Younger*	1546–7
Ulhart, Johann Anton	1579–85

Urach
Fyner, Conrad	1480–8
Ungnad, Ivan	1561–3

Venice
Maler, Bernhard	1478
Ratdolt, Erhard	1478–83
Justus, *de Albano*	1486
Liechtenstein, Petrus	1502–3?
Valgrisi, Vincenzo	1563
Ciotti, Johann Baptist	1587–94
Franciscis, Franciscus de	1594

Vienna
Koblinger, Stephan	1482–5
Winterburg, Johann	1493–1517
Vietor, Hieronymus	1509–30
Vietor, Hieronymus, and Singriener, J.	1510–14
Alantse, Leonardus	1511–16
Alantse, Leonardus and Lucas	1512–17
Alantse, Lucas	1513–22
Singriener, Johann	1514–45
Metzker, Joannes	1518–34
Werlen, Bartholomeus	1519–20
Alantse, Urbanus	1530
Singriener, Matthaeus	1545
Singriener, Johann, *Heirs of*	1546–8
Kohl, Hans, and Adler, Aegidius	1548
Singriener, Johann, *the Younger*	1549–61
Singriener, Matthaeus and Johann, *the Younger*	1549
Adler, Aegidius	1550–2
Kohl, Hans	1550
Zimmermann, Michael	1553–65
Hoffhalter, Raphael	1557–62
Collegium Societatis Jesu	1560–3
Stainhofer, Kaspar	1566–74
Eber, Blasius	1571–2
Kreutzer, Stephan	1577–82
Denecker, Hercules	1579–87
Apffel, Michael	1582–4
Nassinger, Leonhard	1583–9
Apffel, Michael, *Widow of*	1589
Pierius, Nikolaus	1591
Kolb, Franz	1594–8
Formica, Leonhard	1595–9
Hieber, Georg	1597

Weissenfels
Hantzsch, Georg	1561–9

Wesel
Straten, Derick van der	1543–8
Johann, *von Kempen*	1545
Lamprecht, Josse	1554–6?
Braecker, Hans de	1558–67
Druess, Johann	1573

Wessobrunn
Zeissenmayr, Lucas	1505

Wimbschpach
Ringer, Hans	1582

Wittenberg
Sertorius, Enricus	1503–4
Stoeckel, Wolfgang	1504
Rhau–Grunenberg, Johannes	1509–25
Lotter, Melchior, *the Younger*	1519–25
Schirlentz, Nickel	1521–45
Cranach, Lucas, and Doering, Christian	1523–5
Lotter, Melchior, *the Younger* and Michael	1523–4
Lufft, Hans	1523–83
Klug, Josef	1524–52
Barth, Hans	1525–7
Rhau, Georg	1525–49
Weiss, Hans	1525–39
Lotter, Michael	1526–8

Reinhart, Symphorian	1527
Seitz, Peter	1537–50
Frischmut, Hans	1538–40?
Kreutzer, Veit	1541–62
Krafft, Johann	1546–78
Rhau, Georg, *Heirs of*	1550–66
Seitz, Peter, *Heirs of*	1550–8
Klug, Thomas	1554–61
Schwenck, Lorenz	1558–73
Ruelius, Cunradus	1559–62
Heuss, Christoph	1560
Schnellboltz, Gabriel	1560–3
Seitz, Peter, *the Younger*	1560–74
Schram, Christophor	1561
Lucius, Jakob	1563
Selfisch, Samuel	1563–1600
Schwertel, Johann	1565–76
Schleich, Clemens, and Schoene, A.	1569–78
Bruno, Gregorius	1571
Gronenberg, Simon	1579–96
Krafft, Johann, *Heirs of*	1579–99
Schoene, Anton	1579–83
Welack, Matthaeus	1580–93
Lehmann, Zacharias	1581–1600
Schleich, Clemens	1584–8
Krafft, Zacharias	1586–8
Mueller, Georg	1590–9
Axin, Christoph	1591–3
Rabe, Bechtold	1591
Hellwig, Paul	1592–1600
Krafft, Johann, *the Younger*	1593–8
Meissner, Wolfgang	1593–1600
Welack, Matthaeus, *Widow of*	1593–6
Hoffmann, Andreas	1595–9
Berger, Clement	1596–7
Sueberlich, Lorenz	1597–1600
Lobus, Wenceslaus	1598

Wolfenbüttel

Ruedem, Henning	1540–52
Horn, Konrad	1560–1600

Worms

Drach, Peter, *the Younger*	1504
Hans, *von Erfurt*	1520–2
Schoeffer, Peter, *the Younger*	1522–9
Meihel, Hans	1529
Wagner, Sebastian	1535–41
Hofmann, Gregor	1550?–1
Koepfel, Philipp	1560–3

Würzburg

Reyser, Georg	1481–95?
Mueller, Balthasar	1526–41
Weigle, Bernhard	1527
Mueller, Johann	1548–9
Baumann, Hans	1564
Heinrich, *von Aich*	1583–90
Hoffmann, Wolfgang	1586
Heinrich, *von Aich, Widow of*	1592
Fleischmann, Georg	1593–8

Zerbst

Schmidt, Bonaventura	1583–97
Zanach, Jacob	1596–7
Schleer, Johann	1599

Zinna

Cistercian Monastery	1495?

Zittau

Schneider, Nikolaus	1586

Zürich

Werdemueller, Marcus	1518
Froschauer, Christoph	1521–64
Hager, Hans	1524–6
Friess, Augustin	1540–50?
Froschauer, Eustachius	1545
Gessner, Andreas and Jacob	1550–60?
Gessner, Andreas	1551?–60
Gessner, Andreas, and Wyssenbach, Rudolf	1552
Froschauer, Christoph, *the Younger*	1556–88
Eliezer ben Naphtali Herz Treves, and Joseph ben Naphtali	1558
Gessner, Jacob	1560?–6
Gessner, Jacob and Tobias	1561
Froschauer, *House of*	1586–91
Wolf, Johannes	1590–9

Zweibrücken

Wittel, Kaspar	1597–1600

Zwickau

Gastel, Jörg	1523–5
Kantz, Gabriel	1526–9
Meyerpeck, Wolfgang	1530–45

Place uncertain (Germany)

Sporer, Hans	1473
Printer of Lotharius	1474–5?
Printer of Leo I., *Sermones*	1475?
Printer of Voragine, *Sermones*	1484–6
Faust, Hans	1537?
Nassinger, Leonhard	1564
Reyser, Christian	1586

False and fictitious names

Aresdorf
   Philadelphus, Theophilus 1578
Augsburg
   Anonymus, Adam 1545
   Faber, Joannes 1592
Aygenstein
   Jason, Gabriel 1576
Basle
   Emlos, Theophyll 1540?
   Bonifante, Radulphe 1542
   Cousin, M. 1574
   Ray, Pierre de 1574
   Forest, François 1587–97
   Wallemand, Pieter 1573–4
   Sedabonis, Piero de 1576–82
   Le Fèvre, François 1591
   Roy, Louy 1599
Christlingen
   Gutwinus, Ursinus 1584–90
Cologne
   Bertulphus, Hieronymus 1574
   Jobin, Herman 1586
   Coloresco, Alberto 1589
   Accademia Italiana 1598
Constance
   Samius, Theodorus 1592?
Danzig
   Pessus, Gerardus
Emden
   Aurik, Jacob 1534
Heidelberg
   Hopper, Willhelm 1568
Jericho
   Trauth, Thomas 1542
Leipzig
   Hoff, Ubryght 1541

Leyden
   Jobsson, Wernher 1588
   Warnfast, Hiob 1595
London
   Volckwinner, Collins 1554
Lueneburg
   Golsenus, Sebastianus 1533
Magdeburg
   Rausch, Georg 1554
Marburg
   Lufft, Hans 1528–35
Münster
   Willems, Conrad 1533
Naples
   Zangarus, Joannes Baptista 1585
Schlappershausen
   Flederwisch, M. G. 1560?
Southwark
   Trutheall, Christopher 1556
Strasburg
   Foxe, Francis 1530
   Beckenth, Balthasar 1531
   Le Porché, Gillot 1587
   Heugst, Oelboum 1588
Wesel
   Nycolson, Henry 1546
Wittenberg
   Dorcastor, Nicholas 1554
Zurich
   Mazochius, Jacobus 1528
   Jacobson, Oliver 1543
No place named
   Strosack, Joannes [=G. Husner, Strasburg] 1502
   Turone, Franciscus de 1548?
   Fluvius, Rupertus 1595